RULES
FOR
DEPLORABLES

Reviews

"A must read for fighting leftists' socialist/progressive agenda. Cathi's extraordinary journey from hardcore leftist to a conservative pulled me emotionally into her book. She clearly understands what motivates those on both sides of the ideological coin; and how best to confront leftists' arguments." – *Lloyd Marcus, Author, "The Unhyphenated American"*

"Although I was well versed on the Communist Manifesto, the bailiwick of Cloward-Piven added to Alinsky's *Rules for Radicals* equaling Obama's '*fundamental transformation of America*' the book is a terrific refresher course and the affirmation that elections have consequences. I highly recommend studying Rules for Deplorables..." – *Curtis A. Holmes, Commissioner, City of Largo, Florida*

"A thoroughly researched and documented treatise on how the extreme left operates and how conservatives can counter, using the left's own tactics." – *Dr. Bob Cundiff, Councilmember, City of Clearwater, Florida*

"Cathi's research is phenomenal! This book is very well written, very well researched, an easy read and very informative! I would recommend this to every conservative and liberal who wants some background in Socialism! – *Barbara Thomson, former Deputy Commander, 2d Information Operations Battalion*

RULES

FOR

DEPLORABLES

A Primer For Fighting Radical Socialism

CATHI CHAMBERLAIN

BOOK COVER ART BY:
11 YEAR-OLD
BRAYLON LEE NANCE

EDITED BY:
CHRISTY WHITE-CHAMBERLAIN

ACKNOWLEDGEMENTS

- To Lynne, my sister, for her tireless cheerleading through my recovery period that enabled me to pick myself up and open the new door that replaced the old.
- To Joe, my brother, for his non-judgmental and uplifting compassionate words of love and encouragement that helped me get from a point of despair to one of hope for the future.
- To my sister Lori who, through tough love and relentless spiritual sharing, provided timely, inspirational messages that were always received at the most needed moments.
- To my sister-in-law, Christy Chamberlain, for her painstaking eye-for-detail and months of patience as she helped me edit this book to ready it for publication.
- And, lastly, for all those other family members and friends who helped me get from one very painful chapter in my life to this...the next. I've learned that family and friends are indeed everything in life and for *YOU,* I am grateful.

DEDICATED TO:

PRESIDENT DONALD J. TRUMP
...and, the future generation

CONTENTS

Prologue

I BEGIN THIS BOOK WHILE on the road to recovery. On October 26, 2017, I was thankful to be a 20-year-experienced mobile home roof inspector. My income had tripled over the past month with no end in sight after Hurricane Irma made landfall on September 10th in the lower Florida Keys as a Category 4. Living in the Tampa Bay area put me within driving range to handle roofing sales all over the state. But seeing blue tarps everywhere, one couldn't help feeling sick.

Just one day later, my luck changed. While inspecting the first roof of the day, the unimaginable happened. I positioned my ladder against the side of a mobile home as I'd done many times before. Climbing ten feet up, I watched in horror as my ladder slid to the left. With no choice but to let go, I fell backwards onto a concrete slab using my hands to break my fall.

I was flown by helicopter to the nearest Trauma Center, experiencing the most horrific pain of my life. I remember praying to God out loud over and over again, "please don't let it be my back".

After an onslaught of tests over every inch of my body, I learned I had indeed broken my back in two places, as well as both wrists and my left collarbone. Spending three months in and out of hospitals, I was finally allowed to go home with the depressing realization that my life had been forever changed.

Transitioning from being an independent, active 62

year-old woman to what my life had now become was no easy challenge. I wasn't sitting around thinking, *"poor me, why me?"* I was thinking, *"poor me, why NOW? Why the hell did this happen at a time when my income was the best it had ever been?"* This was not going to be easy, not at my age.

As the middle child of a strict Army Officer father, I was the rebel. While my family moved a lot in my early years, we somehow managed to remain in the Washington, D.C. area from the time I was eight until my dad retired. By seventeen, I had moved out of the house. After working five years for the government, growing disgusted by the wastefulness I saw, I quit and moved to California. There I spent the next fifteen years becoming a liberal, radical leftist.

In D.C., I was bombarded with conservative politics. But, in California, *Roe v. Wade,* eighteen missing minutes on an audio tape about something called Watergate, and the Vietnam War were viewed totally different. It was a refreshing change.

Many years living in Los Angeles sealed my anti-establishment sentiment. I found myself in the midst of pro-abortion demonstrations outside clinics. I adored Jane Fonda, voted for Jimmy Carter, protested the Vietnam War and detested Ronald Reagan. Had my father lived past my twenty-first year, I'm pretty sure he'd have been horrified.

My mom, more moderate than dad, reveled in my wild-child life as a photo-girl at Harrah's Casino in Tahoe, and later as a Playboy Bunny in San Diego, then L.A. Had she lived past my thirtieth birthday, she'd have been proud at my becoming a published author of the book, *How To Succeed in Singles' Bars: For Men Only,* and later as owner of the nation's first, all-female construction company (Tool-Timing Babydolls), after obtaining my building contractor's license in Florida. While in L.A., I don't remember meeting many conservatives. My "bubble" of existence included liberal Hollywood-types and "Valley Girls", hardly Sean Hannity, Tucker Carlson or Judge Jeanine Pirro wannabes.

My time was fairly balanced between partying and working my way through California State University, Northridge (back when a college education allowed varying opinions and open debate). I studied my butt off and graduated with nearly straight A's. I also gained a more balanced attitude towards politics. I still disliked Ronald Reagan and his Vice President and successor, George H. W. Bush, but found myself questioning liberalism and became politically adrift ... until I learned of a business-guy named Ross Perot.

Perot's presidential campaign in 1992 probably did more for my disenfranchisement from the Democratic Party than anything else. History likes to say that Perot voters actually enabled a new guy named William Jefferson Clinton get elected. But, I would have voted for Clinton had Perot not been in the mix. Perot's business experience was exactly what I thought our country needed at the time. So, I volunteered for his campaign committee in Sherman Oaks, California.

I left L.A. in 1994, after the Northridge Earthquake destroyed my neighborhood and business. I'd had it with the phony indoctrinations of Hollywood anyway and moved to Dallas, Texas. Two years later, I relocated to Tampa Bay, Florida, where I've remained ever since.

While Perot's loss was a disappointment, I accepted Bill Clinton as our president. But, as scandal after scandal racked up against him and his wife, Hillary, I was losing faith. Then, I heard about a girl named Monica.

I was so offended by Bill Clinton's affair with Monica Lewinsky, a 22-year-old White House Intern, that I was 100% certain everybody else would be, too. Incredibly, they were not. Appalled to learn that a sizeable majority of Americans dismissed Clinton's behavior with a "boys will be boys" attitude, I instantly recognized that this single, morally-corrupt event, and people's acceptance of it, was going to change our country forever.

It wasn't the actual act that angered me. After all, I hadn't been a model citizen myself to that point. What bothered the hell out of me was that this man was given an incredibly privileged position to represent the people of the United States. Getting a blow job in the Oval Office was hardly what the American people had in mind when they voted him in.

With Clinton's actions while representing America, his lying to Congress about it, and the shameful way in which he and Hillary blamed Republicans for what she claimed was "a right-wing conspiracy", my split from the Democratic Party was complete. The Clintons' ridicule of Lewinsky and other female accusers of Bill's lewd behavior (including rape) shocked me. How anyone, knowing the facts, could support Bill or Hillary in their later political endeavors baffles me to this day.

When Barack Obama ran for the presidency in 2008, my political activism flared up once again. By then, I was an informed, critical thinker. I did my homework prior to his election and had no doubt what type of president he'd be. With just one year in the U.S. Senate prior to running for president, Obama was rated the most liberal Member in 2007.[1]

Obama's relationship with the anti-American, radical, racist Reverend Jeremiah Wright, whose church he and his wife attended for twenty years, and were also married in, was well-documented. In addition, his employment with the fraudulently-charged, convicted and now defunct liberal community activist voter group, known as ACORN,[2] (Association of Community Organizations for Reform Now), was credibly linked to him by opponent Senator John McCain, and others, prior to the election. Unfortunately, the voter-fraud perpetuated by ACORN was a complex issue so Americans paid little attention to the sparse reporting it received given its importance.[3]

I'm convinced that had people done research prior to electing Obama, they would have known about his very dubious connections. Those included such activists as Bill Ayers and Bernadine Dohrn of the Weather Underground (a radical, anti-establishment group responsible for hundreds of bombings, at banks, courthouses, police stations and even the Pentagon. One of those killed was a Boston police officer).

---

[1] Brian Montopoli, "National Journal: Obama Most Liberal Senator in 2007, *CBS News*, https://www.cbsnews.com/news/national-journal-obama-most-liberal-senator-in-2007/. (Jan. 31, 2008)
[2] Matthew Vadum, "ACORN, Obama's Ex-Employer, Convicted in Massive Voter Fraud Scam" *The American Spectator* (4-15-2011) https://spectator.org/25788_acorn-obamas-ex-employer-convicted-massive-voter-fraud-scam/.
[3] Jess Henig. "ACORN Accusations: McCain makes exaggerated claims of 'voter fraud.' Obama soft-pedals his connections." *FactCheck* (Last Updated October 21, 2008) https://www.factcheck.org/2008/10/acorn-accusations/.

There was also evidence that Obama associated with Louis Farrakhan (leader of the radical, virulently anti-Semitic Nation of Islam). A photo of the two was only recently released by the photographer who has admitted that a member of the Congressional Black Caucus (CBC) pressured him to suppress it while the President remained in office. Famed attorney, and Democrat, Alan Dershowitz was especially bothered by the photo. According to Brian Montopoli from *CBS News*, "[Dershowitz] declared he never would have campaigned for Obama had he seen him standing next to Farrakhan back then. I'm sure he's not the only one. Muhammad [the photographer], that CBC functionary, and Farrakhan...all knew it: if that picture spread in 2007 or 2008, a whole different history ensues."[4]

In addition to his decades' long relationship with *"Not-God-Bless-America, But-God-Damned-America",* Reverend Wright, Obama's mentor was activist Frank Marshall Davis, a hard-core, card-carrying member of the Communist Party in the '30s and '40s.[5]

Following Obama's election, I educated myself even more in order to warn others about the dangers of his policies. I was determined to do my part in ensuring that he not get elected to a second term. There was no doubt in my mind that Obama's true intention in promising a

---

[4] Vinson Cunningham. "The Politics of Race and the Photo that might have derailed Obama" *The New Yorker* (January 31, 2008) https://www.newyorker.com/culture/annals-of-appearances/the-politics-of-race-and-the-photo-that-might-have-derailed-obama.
[5] John Lund. "Ben Carson: Where Was the Media's Interest in Obama's Relation to the Rev. Wright, Frank Davis, Bill Ayers...?" *National Review* (Nov. 8, 2015) https://www.nationalreview.com/2015/11/ben-carson-media-double-standard-obama/.

total *"transformation of America"* was to turn our country into a socialist state. But nobody would listen. Instead, I was banned from discussing politics at family gatherings.

Shortly after taking office in 2009, Obama shunned protocol when he appointed forty-five, hand-picked individuals to head some of his most important positions without the usual Senatorial vetting. He called his appointees "czars". The very word, according to Merriam-Webster's, means: "1: emperor; specifically: the ruler of Russia until the 1917 revolution, 2: one having great power or authority." Because Russians are communists, I wanted to know why Obama chose this term for his closest advisers. I should have been more concerned with *who* he selected.

Judicial Watch (JW) put out a "Special Report" in 2009. It warned that Obama's appointments amounted to an over-expansion of government without checks and balances. Instead of nominating his staff (as is the precedent), Obama merely appointed them, effectively evading proper vetting and confirmation by the Senate.[6]

Obama's FCC's Diversity Czar, Mark Lloyd, raised alarms from the media and members of Congress when it became known that he had worked "as a senior fellow at the left-wing think tank Center for American Progress" and made comments "on the need to remove white people from powerful positions in the media to benefit minorities".[7] The fact that he had praised "the

---

[6] Thomas Fitton, Christopher L. Farrell, and John Althen. "President Obama's Czars", pg. 14 *Judicial Watch* (Sept. 15, 2011) https://www.judicialwatch.org/wp-content/uploads/2014/02/Special-Report-President-Obamas-Czars.pdf.

[7] Ibid. pg. 16.

incredible revolution of Venezuelan Socialist leader Hugo Chavez" hardly calmed concerns.[8]

Another eyebrow-raising appointment was Kevin Jennings as the Safe and Drug-Free Schools Czar. "Many were taken aback to learn of Jennings past efforts to overtly promote homosexuality in public schools" and to learn that he "has publically [sic] praised Harry Hay, who is associated with the North American Man-Boy Love Association (NAMBLA)." That association, a pedophilia advocacy group, believes it is okay for grown men to be sexually active with small boys. Even after 53 House Republicans demanded he be relieved, Obama refused![9]

Obama's Global Warming Czar for environmental affairs, Carol Browner, "was one of 14 listed leaders of Socialist International's "Commission for a Sustainable World Society." She was forced to step down after being exposed.[10]

Green Jobs Czar, Van Jones, "was involved with San Francisco's radical Marxist revolutionary group, Standing Together to Organize a Revolutionary Movement (STORM). Further, Jones publicly avowed support for cop-killer Mumia Abu Jamal, a death row inmate who was convicted of murdering a Philadelphia police officer in 1981. Among numerous other controversies, Jones signed a petition in 2004 calling for investigations into the claim that the Bush administration intentionally caused the events of September 11, 2001."[11] After exposure by radio talk

---

[8] Ibid.
[9] Ibid, pg. 19.
[10] Ibid, pg. 21.
[11] Ibid, pg. 25.

show host, Glenn Beck, and pressure from Republican Senators, Jones was forced to resign.

Elizabeth Warren deserves special mention, given that's she'll be running for the presidency in 2020. As Consumer Czar, she was especially targeted by *JW* and so controversial that it devoted almost three full pages to her (pp. 25–27). I urge you to read them if you are thinking to vote for her. She, too, was forced to resign once her dubious history was exposed.

Obama's Terrorism Czar, one of President Trump's most vile attackers, is former CIA Director John Brennan. He admitted himself that he voted for a member of the Communist Party for president during the cold war with Russia.[12] He blames it on youthful rebellion. I was a rebel, too, but I can assure you, it never once occurred to me to vote for a Commie. Given some of Brennan's modern day comments, I don't believe for a minute that his views have changed.

The *JW* report goes on and on exposing the most shocking revelations surrounding Obama's staff. If only Americans had paid attention back then.

If you were for Trump from the very beginning, I can almost bet you already knew the damage the Obama administration was about to foist on the American people before he was elected the first time. But, so many did not. I believe that's why some folks just can't accept these truths even today.

Obama was not only elected to a second term, he succeeded in transforming our country beyond his

---

[12] Natalie Johnson. "CIA Director Once Voted for Communist Presidential Candidate" *The Washington Free Beacon* (Sept. 21, 2016) https://freebeacon.com/politics/cia-director-once-voted-for-communist-presidential-candidate/.

wildest dreams. We now have a "deep state" in which the left has successfully infiltrated our most sensitive government agencies, including the FBI and DOJ. We are in deep trouble. If you're reading this, you probably already know it. If you don't, I pray you keep reading, because we are on the brink of losing our country's freedoms by becoming a socialist state. None of us will escape the disastrous results except the uber-rich.

While recovering from my accident, I decided to revisit a book I read years ago. *Rules for Radicals*, written by the "father" of community organizing, Saul Alinsky, is a blueprint for activists to fight the "establishment" in order to create "social justice" (i.e., socialism) using chaos as their means. In it, Alinsky separates the world into two groups: the "haves" and the "have-nots." His thirteen "tactics" give the have-not's guidance on how to take from the haves and keep for themselves, otherwise known as "wealth redistribution".

Rules for Deplorables will expose those tactics and teach effective ways to fight back by interweaving current-day political events so the reader can better understand how the left has been slowly gaining power for decades.

In *Rules for Radicals*, Alinsky devotes his entire second chapter, "Of Means and Ends", to educating his community-organizer students on ethics required to reach their goals. He lists a total of eleven rules "of the ethics of means and ends".[13] They range from high ethical behavior to the left's oft-quoted, *"by whatever means necessary"*. The level of ethics used depends on the importance of the goal to be achieved. *Rules for*

---

[13] Saul Alinsky. pp. 24-47. *Rules for Radicals* (1972)

Deplorables teaches that, at this point in the game, being ethical is like bringing a knife to a gun-fight. Trump doesn't do it and we should be grateful that, finally, a Republican is standing up to the lunacy of the left. This book offers must-know information because the left's end goal is clearly stated as the replacement of our free market society with socialism. And, they are a lot closer than you think.

Capitalism, with all its warts, is better for freedom-loving people than socialism has, historically, ever been. *Rules for Deplorables* will convince even the most hardened defenders of socialism what that type of government would mean to our freedoms. If we succumb, it will take decades to regain control of our country, if ever. For those who have an open mind, *Rules for Deplorables* may be the single most important book you'll ever read.

Alinsky's successful "community organizer" would be just like a Barack Obama, who has been rightfully linked to him for years. Yet, how could Obama learn the strategies if he was only ten when Alinsky died?

Nancy LeTourneau, in a *Washington Monthly* article dated March 15, 2016 entitled "Hillary Clinton, Barack Obama and Saul Alinsky", writes that "Obama's college years in Chicago were spent as a community organizer with a group that based their methods on [Alinsky's] teachings." She further reveals that "Clinton wrote her honors thesis at Wellesley College on his work."[14]

---

[14] Nancy LeTourneau. "Hillary Clinton, Barack Obama and Saul Alinsky" *Washington Monthly* (March 15, 2016) https://washingtonmonthly.com/2016/03/15/hillary-clinton-barack-obama-and-saul-alinsky/.

Rules for Radicals teaches thirteen tactics that students of Alinsky's must master in order to become community organizers. They are today's Progressives, Democratic Socialists of America (DSA), Communists, and many Democrats. (For purposes of this book, they will hereafter be collectively referred to as the "left".)

Nowhere have I seen Alinsky's tactics dissected in such a way as to give Conservatives the tools to combat the ultimate goal of Alinsky's followers, whose 100% aim is to fundamentally transform America into a socialist state. So, I've decided to do it.

Rules for Radicals' eleven ethical rules in politics explain the imbalances between the way Democrats and Republicans govern today. The Dems threw almost all ethics out the window decades ago as some Republicans still insist on using "gentleman's" tactics from the 1800s. That's suicidal and, if the GOP doesn't wake up soon, they will be to blame for the loss of our Republic.

Reportedly, when Benjamin Franklin emerged from having just signed the Constitution, a woman approached him and asked, *"Well, Doctor, what have we got – a Republic or a Monarchy?"* To which he replied, *"A Republic, ma'am. If you can keep it."* *Rules for Deplorables* offers the knowledge and the means to do exactly that.

I've heard that Alinsky's *Rules for Radicals* was the source for yet a third list of rules, entitled: "How to Create a Socialist State". After an exhaustive search, I couldn't find a single source that ties the list to him or any author.[15] Still, I find the list useful in demonstrating just how close our free-market system is to crumbling:

"There are eight levels of control that must be obtained before you are able to create a socialist state.

*1) **Healthcare** – Control healthcare and you control the people.*

*2) **Poverty** – Increase the Poverty level as high as possible, poor people are easier to control and will not fight back if you are providing everything for them to live.*

*3) **Debt** – Increase the debt to an unsustainable level. That way you are able to increase taxes, and this will produce more poverty.*

*4) **Gun Control** – Remove the ability to defend themselves from the Government. That way you are able to create a police state.*

*5) **Welfare** – Take control of every aspect of their lives (Food, Housing, and Income)*

*6) **Education** – Take control of what people read and listen to – take control of what children learn in school.*

*7) **Religion** – Remove the belief in God from the Government and schools*

*8) **Class Warfare** – Divide the people into the wealthy and the poor. This will cause more discontent and it will be easier to take (Tax) the wealthy with the support of the poor."[16]*

While the author of the above list remains unknown, Americans would be wise to stay vigilant as our country is being insidiously taken over by these very controls.

---

[15] David Mikkelson, "Beware the Useful Idiots" *Snopes* (Jan. 21, 2014) https://www.snopes.com/fact-check/how-to-create-a-social-state/.
[16] Ibid.

Helpfully, these controls were studied at length and taught extensively since the 1960s by renowned political activists Richard Cloward (now deceased) and his wife, Frances Fox Piven. As professors at Columbia University, the couple developed strategies to destroy capitalism and replace it with socialism/Marxism.

One of their papers, for example, "The Cloward-Piven Strategy" (CPS), "focused on overloading the United States public welfare system in order to precipitate a crisis, which would ultimately lead to replacing the welfare system with a national system of 'a guaranteed annual income and thus an end to poverty'".[17] Sound familiar?

Because the CPS plays such a key role in shaping recent American history, I've covered it extensively in Chapter One. The reader will discover the left's systematic plan to destroy America from within, and why they are so far succeeding.

Rules for Deplorables familiarizes the reader with Alinsky's tactics by devoting one chapter to each. Chapter One: "Illusion of Power", begins with Alinsky's Tactic #1: *"Power is Not Only What You Have, but what the Enemy Thinks you Have."* It describes how the left manipulates the minority vote and the gullible right into supporting causes designed to destroy our country.

The second chapter, "Viva la Revolución", explores Tactic #2, proving how devastated countries become when leftists succeed in replacing democracies with socialism. If you think our country is too big to fail,

---

[17] Steve Straub. "Is The Cloward–Piven Strategy Being Used To Destroy America?" *US News* (July 5, 2014) https://thefederalistpapers.org/us/is-the-cloward-piven-strategy-being-used-to-destroy-america.

you'd be among the millions of Venezuelans who thought so, too. Regarded as the richest country in Latin America just two decades ago, Venezuela is in shambles today. The average person has lost 20 pounds due to food shortages and there is no relief in sight. Millions of citizens are now in exile.[18]

Once some of the most beautiful and safest cities in America mere decades ago, are now mired in filth, degradation, homelessness, crime, drugs, etc. San Francisco, L.A., Chicago and Detroit are on downward spirals. The common denominator: all have been under Democratic rule for decades. Why do people continue to vote these "leaders" into office again and again? That is the mystery *Rules for Deplorables* will solve.

Donald J. Trump descended the elevators at Trump Tower in New York City on June 16, 2015. From that day forward, there was never a doubt in my mind that he is the only person capable of saving America. For those of you who also believed in him from the beginning, know this: there is hope. For those who jumped on the Trump train later, welcome aboard. For those who simply cannot stand the man, I'm praying you can overlook his personality for the sake of our country's future.

When Hillary Clinton called Trump supporters "Deplorables" during her campaign against him, she had no idea just how much she had galvanized half of America. It's time to fight back, folks.

The main division between Americans today is that Trump and Deplorables believe America is the best

---

[18] Patrick Gillespie, Marilia Brochetto and Paula Newton. "Venezuela: How a Rich Country Collapsed" *CNN Money* (July 30, 2017) https://money.cnn.com/2017/07/26/news/economy/venezuela-economic-crisis/index.html.

country in the world – the most charitable and free. We believe the world would be less safe had we not intervened at critical moments in history. Sure, we've made mistakes. But, we learned from them and became better people for it. We see the glass as half-full. We are also painfully aware that our country has reached an extremely dangerous tipping point in which our freedoms could be lost forever.

The left, on the other hand, don't see things that way at all. They see America as an insult to the world – an evil colonizer that has caused nothing but grief. They believe if they could just reduce our country to the level of the third world, we would be humbled and forgiven. They are globalists. Reparations for America's past victims is their rally cry, without regard to cost. Their true motivation is to further economically implode our country. They see the glass as half–empty and scheme daily to destroy the foundations on which America was built. Chaos is their means, at any cost.

It should come as no surprise, then, that Alinsky acknowledged Lucifer in *Rules for Radicals*. He describes the devil with fondness as *"...the first radical known to man who rebelled against the establishment and did it so effectively that he at least won his own kingdom"*. His book can be found on many colleges campuses. It is one example of why so many millennials have graduated with a skewed version of history and the world today.

Whether you like President Trump or not, whether you are liberal or conservative, Republican, Democrat, socialist or non–political, you owe it to the future generation to at least understand the issues that will determine the path our country takes next.

Rules for Deplorables will cause a wide range of emotions, including shock, disbelief, skepticism, and even anger, as each chapter uncovers the truth about what is going on in our country. We've been under assault for decades and most Americans don't even know it. The book is heavily foot-noted through painstaking research so the reader will not be able to escape a full reading without a better idea of our country's perilous condition.

If you find *Rules for Deplorables* a sensible guide to help President Trump re-strengthen America, share it with family, friends and co-workers. Whether they are like-minded thinkers or not, open-minded readers will come away with a new awareness of how close we really are to losing basic freedoms that our Founding Fathers fought so hard, and sacrificed so much, to give us. Most importantly, both you and they will have the knowledge necessary to fight for our country's survival.

It is my sincere belief that Americans have one last opportunity to save our country in the coming elections of 2020. President Trump may not be perfect, but he is working night and day for us. He's the only President in my lifetime who has actually done what he promised he'd do once in office, even against incredible odds. But he has so much more to do and needs our support. Our military men and women have us covered on the front lines. It's time we did our share here at home.

GOD BLESS AMERICA ... and, may God Bless President Donald J. Trump!

Cathi Chamberlain

RULES
FOR
DEPLORABLES

ILLUSION
OF POWER

TACTIC #1: *"Power is not only what you have but what the enemy thinks you have."*[19]

"I JUST HAVE TWO WORDS for you tonight: five days." Then-candidate Barack Obama was speaking to a group of supporters during a campaign stop in Missouri in October, 2008. *"After decades of broken politics in Washington,"* he promised, *"and eight years of failed policies from George W. Bush, and 21 months of a campaign that's taken us from the rocky coast of Maine to the sunshine of California, we are five days away from fundamentally transforming the United States of America."*[20]

For those who did our homework on Obama prior to the election, we were ecstatic at his transparency. There was little doubt in our minds what he meant when he said he was close to fundamentally transforming our country. "Obama and others of the post-Alinsky generation described their work in the 1990 book 'After Alinsky: Community Organizing' in which Obama

---

[19] Ibid. Alinsky, pg. 127.
[20] Tim Ryan. "In context: What Obama said about 'fundamentally transforming' the nation" *Politifact* (Feb. 6, 2014) https://www.politifact.com/truth-o-meter/article/2014/feb/06/what-barack-obama-has-said-about-fundamentally-tra/.

wrote that he longed for ways to close the gap between community organizing and national politics."[21]

We knew that others didn't know these facts about him and were fearful of their euphoria over Obama's charismatic style. When he made that cryptic announcement so close to the election, we were certain that others would be alarmed, too. That was not to be.

In Alinsky's book, *Rules for Radicals*, his first tactic to beat the "enemy" (his word) was, not surprisingly, all about power. *"Power"*, he believed, *"is not only what you have, but what the enemy thinks you have."*, maintaining that *"Power has always derived from two main sources, money and people."*[22]

So how does Obama's promise above square with his known ties to Alinsky's community organizing institutes of training? You're about to find out.

In that same campaign speech, Obama went on to say, *"In five days, you can turn the page on policies that put greed and irresponsibility on Wall Street before the hard work and sacrifice of folks on Main Street. In five days, you can choose policies that invest in our middle class, and create new jobs, and grow this economy, so that everyone has a chance to succeed, not just the CEO, but the secretary and janitor, not just the factory owner, but the men and women on the factory floor."*[23]

How'd that work out for us?

A review of the policies of the left is not possible without a clear understanding of the aforementioned,

---

[21] Bill Dedman. "Reading Hillary Rodham's hidden thesis" *NBCnews.com* (May 9, 2007)
http://www.nbcnews.com/id/17388372/ns/politics-decision_08/t/reading-hillary-rodhams-hidden-thesis/.
[22] Ibid. Alinsky, pg. 127.
[23] Ibid. Ryan.

little-known, but incredibly influential "Cloward-Piven Strategy" (CPS). "Developed by ... Andrew [sic, first name is Richard] Cloward and Frances Fox Piven, much of their strategy was drawn from Saul Alinsky.... [ACORN] succeeded the National Welfare Rights Organization in the execution of the [C-P] grand tactics of using the poor as cannon fodder to tear down the capitalist system. It was low-income, [24] mostly black and Hispanic people, who were used by ACORN guerrillas to take subprime toxic mortgages."[25]

The CPS paper, entitled: "The Weight of the Poor: A Strategy to End Poverty", was "based on the fact that a vast discrepancy exists between the benefits to which people are entitled under public welfare programs and the sums which they actually receive."[26]

C-P predicted in the very first paragraph of the paper that, "'[I]f this strategy were implemented, a political crisis would result that could lead to legislation for a guaranteed annual income and thus an end to poverty.' And, how did they profess to achieve this? By converging 'civil rights organizations, militant anti poverty groups and the poor'".[27]

What's interesting is that, in her introduction to the CPS paper recently in the very liberal magazine, *The Nation*, Piven felt compelled to include veiled excuses

[24] Ibid. Dedman.
[25] Robert Chandler. "CHANDLER: The Cloward-Piven strategy" *The Washington Times* (Oct. 15, 2008) https://www.washingtontimes.com/news/2008/oct/15/the-cloward-piven-strategy/.
[26] Frances Fox Piven "The Weight of the Poor: A Strategy to End Poverty" *The Nation* (March 8, 2010) https://www.thenation.com/article/weight-poor-strategy-end-poverty/.
[27] Ibid.

regarding the original intent of the study. "'Our objective was not', she insists, 'as later critics of the Glenn Beck variety later charged, to propose a strategy to bring down American capitalism. We were not so ambitious.'"[28]

Really? Let's examine a few assertions C-P made in the original paper.

The CPS called for "'...national programs to eliminate poverty by the outright redistribution of income.'"[29] Sounds an awful lot like socialism to me.

In an attempt to rationalize what the many poverty-stricken people could do if they found collective bargaining power out of reach, C-P wrote that a "'...federal program of income redistribution has become necessary to elevate the poor en masse from poverty.'"[30] Their strategy further asserts that, while several policies were under consideration in 1966, it was not their intention to assess those. However, whichever policy was adopted, they claimed, it "'must include certain features if it is not merely to perpetuate in a new guise the present evils of the public welfare system.'"[31] (I didn't realize my tax dollars were so evil. Next time I pay them, I'll be sure to remember that.)

Notwithstanding the audacity of C-P's language, they go on to demand various mechanisms be put in place for such new programs to be successful. "'First,' they insist, 'adequate levels of income must be assured. ... Second, the right to income must be guaranteed, or the oppression of the welfare poor will not be

---

[28] Ibid.
[29] Ibid.
[30] Ibid.
[31] Ibid.

eliminated.'"[32] Is it any wonder welfare recipients today feel so entitled? The language that leftists use couldn't be more divisive, or insulting, to both the "haves" and the "have-nots". Who, then, is really the "oppressor" here, the capitalists or the socialists? Let's find out.

In the sixties, when the CPS was written, the public welfare program came with conditions. C-P were offended that people '"have been coerced into attending literacy classes or participating in medical or vocational rehabilitation regimes, on pain of having their benefits terminated. Men are forced into labor on virtually any terms lest they forfeit their welfare aid.'"[33]

I don't know about you, but I'm astonished, not only with the content of what C-P write, but also with the words they use to describe it: "oppressed", "entitled", "coerced", "regimes", "pain", "forced". No wonder we're so divided today.

The scary part is what the CPS proves: this indoctrination has been taking place since at least 1966. That's a whole lot of confused people walking around today. Scarier still, is how propagandistic these professors are, *intentionally*. But, it gets even worse.

In the strategy paper, C-P explain how various cities are in need of complete overhauls. Can you guess which ones? While New York is the primary focus, Chicago, Cleveland, Newark and Detroit also top their list.

They cite several studies done in those cities that don't appear at all academic. They include plenty of figures, but very little in the way of concrete science. When describing the cities, C-P use a lot of statistics to

---

[32] Ibid.
[33] Ibid.

conclude the need for more welfare, but their research appears rudimentary, at best. Under a heading entitled, "Basic Assistance for food and rent," for example, the words "probably", "seems", and appears" are used multiple times to draw assertions.

Even more disturbing is that the means by which C-P suggest reaching the end goal for welfare recipients in 1966 are eerily similar to those used for illegal immigrants today: mass educational programs, advocacy groups, lawsuits, militant groups, etc. are the preferred actions to effect social change.

Don't get me wrong, I have lots of respect for those who want to help the down-trodden. I've been there myself; and, I've helped others along the way. But, the overall objective of the CPS, as laid out, leaves me more than a bit skeptical.

Hard to ignore, too, is the eventual history of New York City, given the programs C-P enacted to bloat its welfare rolls. The city's path to economic crisis began in the early 1960s, with Democratic Mayor Robert Wagner's flagrant spending and dubious bookkeeping practices.

The voters barely strayed from policies of the left when they voted for a liberal Republican named John Lindsay in 1965, who served two terms, further embroiling the city in reckless debt and bad accounting. In 1971, Lindsay switched party affiliations to run as a Democrat in the presidential election, but dropped out soon after due to lack of support.

New Yorkers had still not learned their lesson, again electing a big-spending Democrat as Mayor in 1974 named Abraham Beame. Soon after, the Mayor pressed then-President Gerald Ford for a bail-out to which Ford "made no secret of his feeling that New York had created its own problems, and that it was up to New York to solve them."[34] Leftists protested on a grand scale.

Driven almost to bankruptcy by 1975, "[U]rban economist Robert Poole subsequently assessed matters: 'New York City spent and spent, creating a vast city hospital system, a city university open to all at no charge, the highest welfare benefits in the country and a Civil Service system unparalleled in its solicitude toward employees all without concern for its increasingly hard-pressed taxpayers.'[35]

"The political backlash from the nation's mayors, from concerned members of Congress, from Democrats warming up for the 1976 elections was immediate. The [Ford] administration quickly entered into face-saving negotiations. A few weeks later, the government extended $2.3 billion in loans."[36] Of course, that was funded by taxpayer money.

As always, weak-kneed Republicans caved. Alinsky's first tactic, *"Power is not only what you have but what the enemy thinks you have"*, worked. Politicians, big corporations, banks, and others, run scared whenever the left threatens their positions or profits. That's a mistake the country is paying dearly for today. Our leaders are still making wrong-headed decisions under pressure from the left. Not giving in to pressure tactics for fear of losing votes is a lesson the right must learn. Bailing the left out every time their

[34] Richard E. Mooney. "Running on Empty: When New York City faced the consequences of financial finagling" *NY Daily News* (Oct 30, 1975) http://www.nydailynews.com/new-york/new-york-city-stared-big-town-bankruptcy-article-1.2984790#.
[35] Ibid.
[36] Ibid.

policies prove disastrous plays right into the left's hands. It's crazy policy and will further erode our rights. Freedom of speech, the right to bear arms, freedom of religion, to name a few, are under attack and require strong leadership to protect.

President Trump understands that, and is doing what he can to get our country back on track. Unfortunately, too many Republicans, especially never-Trumpers, are not. They are just as dangerous to our Republic as are leftists. It's up to Deplorables to stay strong in our support of Trump so he can return our country to a sensible direction.

The CPS openly states that, to "'generate an expressly political movement, cadres of aggressive organizers would have to come from the civil rights movement and the churches, from militant low-income organizations like those formed by the Industrial Areas Foundation (that is, by Saul Slinky [sic]), and from other groups on the Left.'"[37]

While the professors admit that previous similar movements have failed, they explain why they believe their strategy will not: "'[O]nce eligibility for basic food and rent grants is established', they project, 'the drain on local resources persists indefinitely'".[38] Are they trying to help people, or "drain" our country's resources? Don't worry, they've answered that, too.

Let's review what C-P have to say about how they expect to reach their goals. They've already told us *why:* once in the system, the welfare recipient stays there indefinitely. So, *how* will they make it happen?

---

[37] Ibid. Frances Fox Piven.
[38] Ibid.

Remember when Chicago's Mayor Rahm Emanuel (Obama's former chief of staff) was caught saying, "Never let a good crisis go to waste?" It caused an uproar on the right. He swears he didn't mean that he'd *create* a crisis, but rather would ensure that if one did happen to occur, he'd make the best of it. Right, Rahm.

Surely, Emanuel would agree with C-P's assessment that, "'[w]e ordinarily think of major legislation as taking form only through established electoral processes,'" the sociologists wrote (apparently referencing the concept of the rule of law as set forth by our prescient Founding Fathers). "'[W]e tend to overlook the force of crisis in precipitating legislative reform....'"[39]

Further, they claim that by "'crisis we mean a *publicly visible* [emphasis theirs] disruption in some institutional sphere. Crisis can occur spontaneously (e.g., riots) or as the intended result of tactics of demonstration and protest, which either generate institutional disruption or bring unrecognizable eruption to public attention.... Because crisis usually creates or exposes conflict, it threatens to produce cleavages in a political consensus which politicians would ordinarily act to avert.'"[40] They got that right.

"'When, however,'" C-P caution, "'a crisis is defined by its participants—or by other activated groups—as a matter of clear issues and preferred solutions, terms are imposed on the politicians' bid for their support.'"[41]

Is this what former President Obama had in mind when he told us he was going to *"fundamentally transform America"?* Did he have these "other activated

---

[39] Ibid.
[40] Ibid.
[41] Ibid.

groups" waiting, behind the scenes, after he left the White House? Is this how Antifa, Black Lives Matter and the "deep state' originated? Are the leftists really that evil? It's not a stretch for me to believe. If it is for you, and you stay open to facts, this book will change your opinions forever.

While it's no secret that blacks have been voting for Democrats in record numbers for a very long time, the left has been intentionally plotting for that group's allegiance for decades. Oftentimes, it was done to the minority's detriment with little concern for improvement in their lives. "'Democratic leadership', according to C–P, 'is alert to the importance of the urban Negro vote, especially in national contests where the loyalty of other urban groups is weakening. Indeed, they wrote, 'many of the legislative reforms of the Great Society can be understood as efforts, however feeble, to reinforce the allegiance of growing ghetto constituencies to the national Democratic Administration.'"[42]

As C–P observe, while the black community was growing more restless due to inaction by the Democratic Party, small concessions were keeping them at bay. The "ever-compassionate" C–P had an answer to the Democrat Party's apathy back then: create a crisis, of course.

"'Legislative measures to provide direct income to the poor would permit national Democratic leaders to cultivate ghetto constituencies without unduly antagonizing other urban groups, as is the case when

---

[42] Ibid.

30

the battle lines are drawn over schools, housing or jobs.'"[43] You have to admit, these leftists are organized.

Finally, C-P says it all in the last few sentences of their strategy. "'If organizers can deliver millions of dollars in cash benefits to the ghetto masses, it seems reasonable to expect that the masses will deliver their loyalties to their benefactors. At least, they have always done so in the past.'"[44]

How successful, then, was the former community-organizer-turned-president, Barack Obama, in his eight years in the White House with the all-important lessons from Saul Alinsky and C-P? Not very.

While Obama proved adept at creating numerous crises in order to get new laws passed (i.e., the Fast and Furious operation), like so many attempts under his leadership to further the left's cause, he utterly failed with major legislation, like gun-control.

Federal welfare spending, on the other hand, was another matter. Not a surprise, given that is a community organizer's area of expertise. "'[S]ince President Obama took office, federal welfare spending ... increased by 41 percent, more than $193 billion per year,' according to a study by the Cato Institute in 2012. [P]art of the program's growth is due to conscious policy choices by [Obama's] Administration to ease eligibility rules and expand caseloads."[45] That's straight out of the C-P strategy paper. But, the "federal government is not making much headway reducing poverty", the article

---

[43] Ibid.
[44] Ibid.
[45] Matt Cover. "Study: More Than Half a Trillion Dollars Spent on Welfare But Poverty Levels Unaffected". *CNS News* (June 25, 2012) https://www.cnsnews.com/news/article/study-more-half-trillion-dollars-spent-welfare-poverty-levels-unaffected.

continues. "The poverty rate has remained relatively constant since 1965, despite rising welfare spending."[46]

Obama assured his supporters in '08 that in "*five days, you can turn the page on policies that put greed and irresponsibility on Wall Street before the hard work and sacrifice of folks on Main Street.*" That sounds great, but, "[W]ith Obama as president, the U.S. stock market, as measured by the S&P 500, returned 235%, or 16.4% annualized...trouncing the stock market of his presidential predecessor, George W. Bush, which fell 30.6% from January 20, 2001 to January 20, 2009."[47]

We can chalk that up as one for Wall Street.

Not surprisingly, given Obama's aversion to all things non-renewable, oil and natural gas stocks plummeted. But, with "the Obama Administration providing solar subsidies ... the largest U.S. solar equipment producer" fell 74%. This was totally unexpected by his supporters since Obama, "has particularly promoted solar energy".[48]

The left doesn't understand that renewable energy is preferred by a majority of Americans, it's just not feasible yet, nor is it affordable by the average person. No amount of strong-arming by the radical left politicians, out to win votes, is going to make it any more so. Not even someone as persuasive as Obama.

Promises made, promises broken.

How about Obama's second promise during that campaign speech: *"In five days, you can choose policies*

---

[46] Ibid.
[47] Nathan Vardi. "Inside the Obama Stock Market's 235% Return" *Forbes* (Jan. 17, 2017) https://www.forbes.com/sites/nathanvardi/2017/01/17/inside-the-obama-stock-markets-235-rise/#2af597f816d1.
[48] Ibid.

that invest in our middle class"? According to an article by the extreme far left magazine, *Jacobin*, Obama dismally failed the middle class. They say that, "the nation's first African-American president was a disaster for black wealth."[49] *Ouch.*

Indeed, *Jacobin Magazine* puts the blame squarely on Obama, attributing the failures to lax oversight from his Treasury Department and DOJ, going so far as to call their actions "chicanery" and "illegal". "The Administration's aim," they assert, "was to 'foam the runway' for the banks"; and, they offer compelling evidence that such Obama's top aides as Elizabeth Warren knew it. "Obama's approach failed cataclysmically", according to *Jacobin*."[50] *Double ouch.*

Promises made, promises broken.

The above-noted article strengthens the case as to why black Americans' support for President Trump doubled in his first two years.

Surely, President Obama succeeded in keeping his third promise, regarding jobs, made during his Missouri campaign speech. It seemed simple enough given the condition of the economy when he first entered the White House. There was really only one way for jobs to go but up, right? Not so, if you're a leftist. All Obama had to do, after all, was to *"create new jobs"*. He didn't say by how many, or how fast. He just said he'd do it.

"Huge numbers of jobs were destroyed from 2008 to 2009", according to an article in Forbes, "...and since

---

[49] Matt Bruenig and Ryan Cooper. "How Obama Destroyed Black Wealth" *Jacobin Magazine* (December, 2017) https://jacobinmag.com/2017/12/obama-foreclosure-crisis-wealth-inequality.
[50] Ibid.

then there has been disappointingly slow job creation." The writer points to "Economic Innovation Group figures showing that net new businesses fell from 421,000 (1992-1996) and 405,000 (2002-2006) to 166,500 (2010-2014). That indicates a shocking decline...."[51]

The author goes on to explain why the sluggish job growth occurred under President Obama. "Higher federal tax rates have hurt, and high-tax states have seen businesses flee to low-tax places such as Texas. Taking money away from existing enterprises and potential entrepreneurs to pay for skyrocketing pensions for retired public-employee union members is not a recipe for job growth." Additionally, the author blames Obama's over-regulating businesses, higher minimum wages, increased benefits and leave time.[52]

While other sources are more kind, claiming Obama did have job growth, we'll rate this one: promises made, promises, barely kept.

How about Obama's promise to *"grow this economy"?* "One of the biggest criticisms of Obama's economy is that growth has been so slow. Historically, the U.S. economy has expanded 3% or more a year, on average," according to *CNN Money.* The author concedes that the "Great Recession was a meat-cleaver on the economy. Since then, the U.S. has struggled to grow at much more than 2% a year under President

---

[51] Michael Barone. "Why We Have - and Probably Will Keep Having - Sluggish Job Growth" *National Review* (June 20, 2016) https://www.nationalreview.com/2016/06/job-creation-economic-growth-under-obama-slow/.
[52] Ibid.

Obama."[53] Never in the history of our country has any president grown our GDP at less than 2% for every year in office.

I get it that Obama inherited a recession. But, how does that explain that, in his last quarter in office after eight years, the GDP fell to 1.6%? That he and his supporters are trying to take success from President Trump's GDP success is almost laughable given Obama's under-performance.

Even so, I'll rate this as promises made, promises sort-of, kind-of kept.

Did Obama come through on his promise that everyone would have *"a chance to succeed, not just the CEO, but the secretary and janitor, not just the factory owner, but the men and women on the factory floor"? FactCheck* sums it up nicely: "Corporations did much better than workers during Obama's time".[54]

Promises, promises.

Still, I'm sure Frances Fox Piven was giddy at Obama's increased spending on welfare programs. Had Hillary taken the reigns, instead of Trump, no doubt in my mind we'd be a lot closer to socialism today.

A lot of Obama's legacy is now being dismantled, thanks to Trump. Not because Obama didn't try. In fact, he got very close to succeeding in totally transforming America. The only reason Obama's goals are slipping away is because his methods were weak.

---

[53] Heather Long. "The Obama economy in 10 charts", *CNN Money* https://money.cnn.com/gallery/news/economy/2017/01/06/obama-economy-10-charts-final/3.html.
[54] Brooke Jackson. "Obama's Final Numbers" *FactCheck.org* (Sept. 29, 2017) https://www.factcheck.org/2017/09/obamas-final-numbers/.

Obama refused to follow long-held Constitutional tenets and, instead of getting his legislation passed through Congress, he shoved it down the American peoples' throats with the click of a pen. (Remember his flippant, *"I've got a pen, and I've got a phone"* quip?) Thanks to his arrogance, we are now witnessing the systematic reversal of every one of his destructive executive orders and regulations. The rule of law is the only thing that prevents America from becoming a banana republic.

Obama was handed a lot of power when Americans gave him the White House twice. Deplorables understood the damage he did. Fortunately for us, he was weak, both domestically and globally. The power he was given was just an illusion. A stronger candidate could have destroyed our democracy in eight years. Luckily, America has been given yet one more chance to save herself.

Complacency is the real enemy in the political landscape today. Americans can't sleep through the election of 2020. The price is too great. The 2018 midterms gave the left the House majority and now Trump will have more pushback, more investigations, less legislation and more interference. Even with all those fighting him from so many directions in his first two years, Trump is just getting warmed up.

The left understands that *"power is not only what [they] have but what the enemy [Republicans] think [they] have"*. If Republicans continue to be conned into believing the left holds more power than they actually do, the left already wins. Recognizing that the power the left threatens over the right is many times more powerful than the actual power they hold, is only half the battle. We must stand up to them, no matter how insignificant or ridiculous their demands may seem.

President Trump knows this tactic well and uses it masterfully against the left. Especially when he derides those trying to hurt him by publicly calling them out. The only problem is that Republicans who should be on his side, the "holier-than-thou", never-Trumpers like Mitt Romney, Bob Corker and Jeff Flake, turn on Trump and diminish his power. That's insane. Never-Trumpers and those in the "swamp" don't understand the gravity of what's at stake. If they do not pull together and support Trump in the next two years, they'll be more to blame for our country's demise than anyone on the left.

When we allow the Dems to get away with the tiniest of leftist triumphs, we strengthen their power and allow them to further erode our freedoms. Make no mistake about it, our freedoms are exactly what's at stake.

If you don't believe me, read Chapter Two, "Viva la Revolución". You'll learn that the left's master plan is to destroy our democratic way of life and replace it with a socialistic, even communistic, society. Before you laugh, read on to find out who in Venezuela isn't laughing now.

VIVA LA REVOLUCIÓN

TACTIC #2: *"Never go outside the experience of your people."*[55]

"'UNEMPLOYMENT IS LOW BECAUSE everyone has two jobs,' protested self-described Democratic Socialist Alexandria Ocasio-Cortez (AOC) during an interview on the PBS show Firing Line. *'Unemployment is low because people are working 60, 70, 80 hours a week and can barely feed their family.'"*[56]

Not surprisingly, *Politifact's* "Truth-O-Meter" rated the newly-elected, U.S. Congresswoman from Bronx, New York, off-the-charts, "Pants on Fire". *Politifact* notes that "by the official statistics, multiple job holders account for a tiny fraction of American workers" and "the people working 70 or 80 hours a week amount to a tiny percentage...."[57] Democratic National Committee chair, Tom Perez, called the 28-year-old, who was barely heard of less than a week before, "'the future of our

---

[55] Ibid. Alinsky, pg. 127.
[56] Louis Jacobson. "Alexandria Ocasio-Cortez wrong on several counts about unemployment." *Politifact*
https://www.politifact.com/truth-o-meter/statements/2018/jul/18/alexandria-ocasio-cortez/alexandria-ocasio-cortez-wrong-several-counts-abou/.
[57] Ibid.

Party.'"[58] During the following months, the Dems paraded her around as their newest secret weapon. They apparently had forgotten Alinsky's Tactic #2: *"Never go outside the experience of your people"* ... it causes fear, confusion and retreat. That oversight may cost them dearly.

AOC has been flubbing facts on almost every appearance since her win in July, 2018. When she called Palestine a "state", it was shrugged off by the left because she is only a local representative from a very small district and is young, after all. *Really?*

I'd let that slide if it weren't so alarming that the college graduate, like a lot of millennials, has been indoctrinated by left-wing, liberal professors who have re-written American history to suit their ideologies, or they don't teach it at all. That's just plain dangerous.

With AOC's primary defeat of one of the Dems' highest ranking members, the radical left became emboldened. This could become a rift in the party that may not be repairable. Ignorance like hers may be just what Republicans need to win in 2020.

I wasn't surprised to learn that AOC graduated from the liberal Boston University. While there, she was a strong proponent for social justice. I literally laughed out loud, however, upon learning she received her degrees in economics and international relations![59] Her

---

[58] Aleza Relman. "The chair of the Democratic Party just embraced Progressive insurgent Alexandria Ocasio-Cortez, calling her 'the future of our party'" *Business Insider* (July 3, 2018). https://www.businessinsider.com/dnc-tom-perez-alexandria-ocasio-cortez-democratic-socialist-future-2018-7.
[59] Alana Levee. "Alexandria Ocasio-Cortez Championed social justice at Boston University" *The Globe* https://www.bostonglobe.com/news/politics/2018/06/27/alexandri

comments in both areas have been dead wrong. While I admire her enthusiasm and sheer guts, I fear her naïveté and sway over other millennials who may hold a romantic view of socialism.

Because of the indoctrination of college students for decades, there are millions of AOC think-a-likes, whose main goal is to establish socialism in capitalism's place. They're out to take Obama's *"transformation of America"* one step further to the left. You think I'm exaggerating?

The coming years will be a fight for our freedoms that have already been so damaged by eight years of Obama. With the indoctrinated millennials coming of age, our intelligence agencies, educational institutions and the media will become even more populated by utopian socialists. This dangerous shift is going to take a generation or more to reverse, if it's even possible.

According to a disturbing article from the *Daily Wire* recently, "professors at 51 of the 66 top-ranked liberal arts colleges in the U.S. published by the National Association of Scholars found that the ratio of faculty members registered as Democrats compared to those registered Republican is now a stunning 10.4 to 1."[60] Even more alarming is "that nearly 40% of the colleges in the study had zero faculty members who were registered Republican. Not a single one. Nearly 80% of

---

a-ocasio-cortez-championed-social-justice-boston-university/hijSs266a6aQe6cSR1E1ul/story.html.
[60] James Barrett. "How Politically Biased Are Colleges? New Study Finds It's Far Worse Than Anybody Thought" *Daily Wire* (May 9, 2018) https://www.dailywire.com/news/30222/how-politically-biased-are-universities-new-study-james-barrett/

the 51 colleges had so few Republican faculty members that they were statistically insignificant."[61] Parents should think hard before sending their child to one of these biased institutions. Many realize their mistake when, four years and a fortune later, their kid returns as a brainwashed leftist. They come home looking for socialist causes on which to waste the very education their parents worked so hard to give them.

Take time to research your alma mater before making donations, too. Find out if it's hiring liberal professors and backing programs that turn our next generation into "Snowflakes". You could, unknowingly, be contributing to the destruction of our country.

The good news is that some parents are already responding. "Evergreen State College enrollment plummeted after fallout from the controversial 'Day of Absence' in May 2017 when all white people were asked to leave the campus."[62] The situation worsened when a self-described, "deeply progressive", professor at the *publicly-funded* college questioned the event. He "ultimately lost his job and was labeled a 'racist' and 'white supremacist'"[63] Ironic, since he is the very type professor who has contributed to the left's craziness propagated on college campuses today.

Tucker Carlson, of *FOX News*, deserves our thanks for bringing this subject to our attention. If you haven't watched his show, especially the segment called

---

[61] Ibid.
[62] Caleb Parke. "Evergreen State see's 'catastrophic' drop in enrollment after social justice meltdown" *FoxNews.com* (Sept. 12, 2018) http://www.foxnews.com/us/2018/09/12/evergreen-state-sees-catastrophic-drop-in-enrollment-after-social-justice-meltdown.html.
[63] Ibid.

"Campus Craziness", I highly recommend it. You'll be alarmed at the current state of our educational system. I predict a drop in college enrollments for decades to come. Specialty trade schools and conservative-backed, private institutions will become the preferred path for students. They provide better educations for critical thinkers who will face little competition from "Snowflakes" entering the workplace.

Hillsdale College, for example, which follows a secular approach, and Biola University, more Judeo-Christian, are excellent examples of those that will see increasing growth in enrollments. That will only hold true, however, if the left's march to socialism is totally exposed. Once its spread becomes better understood, more parents will take notice and ensure their kids get balanced educations, for the same reasons home-schooling became popular.

Donald Trump Jr., the President's son, spoke for a lot of us when he tweeted on August 9, 2018, about the newly-elected Democratic Socialist Ocasio-Cortez: "OMG this is insane and yet the liberal campaign to make her the rockstar [sic] face of the left will continue...let's face it, I guess they don't have much else. It's amazing the illusions libs can create with the MSM [Mainstream Media] in their back pocket...." Is AOC an anomaly?

Glenn Beck was once my favorite radio personality, before he became a never-Trumper. He taught me a lot about critical thinking in politics. Recently, Beck was quoted by *Jacobin Magazine* writer for DSA, Meagan Day. "'Democratic Socialists will not be covered as the radicals that they are,' Glenn Beck said on his show. 'They'll be covered as 'innovative, millennial-friendly upstarts with fresh ideas' when they are really diet-Communism.'"[64]

In her article, Day responded to Beck's comments: "In the long run, democratic socialists want to end capitalism. And we want to do that by pursuing a reform agenda today in an effort to revive a politics focused on class hierarchy and inequality in the United States. The eventual goal is to transform the world to promote everyone's needs rather than to produce massive profits for a small handful of citizens."[65]

That is the true goal of DSA. They've been moving our country ever closer to global socialism for decades, with America as the piggy bank. We'll be brought down to third world status and the poor will become worse off without U.S. support. Americans are way behind in their understanding of this movement.

To further understand the DSA, I googled the word 'Jacobin', the name of the liberal magazine quoted from above. What I found astounded me. *Merriam-Webster Dictionary* defines it as: "a member of an extremist or radical political group; *especially:* a member of such a group advocating egalitarian democracy and engaging in terrorist activities during the French Revolution of 1789".

Since that sounded rather ominous, I went straight to an encyclopedic definition. During times of economic hardship, the impoverished French population were growing increasingly impatient with

---

[64] Meagan Day. "Democratic socialism, explained by a democratic socialist" *VOX* (August 1, 2018)
https://www.vox.com/first-person/2018/8/1/17637028/bernie-sanders-alexandria-ocasio-cortez-cynthia-nixon-democratic-socialism-jacobin-dsa.
[65] Ibid.

King Louis XVI. Seeking to limit his powers, a "resistance" grew. The Jacobins were one such political group, led by Maximilien Robespierre, and "were the most radical and ruthless of the political groups formed in the wake of the French Revolution ... [and were] responsible for the Reign of Terror of 1793-4."[66] Isn't that comforting?

The Jacobins' main opponent was a more moderate group called the Girondins, who felt that the final decision about the king's punishment should be left to majority rule. Robespierre disagreed. The Jacobins' Reign of Terror left many dead, including counter-revolutionaries like the Girondins. Eventually, Robespierre was himself turned against and executed.

Today's DSA mirrors that of the Jacobins. *Jacobin Magazine* explains that, "[A]ddressing the Assemblee nationale on December 28, 1792, Robespierre claimed that, in attesting to the truth, any invocation of a majority or minority is nothing but a means of reducing 'to silence those whom one designated by this term ... [The] minority has everywhere an eternal right: to render audible the voice of truth.' It is deeply significant that Robespierre made this statement in the *Assemblee* apropos the trial of the king. The Girondins had proposed a 'democratic' solution: in such a difficult case, it was necessary to make an 'appeal to the people', to convoke local assemblies across France and ask them

---

66 Encyclopedia.com. *Oxford University Press* (2006) https://www.encyclopedia.com/history/modern-europe/french-history/jacobins.

to vote on how to deal with the king – only such a move could give legitimacy to the trial."[67]

Jacobins believed that their minority vote should prevail because their "truth" was the real truth. Their opponents, the Girondins, believed in majority rule. Once achieving control through violence, not surprisingly, the Jacobins did not allow a democratic rule of law. They evolved into a rule of terror and dictatorship. Recall the left's de-legitimatization of President Trump's election and Justice Kavanaugh's confirmation and you'll begin to see the similarities.

While many Conservatives believe the same could never happen in our society, it already has. Just as the Jacobin membership exploded after the king's capture, DSA grew from 6,000 prior to Trump's election, to over 45,000 a year and a half later.[68] The left had much to do with that growth by their demonization of Trump.

DSA, and a growing shift towards minority rule, was exactly how Obamacare divided the American people. Then-President Obama and Dems made it sound great. Who wouldn't want free health care, or at a reduced cost? And, everyone knows somebody with a pre-existing condition. Trump and his supporters also agree that it's inhumane to deny coverage. So, what's not to like about what they told us we could get? Try the fine print. As Nancy Pelosi so famously said, "we have to pass the [health care] bill so that you can find out what's in it." What the Obama Administration purposely omitted

---

[67] Slavoj Zizek. "The Jacobin Spirit" *Jacobin Magazine* (May 26, 2011) https://www.jacobinmag.com/2011/05/the-jacobin-spirit.

[68] Steve Peoples. "Democratic socialism on the rise in the Trump era" *The Christian Science Monitor* (July 23, 2018) https://www.csmonitor.com/USA/Politics/2018/0723/Democratic-socialism-on-the-rise-in-the-Trump-era.

telling the American people was that price increases for premiums would be phased in so they wouldn't hit until after he left office. Also, many more young folks "opted out" than was expected for the plan to succeed, something the Obama administration didn't anticipate. Predictably, premiums for the ACA have skyrocketed.

Topping the list of DSA's priorities is single-payer health care (100% government-controlled). Joining Bernie Sanders in supporting this goal are some of 2020's biggest Democratic presidential contenders: Senators Kamala Harris, Elizabeth Warren, Cory Booker and Kristen Gillibrand, among others. "A key author of the Affordable Care Act [ACA], former Sen. Max Baucus of Montana, also supports it."[69] Americans had been promised again and again that the ACA would never become single-payer.

` In 2009, for example, Obama told the American Medical Association, "'[W]hen you hear the naysayers claim that I'm trying to bring about government-run health care, know this. They are not telling the truth".[70] Yet in 2018, in a speech in Illinois, he told his audience that Democrats are now "'running on good new ideas like Medicare for all.'"[71] In other words, single-payer. Obama lied to get the ACA passed. The article rightfully asserts that, "Democrats really did view Obamacare as a stepping stone to single-payer healthcare. This is also

---

[69] Ibid.
[70] "EDITORIAL: Obama reverses on Medicare-for-all" *Las Vegas Review-Journal* (Sept. 10, 2018)
https://www.reviewjournal.com/opinion/editorials/editorial-obama-reverses-on-medicare-for-all/.
[71] Ibid.

evidence that Obama knew his 'if you like your health care plan, you can keep it' line was a lie from the start."[72]

There is plenty of evidence that single-payer was Obama's real goal. Lying to the American people by the left is an acceptable part of their strategy. It follows Alinsky's mantra, "by any means necessary." Republicans must stop allowing rational thinking to guide their compromises with the Dems. There is no logic to their madness, except power. Former Attorney General Jeff Sessions fell into that trap, as have Senators Ben Sasse, Mitt Romney, and former Senators Jeff Flake and Bob Corker. It's just plain naïve. Thanks to never-Trump Republicans, given their majority in Congress under Trump's first two years, the opportunity to stop single-payer has come and gone ... possibly, forever.

In 2017, the very liberal California State Senate "passed a single-payer bill without a plan to pay for it. That was a concern, because the nonpartisan Legislative Analyst's Office estimated it would cost $400 billion a year. That's more than double California's budget. To pay for its share of that tab, around $200 billion, California would have needed to increase its sales tax from 8.5 percent to almost 37 percent. The Democrat Assembly speaker eventually had to pull the bill."[73] Together with current sales taxes already collected, single-payer health care would have cost Californians a whopping 45.5 percent of every purchase they make! Maybe economist Ocasio-Cortez can explain that one.

The real tragedy is that an Independent Payment Advisory Board (IPAB) would surely be included in a

---

[72] Ibid.
[73] Ibid.

single-payer system. It's often called a death panel because "[t]he unelected 15-member board would ultimately have the power to cut Medicare spending without Congressional review, impacting the health access of more than 55 million seniors".[74]

Doug Schoen, Democratic political strategist, had this to say about the unfairness of an IPAB: "I have long been a critic of IPAB because it takes the Medicare decision-making process away from doctors and gives it to an unelected, unaccountable advisory board of bureaucrats. IPAB also threatens the quality of medical treatments and services for Medicare beneficiaries."[75]

Imagine if, for cost-cutting purposes, an IPAB decided to discontinue paying for open-heart surgeries for all those over the age of 70. Countless Americans have had those surgeries at that age and continue to live productive, happy lives for another ten years or more. If, however, an IPAB votes to end that medical necessity to save older people's lives, they would die much earlier. While the Republicans failed to repeal and replace the ACA, as promised to voters, they were able to, at least, kill the IPAB amendment in early 2018.

Even the AARP advised against an IPAB citing a similar model in Britain. "The British health system has a controversial board with exactly that kind of power...older people would be unwise to allow a strong, unelected board to take the place of their doctor in

---

[74] Hadley Heath Manning. "There's still time to repeal, replace ObamaCare's Medicare board" *The Hill* (Nov. 2, 2017) https://thehill.com/opinion/healthcare/358307-theres-still-time-to-repeal-replace-obamacares-medicare-board.
[75] Doug Schoen. "Now is the Time to Finally Get Rid of IPAB" *Forbes* https://www.forbes.com/sites/dougschoen/2017/09/14/now-is-the-time-to-finally-get-rid-of-ipab/#64450e786f2d.

deciding what the best treatment is. The question is who gets to decide how a reined-in Medicare budget will be spent. ...It means the government decides what your doctor will be paid and, ultimately, what health care you will get. The alternative vision has no board because each older person would have the right to decide either which health plan, or which doctor and hospital, will get that person's portion of the Medicare budget."[76]

You don't have to be in your sunset years to fear a death panel. In October, 2016, a British couple's newborn baby, named Charlie, was diagnosed with a rare genetic disease. An American neurosurgeon offered an experimental treatment that would not only have given the boy a small chance of survival, but would have also given him relief from suffering. The parents raised enough money, through private donations to GoFundMe, to pay all costs for little Charlie to travel to the U.S. and receive the treatment. Unfortunately, it wasn't the parents' decision to make. British "doctors and the government [wouldn't] let the eight-month-old out [of the London hospital], defying his parents' wishes and insisting he be transferred to end-of-life care."[77]

Little Charlie died soon after. Yet, somehow the Dems profess to be the humane ones. You can bet death

---

[76] Stuart Butler Ph.D. "Option: Strengthen the Independent Payment Advisory Board (IPAB)" *AARP* (June 7, 2012) https://www.aarp.org/content/dam/aarp/research/public_policy_ins titute/health/option-strengthen-the-independent-payment-advisory-board-AARP-ppi-health.pdf.

[77] Selwyn Duke. "This 8-Month-Old British Baby Is Getting a Death Sentence" *Observer* (May 2, 2017) https://observer.com/2017/05/chris-gard-connie-yates-baby-charlie-mitochondrial-depletion-syndrome/.

panels won't be just for granny when a single-payer system is adopted by a pro-DSA Democratic Party.

Code words were once used by the radical left to conceal their true socialist agenda. Now, they no longer hide their goals. That is a scary testament to how close they believe they are to achieving their ideology.

Just listen to the words of self-described, DSA member, Megan Day: "So why are democratic socialists not demanding an NHS [National Health System, like in Britain] right now? Because", she answers with no equivocation, "we currently don't have the support to push for and win such an ambitious program. Social democratic reforms like Medicare-for-all are, in the eyes of DSA, part of the long, uneven process of building that support, and eventually overthrowing capitalism."[78]

"The prerequisite for an ideology," Alinsky writes, "is possession of a basic truth. For example, a Marxist begins with his prime truth that all evils are caused by the exploitation of the proletariat by the capitalists. From this he logically proceeds to the revolution to end capitalism, then into the third stage of reorganization into a new social order or the dictatorship of the proletariat, and finally the last stage – the political paradise of communism."[79] We are already in stage two.

Alinsky's *"[T]enth rule of the ethics of means and ends is that you do what you can with what you have and clothe it with moral garments"*. To prove his point, he quotes Lenin: "'The task of the Bolsheviks is to overthrow the Imperialist Government. But this government rests upon the support of the Social

---

[78] Ibid. Meagan Day.
[79] Ibid. Alinsky, pg. 10.

51

Revolutionaries and Mensheviks, who in turn are supported by the trustfulness of the masses of people. We are in a minority. In these circumstances there can be no talk of violence on our side.' The essence of Lenin's speeches during this period was 'They have the guns and therefore we are for peace and reformation through the ballot. When we have the guns then it will be through the bullet.' And it was."[80]

Lenin's brutality, once in power, set the stage for the mass genocide created by his even crueler successor, Stalin. "A Soviet weekly newspaper [in 1989] published the most detailed accounting of Stalin's victims yet, ... indicating that about 20 million died in labor camps, forced collectivization, famine and executions."[81]

Throughout history, the end result of socialism has been communism and dictatorship. DSA's recent explosive growth should concern us all. But it won't, unless you consider the plight of another once-wealthy capitalist country that followed Alinsky's tactics.

Once the richest country in Latin America, Venezuelans voted for a new leader in the late 1990s. Hugo Chavez promised everything for free, much like the DSA are doing now. Ocasio-Cortez and her Democratic Socialist comrades (Kirsten Gillibrand, Elizabeth Warren, Bernie Sanders, Keith Ellison and Kamala Harris, to name a few) are touting free college and health care, a raise in the minimum wage, free

---

[80] Ibid. Alinsky. pp. 36–37.
[81] Bill Keller. "Major Soviet Paper Says 20 Million Died As Victims of Stalin" *The New York Times* (Feb. 4, 1989) https://www.nytimes.com/1989/02/04/world/major-soviet-paper-says-20-million-died-as-victims-of-stalin.html.

income, guaranteed jobs, etc. Not once have I seen a plan on how they intend to pay for these freebies. But that didn't stop Venezuelan voters either. The majority voted for Chavez and within several years, his government took over control of the oil industry, source of the country's major wealth, and ran it into the ground. Chavez also socialized the media, educational system, health care, private industries, and the military. By the time people woke up, it was too late. They watched helplessly as their country became so poor that today they are reduced to eating grass (literally) because food is so scarce; and, they can't even find toilet paper except on the black market.[82] We aren't far behind if we don't wake up soon. Think that can't happen here?

Aside from positioning our health care to become single-payer once they gain enough control, the left has already flooded our universities with radical professors, most of whom are tenured, so it's nearly impossible to fire them. The "fake news" media is entrenched with a majority of leftist sympathizers, too. Our military and intelligence agencies were drained of Conservatives and replaced with leftists, like former CIA Director John Brennan, under Obama. If the Dems succeed in stripping us of our gun rights, which is exactly what they are determined to do through gun control, any chance to save our country will be gone forever.

Hitler understood the power of removing guns from German citizens prior to WWII. "As has been typical of tyrannies since the dawn of time, arms prohibition has

---

[82] Patrick Gillespie, Marilia Brocchetto and Paula Newton. "Venezuela: How a rich country collapsed" *CNN Money*
https://money.cnn.com/2017/07/26/news/economy/venezuela-economic-crisis/index.html.

aided in the suppression of dissent."[83] Under Hitler's regime, it is now estimated that up to 20 million died. Venezuelan dictator Chavez understood the importance of gun control for his survival, too. Under the guise of controlling crime in "2012, the communist-dominated Venezuelan National Assembly enacted the 'Control of Arms, Munitions and Disarmament Law.' The bill's stated objective was to 'disarm all citizens.' The new law prohibited all gun sales, except to government entities. The penalty for illegally selling or carrying a firearm is a prison sentence of up to 20 years."[84] The citizens' opportunity to defend their country ended that day. Chavez's successor, Nicolas Maduro, beefed up citizen militias loyal to his regime who now behave like the "Brownshirts" of Hitler's day. They're heavily armed, as is the military. Most have become the criminals, robbing innocent civilians and murdering dissenters.

Climate change is another great example. Does the climate change? Of course it does. Is that change caused by man? Probably. To what degree remains debatable. We must be careful not to create millions of deaths by disastrous, irresponsible agricultural and economic policies, as happened under Stalin and Mao Zedong. Together, they account for over 100 million deaths.

At the United Nations Climate Change Conference in Copenhagen in 2009, Chavez unapologetically told a reporter, "We must reduce all the emissions that are destroying the planet. However, that requires a change

---

[83] David Kopel and Vincent Harinam. "In the wake of a gun ban, Venezuela sees rising homicide rate" *The Hill* (April 19, 2018) https://thehill.com/opinion/campaign/383968-in-the-wake-of-a-gun-ban-venezuela-sees-rising-homicide-rate.
[84] Ibid.

in lifestyle, a change in the economic model: We must go from capitalism to socialism."[85] When the reporter asked how much emissions he was willing to reduce, Chavez answered, "100%"! When she asked how he believed capitalism would be replaced by socialism, he replied, "[T]he way they did it in Cuba.... The same way we are doing it in Venezuela: giving the power to the people and taking it away from the economic elites. You can only do that through a revolution."[86]

Alinsky would have agreed. In his book, he referenced Abraham Lincoln's statement of May 19, 1856: "'Be not deceived. Revolutions do not go backward.'"[87] We would all be wise to keep that in mind.

A look at history, however, tells us that Chavez's idol, Cuba, didn't fare too well by replacing capitalism. "After decades of relying on Moscow for oil, chemical fertilisers, pesticides and a large chunk of its food, Fidel Castro's government faced a crisis. The economy shrank and strict food rationing was imposed. There was an acute shortage of fuel for tractors. Calorie intake fell by a third. The Cuban government responded by creating urban farms: agriculture went local, small scale and – by necessity – organic. Food production became less oil-intensive, as every possible scrap of land was exploited ... Cuba provides [a] sketch of what could be in store if the transition from a fossil fuel world to one running on

[85] Amy Goodman. "VIDEO: Venezuelan President Hugo Chávez on Climate Change: 'We Must Go from Capitalism to Socialism' *Democracy Now* https://www.democracynow.org/2012/12/12/video_venezuelan_president_hugo_chavez_on_climate_change_we_must_go_from_capitalism_to_socialism.
[86] Ibid.
[87] Ibid. Alinsky, pg. 10.

renewable energy does not go according to plan.... The grow-your-own drive has only been partially successful: a quarter of a century later, food is still rationed in Cuba."[88]

As the youngest Congresswoman ever elected, new darling of the left, Ms. Ocasio-Cortez, was pushing hard for socialist policies even before her first day on Capitol Hill. "In a draft resolution to create a House select committee that would be responsible for writing the Green New Deal legislation, [AOC] outlines the primary goals of her plan. Among them, [she] proposes eliminating all fossil-fuel-powered electricity, closing every coal and natural gas power plant in the country, thus destroying the hundreds of thousands of jobs related to these businesses. Even more stunning, all this would occur by 2030, just 10 years after [she] expects the legislation to be completed.

"In its place, nearly all energy would be produced by renewable sources of power, especially wind and solar. This goal would create massive economic harm.

"Although economists have yet to provide an analysis of [AOC's] proposal to eliminate all fossil fuels, other studies have found less-extreme policies would be absolutely devastating. A study published in October 2018 by Capital Alpha Partners on behalf of the Institute for Energy Research found a national tax on carbon dioxide would cost the U.S. economy $4.21 trillion to $5.98 trillion, depending on the tax level chosen, in just the first 10 years of the tax scheme. By 2040, as much

---

[88] Larry Elliott. "Can the world economy survive without fossil fuels? *The Guardian* (April 8, 2015) https://www.theguardian.com/news/2015/apr/08/can-world-economy-survive-without-fossil-fuels.

as $12.32 trillion would be lost. Nearly one-quarter of the country's GDP, relative to what it would otherwise be, could be lost as a result of a nationwide carbon-dioxide tax. And this far left-wing plan is nowhere near as radical as Ocasio-Cortez's Green New Deal."[89]

We live in dangerous times which require extreme measures to correct this socialist trend if we want to hold on to the Republic so generously given us by our Founding Fathers. President Trump recognizes that and, thank God, he's in office. I truly believe he's our last best chance of reversing this trend. But, he can't do it without our support. We can't fall victim to the sinister plots of the left who want to keep our attention focused on what they want us to believe are Trump's "faults". Don't buy it. Trump understands the left well; and, everything he is doing tells me he is fighting them at every front on our behalf. It's up to us whether or not we really want to keep our Republic the way it was designed to be.

The good news is that the left is not only transparent now, they are a product of their own design. Their constituents, and colleagues, have been dumbed down by the left's ideologies and tactics. Now that the Dems have won back the majority of the House, their leaders have a helluva mess on their hands trying to keep their newest, far-left members under control. It's becoming more difficult for Dems to "*[n]ever go outside the expertise of [their] people*", because it exposes the true intent of the left. AOC and her like-minded radicals,

---

[89] Justin Haskins. "If Ocasio-Cortez's 'Green New Deal' succeeds in 2019 it will be the most radical plan offered in decades" *FOX News* (Dec. 31, 2018) https://www.foxnews.com/opinion/if-ocasio-cortezs-green-new-deal-succeeds-in-2019-it-will-be-the-most-radical-plan-offered-in-decades.

have successfully divided the Dems in two. That is a gift for Republicans. It's up to Conservatives now to demand that our Congress, men and women, call the Dems out for their socialist agendas.

Trump needs all the help he can get, as you'll discover in the following chapter: "Collusion Delusion". Never have I witnessed a president so falsely attacked from so many directions. When you find out how Trump has been set up with the Russia–Trump collusion witch hunt, since before he was even elected, you'll realize just how much danger our Republic is in.

COLLUSION DELUSION

TACTIC #3: *"Whenever possible, go outside of the experience of the enemy."*[90]

'"SHOW ME THE MAN and I'll show you the crime.' So said Lavrentiy Beria, "the most ruthless and longest-serving secret police chief in Joseph Stalin's reign of terror in Russia and Eastern Europe," bragging that he *'"could prove criminal conduct on anyone, even the innocent'....*

"...Beria targeted 'the man' first, then proceeded to find or fabricate a crime. Beria's modus operandi was to presume the man guilty, and fill in the blanks later. By contrast, under the United States Constitution, there's a presumption of innocence that emanates from the 5th, 6th, and 14th Amendments, as set forth in Coffin vs. U.S. (1895)."[91]

You wouldn't know that if you've been following the Trump-Russia collusion special counsel investigation or with the confirmation process of Judge Kavanaugh for the Supreme Court.

When Saul Alinsky discusses Tactic #3, *"Whenever possible, go outside of the experience of the enemy"*, he

---

[90] Ibid. Alinsky. pg. 127.
[91] Michael Henry. "Show me the man and I'll show you the crime." *Oxford Eagle.* https://m.oxfordeagle.com/2018/05/09/show-me-the-man-and-ill-show-you-the-crime/.

claims its intent is to cause confusion, chaos, fear and retreat on the part of one's opponent. The first two years of Trump's presidency has been filled with that. But, has it all been his doing?

While both parties have their fair share of corrupt politicians, Republicans play more by the rule of law, naïvely assuming the same of their opponents. The Dems closely follow Alinsky's advice that the end justifies the means, even if the means are unethical and destroy lives.

The *"second rule of the ethics of means and ends"*, for example, *"is that the judgment of the ethics of means is dependent upon the political position of those sitting in judgment.* If you actively opposed the Nazi occupation and joined the underground resistance," he claims, "then you adopted the means of assassination, terror, property destruction, the bombing of tunnels and trains, kidnapping, and the willingness to sacrifice innocent hostages to the end of defeating the Nazis."[92]

Nothing could better explain why the left and their "fake news" media arm work so tirelessly and in tandem to get Americans to believe that Trump is Hitler and Deplorables are his Nazis. The Dems don't really believe that themselves; but, if they can whip enough voters into a frenzy with that mantra, they've won. The left knows they are following Alinsky's tactics and have said so themselves, not overtly, of course. But, if you pay attention to them closely enough, you'll find that they use identical language, practices, and tactics that are prevalent throughout his book. Fortunately for us, Trump uses them, too. That is precisely why never-

---

[92] Ibid, Alinsky, pp. 26–27.

Trumpers can't accept him. They believe themselves to be "holier-than-thou". But, in reality, they are causing great harm to our American way of life.

Were there ever a *"show me the man and I'll show you the crime"* scenario, Special Counsel Robert Mueller's Trump-Russia collusion investigation is it; and, Mr. Mueller is Trump's Beria.

The left hoped that Americans would never get wind of their sinister plot to take Trump down. Had Hillary won, we would probably never have known. His win put all that secrecy in jeopardy. If you, like so many other Americans, can't keep up with the details of this complex investigation, you are going to be shocked with what you are about to read.

The Trump-Russia inquiry was being ramped up just months before the 2016 election. It was handled by a group of FBI senior level personnel at headquarters, rather than at field offices, as is the norm. The key players were then-FBI Director James Comey, his then-Deputy Director Andrew McCabe, then-Deputy Assistant Director of Counterintelligence Peter Strzok and then-FBI lawyer, Lisa Page (all since fired or, in Lisa Page's case, voluntarily left). DOJ Deputy Director Rod Rosenstein and then-Associate Deputy Attorney General Bruce Ohr had roles that have, so far, not been completely revealed. Former CIA Director John Brennan kicked the entire investigation into action.

According to *The Guardian*, as far back as late 2015 through the summer of 2016, the British spy agency GCHQ (equivalent to our NSA), along with other foreign allied agencies known as the "Five Eyes", began passing highly sensitive information to their US counterparts. GCHQ supposedly became aware of "suspicious 'interactions' between figures connected to Trump and known or suspected Russian agents, a source close to UK intelligence said."[93] Or, did they?

"GCHQ's then head, Robert Hannigan, passed material in summer 2016 to CIA chief, John Brennan." Brennan used that information to "launch a major interagency investigation. ...both US and UK intelligence sources acknowledge that GCHQ played an early, prominent role in kick-starting the FBI's Trump-Russia investigation, which began in late July 2016."[94] But, why?

Joe DiGenova, former US Attorney for the District of Columbia, reported on a "Lou Dobbs Tonight" episode of *FOX News Business* (October 16, 2018), that they did so because it was illegal for American agencies to spy on American citizens. The Obama administration, via his FBI and DOJ asked the UK for assistance, and GCHQ complied. The first of several American citizens GCHQ spied on was a young, naïve, Trump foreign policy aide named George Papadopoulos who travelled frequently to London on business.

In April 2016 while in London, Papadopoulos met Joseph Mifsud, a "London-based professor with links to the Russia government". Mifsud told Papadopoulos "he learned the Russians had possession of 'thousands' of Clinton-related emails. That conversation would,

---

[93]Luke Harding, Stephanie Kirchgaessner and Nick Hopkins. "British spies were first to spot Trump team's links with Russia" *The Guardian.* https://www.theguardian.com/uk-news/2017/apr/13/british-spies-first-to-spot-trump-team-links-russia.
[94] Ibid.

conveniently, spark the FBI's investigation into Russian interference in the presidential campaign."[95]

A month later, Papadopoulos was introduced to Australian High Commissioner to the United Kingdom, Alexander Downer (a Trump-hater), who had previously arranged a $25 million grant to the Hillary Foundation.[96] "During a barroom conversation at Kensington Gardens, Papadopoulos told Downer about the emails Mifsud mentioned to him. [Hence, the Trump-Russia collusion "link" was secured.]

"After WikiLeaks published a trove of stolen DNC emails in July 2016, Australian government officials told the FBI about Downer's interaction with Papadopoulos. The bureau opened its counter-intelligence investigation July 31, 2016."[97]

Unfortunately for Papadopoulos, the "spies" weren't done with him yet.

"Two months before the 2016 election, George Papadopoulos received a strange request for a meeting in London...from Stefan Halper, a foreign policy expert and Cambridge professor with connections to the CIA and its British counterpart, MI6."[98] In an email to Papadopoulos on September 2, 2016, Halper offered him "$3,000 to write a policy paper on issues related to

---

[95] Chuck Ross. "EXCLUSIVE: A London Meeting Before The Election Aroused George Papadopoulos's Suspicions" *dailycaller.com* https://dailycaller.com/2018/03/25/george-papadopoulos-london-emails/ (Mar. 25, 2018)
[96] John Solomon. "Did FBI get bamboozled by multiple versions of Trump dossier?" *The Hill* (July 10, 2018) https://thehill.com/hilltv/rising/396307-Did-FBI-get-bamboozled-by-multiple-versions-of-Trump-dossier%3F.
[97] Ibid. Chuck Ross.
[98] Ibid.

Turkey, Cyprus, Israel...",[99] plus a free, three-day trip to London. Papadopoulos jumped at the opportunity.

While there, Papadopoulos was said to have been surprised when Halper asked about his knowledge of DNC emails hacked by Russia. Papadopoulos supposedly denied any knowledge. Looking back on the unusual request for the assignment must now seem perplexing to the young aide, especially given that to-date "[t]here are no public records of Halper releasing reports on Turkey, Cyprus and Israel."[100] Coincidentally, Halper is known to have close associations not only with British and American intelligence officials, but also with the DOJ. Papadopoulos had no known connection to Russia ... until meeting the above-mentioned men. Were they "chance" meetings? Most think not.

John Solomon, awarding-winning investigative journalist for *The Hill*, says that "[t]he FBI formally opened the Trump campaign probe — code-named Crossfire Hurricane — on July 31, 2016, based on [the] Australian diplomat's claim that Papadopoulos appeared to have prior knowledge that Russia had derogatory information it planned to release on Hillary Clinton. ... Agents feared Papadopoulos might be looking to create contacts in Moscow to gain access to that Clinton dirt. ... The FBI's own account in court records shows agents suddenly seemed to lose a sense of urgency about the Papadopoulos allegation."[101]

More than two years after the investigation began, and after putting Papadopoulos through hell, Special Counsel Mueller only charged him with lying to federal

---

[99] Ibid.
[100] Ibid.
[101] Ibid. Solomon.

agents about the meetings and gave him a fourteen day sentence. That should make every American angry. Papadopoulos now feels certain he was set up. He has admitted that he lied to the FBI, but only out of fear that the meetings in London would hurt then-candidate Trump. It's now widely believed that he was entrapped by Downer to become the first fall guy of a soft-coup against our president, in case he won.

According to Solomon, the reason the FBI's focus shifted away from Papadopoulos was because of a former British MI6 agent named Christopher Steele.

The day before the July 31st "Crossfire" probe against Trump was launched, a breakfast meeting took place in Washington, D.C. between some very unsavory diners. Glenn Simpson met with Bruce and Nellie Ohr to discuss a report now known to have been commissioned and funded by Hillary Clinton and the DNC to dig up dirt on Trump. Simpson's firm, Fusion GPS, created the report now known as the "Steele dossier". Nellie Ohr was an employee of Fusion GPS, whose husband, Bruce Ohr, happened to be then-Associate Deputy Attorney General at the DOJ. He was also, conveniently, friends with Christopher Steele.

Steele, with his connections to the global intelligence community, was hired by Fusion GPS to "find dirt on Trump in Russia".[102] Nellie Ohr was well-compensated for her "connection", husband Bruce Ohr ensured its delivery to the FBI. They all had one thing in common: hatred for Donald J. Trump.

The dossier included a preposterous, and now known to be false, story that, while in Russia some years

---

[102] Ibid.

ago, Trump hired prostitutes to pee on the hotel bed on which, presumably, the Obamas had slept. You'd think Steele could have come up with something more believable than that. Only the most rabid anti-Trumpers bought in, along with those who are sleeping.

It has since been determined that the FBI received no fewer than three versions of the dossier, "[e]ach arriving from a different messenger: [Republican Senator] John McCain, Mother Jones reporter David Corn, Fusion GPS founder (and Steele boss) Glenn Simpson."[103] The known similarities between the three men and the three versions, were that all versions included the den-of-prostitutes story ... and, all three men hated Donald J. Trump.

"It's exactly the sort of circular intelligence-gathering and political pressure that the FBI is supposed to reject,"[104] Solomon says. In other words, using opposition research bought and paid for by the DNC, funneling it to the FBI via avowed political enemies of the president, leaking it to a reporter, then using all three sources to give the dossier credibility, is highly suspect and irregular. Yet, the FBI did just that.

Kimberly Strassel, member of the *Wall Street Journal* editorial board, laid out John Brennan's involvement better than I ever could: "In a late August [2016] briefing, [Brennan] told the [Democratic] Senate minority leader [Harry Reid] Russia was trying to help Mr. Trump win the election, and that Trump advisers might be colluding with Russia.

---

[103] Ibid.
[104] Ibid.

"...Within a few days of the briefing, Mr. Reid wrote a letter to Mr. Comey, which...immediately became public. 'The evidence of a direct connection between the Russian government and Donald Trump's presidential campaign continues to mount,' wrote Mr. Reid, going on to float Team Clinton's the-Russians-are-helping-Trump theory. Mr. Reid publicly divulged at least one of the allegations contained in the infamous Steele dossier, insisting that the FBI use 'every resource available to investigate this matter.'

"The Reid letter marked the first official blast of the Brennan–Clinton collusion narrative into the open. Clinton opposition-research firm Fusion GPS followed up by briefing its media allies about the dossier it had dropped off at the FBI. On Sept. 23, Yahoo News's Michael Isikoff ran the headline: 'U.S. intel officials probe ties between Trump adviser and Kremlin.'...Not only was the collusion narrative out there, but so was evidence that the FBI was investigating."[105]

What do the above players all have in common? Their hatred for Donald J. Trump.

The Guardian concurs with Strassel's account, adding further insight: "In late August and September 2016, Brennan gave a series of classified briefings to the Gang of Eight, the top-ranking Democratic and Republican leaders in the House and Senate. He told them the agency had evidence the Kremlin might be trying to help Trump to win the presidency...." At the time, Brennan did not tell the committee who his

---

[105] Kimberley A. Strassel. "Brennan and the 2016 Spy Scandal" *Wall Street Journal* (July 19, 2018) https://www.wsj.com/articles/brennan-and-the-2016-spy-scandal-1532039346.

sources were, only that they came from America's allies. Much later, however, Trump learned that the source was the GCHQ.[106] In fact, Trump blamed them later in his infamous wiretap tweet for secretly surveilling him in Trump Tower. He's not looking so crazy anymore, is he?

In mid-October, 2016 (two and a half months after "Crossfire" was launched and just weeks before the election), a Foreign Intelligence Surveillance Act (FISA) order was approved to spy on an American for supposed criminal activities with Russia. A large part of the evidence supporting that warrant was based on the "Steele dossier" and the Yahoo article by Michael Isikoff.

A graduate of the U.S. Naval Academy and self-professed volunteer for the FBI whenever he could to serve his country, businessman Carter Page had no idea the mess about to infiltrate his life. For two years, he was spied on by the FBI looking for a crime that didn't exist. After spending a fortune defending himself, ever claiming his innocence, Page hasn't been charged with one single crime. But like so many other innocent Americans caught up in this dirty plot, his reputation has been forever tarnished. Of course, that doesn't matter to the left. Whatever means necessary to impeach Trump is all that matters to them. The Russia-Collusion narrative has proved the perfect weapon to do just that.

The DOJ Inspector General, Michael Horowitz, announced on January 12, 2017 that he was opening a probe into the FBI's mishandling of the investigation into Hillary's private email server. His mission was to investigate the FBI's role in the "Mid-Year Exam" (MYE), FBI code-name for the probe into Hillary's private server

---

[106]Ibid. Luke Harding, et al.

and handling of her emails. This was demanded by both parties because Comey broke protocol when, just weeks before the election, he announced finding Clinton's supposed lost emails, then quickly cleared her of any wrongdoing. Curiously, the MYE was handled by the exact same group of senior FBI leaders that went on to handle Crossfire.

On June 14, 2018, seventeen months after he began his investigation, Horowitz was in front of Congress announcing his findings along with FBI Director, Chris Wray. Wray had replaced Comey, who was fired by Trump in May, 2017.

According to *RealClear Politics*, who published a full transcript of the testimony, IG Horowitz said, "We found the implication that senior FBI employees would be willing to take official action to impact the presidential candidates [sic] electoral prospects to be deeply troubling and antithetical to the core values of the FBI and the Justice Department. ... We identified the inappropriate text and instant messages discussed in the report ... the OIG's painstaking forensic examinations recovered thousands of text messages that otherwise would have been lost...."[107]

According to an updated report issued nearly six months later by the DOJ's internal watchdog, those lost texts were, supposedly, caused by "a technical glitch for a swath of missing text messages between anti-Trump ex-FBI officials Peter Strzok and Lisa Page -- and

---

[107] Tim Hains. "Full Replay: DOJ Inspector General, FBI Director Wray Testify On IG Report At Senate Judiciary Committee" *RealClear Politics*
https://www.realclearpolitics.com/video/2018/06/18/watch_live_do j_inspector_general_fbi_director_wray_testify_on_ig_report_at_senate _judiciary_committee.html.

revealed that government [iPhones] issued by Special Counsel Robert Mueller's office to Strzok and Page had been wiped completely clean after Strzok was fired from the Russia probe. ... The DOJ's Inspector General (IG) said that, with help from the Department of Defense, it was able to uncover thousands of missing text messages written by Strzok and Page and sent using their FBI-issued Samsung phones from December 15, 2016, through May 17, 2017, 'as well as hundreds of other text messages outside the gap time period that had not been produced by the FBI due to technical problems with its text message collection tool.'[108]

"[W]hen the IG went looking for the iPhones separately issued to Strzok and Page by the Mueller team, investigators were told that '[Strzok's] iPhone had been reset to factory settings and was reconfigured for the new user to whom the device was issued.' ... The records officer at the special counsel told the IG that 'as part of the office's records retention procedure, the officer reviewed Strzok's DOJ issued iPhone' on September 6, 2017, and 'determined it contained no substantive text messages' before it was wiped completely -- just weeks after Strzok was fired from Mueller's team for anti-Trump bias and sending anti-Trump text messages."[109] That is, quite literally, unbelievable. There is a disturbing pattern with the left illegally concealing evidence. That can no longer be ignored; and, we should pray that Trump digs deep.

---

[108] Gregg Re. "Giuliani suggests Mueller cover-up..." *FOX News* (Dec. 31, 2018) https://www.foxnews.com/politics/giuliani-dems-could-have-prevented-cops.
[109] Ibid.

Regarding Comey's surprise announcement just prior to the 2016 election that Hillary's "lost" emails had been found, during his testimony in front of Congress, the IG said, "'we found the FBI's explanations for its failures to take immediate action after discovering the Weiner laptop to be unpersuasive....'"[110] Anthony Weiner was the disgraced pedophiliac husband of Hillary's closest aide, Huma Abedin. Hillary's purposely destroyed emails, regarded as evidence to be preserved, were discovered on Weiner's laptop less than two months before the election during the FBI's investigation of him. Comey sat on the evidence for a full month before finally releasing them, only after pressure from field agents concerned about protocol.

Horowitz also testified that, "'we did not have confidence that the decision of Deputy Assistant Direct[or] Strzok to prioritize the Russia investigation [over MYE] ... *was free from bias in light of his text messages* [emphasis mine]. ... We also found that in key moments then FBI Director Comey clearly departed from FBI and department norms, and his decisions negatively impacted the perception of the FBI and the Justice Department as fair administrators of justice.'"[111] Horowitz believed that Comey rushed to prematurely shut down MYE and open the Crossfire investigation against Trump.

The IG found Comey's conduct to be "deeply troubling" by intentionally re-characterizing Hillary's conduct from "grossly negligent" to "extremely careless"

---

[110] Ibid. Tim Haines.
[111] Ibid.

in his final report, ensuring that she'd be protected from criminal prosecution.

Also revealed in the IG's original report, as everyone now knows, were the thousands of "lost", then recovered, clearly biased, text messages between Peter Strzok and Lisa Page of the FBI. It was revealed that the two had an ongoing extramarital affair throughout the period in question. The American people can be thankful for that. Without those texts from their government-issued phones, prior to the phones they used after joining the Mueller team, we may have never known about the depth of their anti-Trump bias. Nor would we likely have known about the attempts to thwart his presidency.

Their texts were **BIASED**: 3/4/2016, PAGE: "God Trump is [sic] loathsome human" - STRZOK: "God Hillary should win. 100,000,000-0."; **REVEALING**: 5/4/2016, PAGE: "And holy sh-t Cruz just dropped out of the race..." - STRZOK: "Now the pressure really starts to finish MYE...and K. Rybicki just sent another version...He changed President to 'another senior government official' [leading many to believe then President Obama was wanting cover]"; and, **INFANTILE**: 8/26/16, STRZOK: "Just went to a southern Virginia Walmart. I could SMELL the Trump support...."[112]

According to Debra Heine of *pjmedia.com*, "one text regarding a strategy session that had taken place in

---

[112] Catherine Herridge. "Read FBI's Strzok, Page Texts about Trump" *FOX News*
http://www.foxnews.com/politics/2018/01/21/ex-mueller-aides-texts-revealed-read-them-here.html.

Andrew McCabe's office has really stood out: 'I want to believe the path you threw out for consideration in Andy's office—that there's no way he gets elected—but I'm afraid we can't take that risk. It's like an insurance policy in the unlikely event you die before you're 40,'" Strzok texted to Page in August, 2016.[113]

That "insurance policy" is widely believed to be the Russia–Trump investigation leading to impeachment.

While some Republican lawmakers have done a good job of trying to get more documents related to Crossfire unredacted from the FBI, they have largely been stonewalled, by both the DOJ and some of their own colleagues, never-Trumpers, of course. The DOJ says the documents are highly–classified. Yet, when Congress does receive them, in small increments at a time, the unredacted versions prove they weren't classified for their secrecy at all. Rather, they were simply embarrassing to those involved.

On September 17, 2018, President Trump finally "ordered the declassification of the Carter Page FISA application and the public release of 'all text messages relating to the Russia investigation, without redaction, of James Comey, Andrew McCabe, Peter Strzok, Lisa Page, and Bruce Ohr.'"[114]

Heine says that, according to House Permanent Select Committee on Intelligence member, Devin Nunes (Republican), "'[t]hose are significant not just because of the Carter Page FISA but also because it shows the

---

[113] Debra Heine. "Nunes: Declassifying the 20 Redacted Pages will Reveal Peter Strzok's 'Insurance Policy'" *pjmedia.com* (9-18-2018) https://pjmedia.com/video/nunes-declassifying-the-20-redacted-pages-will-reveal-peter-strzoks-insurance-policy/.
[114] Ibid.

interaction between Christopher Steele, Fusion GPS, and many other rotten apples within the FBI that were up to no good,.... Finally, there's exculpatory information that the president has ordered declassified,' he explained. Nunes has been saying for months now that when the American people see this information, they will be shocked."[115]

While Trump has since put his request to declassify the documents on hold, you can bet he's keeping that ace in his back pocket for later leverage against his enemies. Trump has Alinsky's tactics down.

The evidence suggests that the senior-level people who headed our most trusted agencies, the FBI and DOJ, concocted the Trump-Russia collusion narrative in order to deflect the public's attention from what was real collusion with Russia between the FBI and DOJ, and Hillary and the DNC in order to bring down a duly-elected president. They hid behind their powerful positions and took advantage of our trust by believing they were going outside the experience of their "enemy", the American people. But, the truth always comes out; and, it soon will, to the disgrace of the Democratic Party.

One of Strzok's texts indicated that he originally didn't want to join the Mueller investigation because he felt there was no "there, there". Yet, his passion to bring down the president proved too tempting. It was only after the discovery of his biased texts that he was demoted and removed from Mueller's team. Fortunately for America, these rats left quite a trail for what is about to implode into one of the most massive scandals in the history of our country.

---

[115] Ibid.

On October 3, 2018, John Solomon reported that former FBI general counsel James Baker testified before Congress that he met with Michael Sussman (lawyer for Perkins Coie, the DNC's private law firm) during 2016. (Solomon, who has been the frontrunner on the Russia-Trump collusion narrative, along with Sara Carter, deserves great credit from the American people for uncovering much of the truth we've learned.)

Perkins Coie is "the law firm used by the DNC and Hillary Clinton's campaign to secretly pay research firm Fusion GPS ... to compile a dossier of uncorroborated raw intelligence alleging Trump and Moscow were colluding to hijack the presidential election.

"It means the FBI had good reason to suspect the dossier was connected to the DNC's main law firm and was the product of a Democratic opposition-research effort to defeat Trump – yet failed to disclose that information to the FISA court in October 2016, when the bureau applied for a FISA warrant to surveil Trump campaign adviser Carter Page."[116]

Had Hillary won the presidency, the left would have continued corrupting our system unchecked. Had Trump's former Attorney General Jeff Sessions not recused himself from everything "Russia" almost from day one, or had he at least informed the president of his plans to do so prior to accepting the appointment, there likely would have been no special counsel.

Regardless, we now know that what Comey himself called a "salacious and unverified" dossier on a sitting

---

[116] John Solomon. "Collusion bombshell: DNC lawyers met with FBI on Russia allegations before surveillance warrant" *The Hill* (Oct. 3, 2018) https://thehill.com/hilltv/rising/409817-russia-collusion-bombshell-dnc-lawyers-met-with-fbi-on-dossier-before.

president was leaked and led to a special counsel to investigate unsubstantiated claims against Trump.

The FISA application and its three extensions, approved by FISC (Foreign Intelligence Surveillance Court) judges, appears to have omitted exculpatory evidence regarding George Papadopoulos and Carter Page. If true, the signatories, including Rod Rosenstein and Andrew McCabe, have a lot of explaining to do.

Special Counsel Mueller received a virtually unlimited scope for his collusion investigation and hired thirteen prosecutors for his team, *all* of whom are Democrats and proven supporters of, and donors for, Hillary. He was also appointed by Rosenstein who, by virtue of his FISA authorization, should have recused himself. Mueller should have recused himself as special counsel, as well, for having been interviewed, and passed over, by Trump to replace Comey at the FBI. Instead, the naïve Jeff Sessions played right into the left's hands when he allowed the Dems to pressure him into recusal of all things Russia. The left went "outside the experience of the enemy" and, it paid off. Until Trump fired him two years later, Sessions still didn't understand that the left played him like a chump. Thanks to him, Trump has had to endure his first two years embroiled in a totally unsubstantiated investigation, led by a ruthless special counsel who would never have been appointed had the GOP stood its ground and defended its president. And, Trump had to fight his enemies without protection of an AG.

According to an article in the *Wall Street Journal*, "[n]o evidence has emerged of Trump-Russia collusion, and Mr. Mueller has yet to bring collusion-related charges against anyone...Given the paucity of evidence, it's staggering that the FBI would initiate a counterintelligence investigation, led by politically biased staff, amid a presidential campaign....

"All special-counsel activities — investigations, plea deals, subpoenas, reports, indictments and convictions — are fruit of a poisonous tree, byproducts of a violation of due process. That Mr. Mueller and his staff had nothing to do with Crossfire's origin offers no cure."[117]

In mid-December, 2018, Michael Isikoff, the *Yahoo News* reporter who broke the information fed to him by Fusion GPS about the dossier, has publicly stated that, "'[W]hen you actually get into the details of the Steele dossier, the specific allegations, we have not seen the evidence to support them, and, in fact, there's good grounds to think that some of the more sensational allegations will never be proven and are likely false.'"[118]

On four separate occasions, "the FBI suggested to the [FISA] court, the article by Michael Isikoff was independent corroboration of the salacious, unverified allegations against Trump in the infamous Steele dossier. Federal authorities used both the Steele dossier and Yahoo News article to convince the FISA court to authorize a surveillance warrant for Page."[119]

The difference in the treatment of those who worked on Trump's campaign, i.e., retired Lt. General

---

[117] David B. Rivkin Jr.and Elizabeth Price Foley. "Mueller's Fruit of the Poisonous Tree" *Wall Street Journal* (June 22, 2018) https://www.wsj.com/articles/muellers-fruit-of-the-poisonous-tree-1529707087.
[118] Gregg Re. "Reporter who broke news of Steele dossier used to surveil ex-Trump aide calls its claims largely 'false'" *FOX News* (Dec. 18, 2018) https://www.foxnews.com/politics/likely-false-steele-dossier-faces-new-credibility-challenges-from-cohen-isikoff.
[119] Ibid.

Michael Flynn (a 33-year veteran), Paul Manafort, Carter Page, George Papadapoulas, Michael Cohen and others, versus that given to Hillary and her people, is simply staggering. These men have lost fortunes defending themselves against a group of biased, cut-throat, politically-motivated and power-hungry individuals. That's the real crime; and, we should all be outraged.

If we aren't, the left will again resume power, corruption will return in record speed, and Hillary and every other cheat will be back in business. Just because they *"go outside of the experience of the enemy"*, doesn't mean we can't fight back. But it does mean that we must start paying closer attention to what they say and do. Our very rule of law is at stake.

We don't have to look far to find out what our future will be if we don't start holding the Dem's feet to the fire. The next chapter, "White Men Can't Judge" reveals the extremes Democrats will go to in order to bring down an innocent, well-respected servant of the courts...all for the sake of increasing their power. It will shake you to your core.

WHITE MEN CAN'T JUDGE

TACTIC #4: *"Make the enemy live up to their own book of rules."*[120]

"'GUESS WHO IS PERPETRATING all of these kinds of actions?' Sen. Mazie Hirono (D-HI) asked on September 18, 2018, responding to reporters' questions about accusations of sexual misconduct levelled at the nominee to the Supreme Court. *'It's the men in this country...I just want to say to the men in this country: Just shut up and step up. Do the right thing for a change.'"*[121]

She called on all *"enlightened"* men across the country to *"'rise up to say we cannot continue the victimization and the smearing of someone like Dr. Ford...she is under no obligation to participate in the Republican efforts to sweep this whole thing under the rug, to continue this nomination on the fast track....'"*[122]

Talk about emotional abuse!

My initial reaction to what Hirono said bordered on incredulity. Her intonation clearly blamed all men for all things accused. They were guilty and needed to just *"shut up"*. What kind of person talks like this?

---

[120] Ibid. Alinsky. pg. 128.
[121] Eli Rosenberg. "'Shut up and step up.' This senator's message to men in the wake of the Kavanaugh accusation" *latimes.com* http://www.latimes.com/nation/politics/la-na-pol-kavanaugh-hirono-20180919-story.html.
[122] Ibid.

Hirono's comments came a mere two days after Dr. Blasey Ford's sexual accusations were "outed"; and, one day after Judge Brett M. Kavanaugh vehemently denied them. No evidence. No trial. No basis at all that either were lying...or, telling the truth. The timing, just prior to the cloture vote, left much to question.

"In an interview with *The Washington Post*, Ford alleged that Kavanaugh corralled her into a bedroom during a gathering in Maryland when she was in high school, and pinned her to a bed, groped her over her clothes and attempted to pull off the clothing she was wearing. She said he held his hand over her mouth when she tried to scream. Kavanaugh has denied the accusation, saying in a statement Monday he'd never done anything like what she described 'to her or to anyone.'"[123] Yet, apparently, Kavanaugh is guilty as hell, and Ford deserves our undivided loyalty.

The *Los Angeles Times* story gives us a window into what motive the liberal Democrat Hirono might have had in her premature accusatory ramblings. She said that "'if Kavanaugh is not nominated — and Democrats win the Senate in November — Republicans should nominate a more moderate judge or the seat could be held open until the 2020 election, a tactic Republicans deployed with Antonin Scalia's seat in 2016.'"[124]

The very liberal *HuffPost* laments over why the outgoing two-term President Obama never got a replacement justice confirmed for the late Justice Scalia. "Majority Leader Mitch McConnell (R-Ky.) ... refused to give Obama's nominee, Merrick Garland, a shot at filling

---

[123] Ibid.
[124] Ibid.

the seat ... Garland never got a confirmation hearing or a vote; ... McConnell pushed the argument that the next president should get to choose the next justice."[125]

Kudos to McConnell and the other Republicans for finally playing hardball...it works!

In *Rules for Radicals*, Alinsky's fourth tactic, "*Make the enemy live up to their own book of rules*", is recommended to attack a person's credibility and reputation. "For example, since the Haves publicly pose as the custodians of responsibility, morality, law, and justice..., they can be constantly pushed to live up to their own book of morality and regulations. No organization, including organized religion, can live up to the letter of its own book. You can club them to death with their 'book' of rules and regulations."[126]

By delaying Scalia's replacement, Republicans turned the tables on the Dems. Was it fair? You bet it was. Republicans were not the ones who started the dirty games in the judicial branch nomination process.

In 2003, former President George W. Bush enjoyed a majority Republican Senate when he nominated a well-qualified man to the D.C. appeals court. Unbeknownst to Bush and his administration, the Dems were plotting, in secret, to keep Miguel Estrada off the bench.

"This extraordinary design," led by Sen. Edward M. Kennedy, "without precedence in two centuries of judicial nominations, was launched January 30 in the office of Senate Minority Leader Tom Daschle. Present

---

[125] Igor Bobic, Amanda Terkel, and Jennifer Bendery. "Democrats Regret Not Fighting Harder For Obama's Supreme Court Pick" *HuffPost* (June 27, 2018)
https://www.huffingtonpost.com/entry/democrats-merrick-garland_us_5b33b0efe4b0b5e692f38738.
[126] Ibid. Alinsky, pg. 152.

were Assistant Leader Harry Reid and six Senate Judiciary Committee Democrats. With all pledged to secrecy, the fateful decision was made to filibuster Estrada's nomination."[127] At the time, it took sixty votes in the Senate to end a filibuster. In 2003, there were 51 Republicans and 49 caucused Democrats.

Estrada would have been the first Hispanic to sit on the DC court. After two years of the Dems filibustering tactics, out of frustration, he withdrew. So much for Democrats supporting minorities.

But the Dem's secret scheme didn't end there. *CNN* noted at the time that, "[I]nternal Senate sources depict a Senate minority on an audacious mission. Rare use of the filibuster to keep a judicial nominee off the bench is only the tip of the iceberg. Multiple filibusters would generate the first full-scale effort in American history to prevent a president from picking the federal judges he wants."[128] And, that's what the Dems went on to do.

In 2005, after two years of the Dem's filibustering confirmations of ten well-qualified Bush federal appellate nominees, the GOP majority Senators had enough. They threatened to deploy the "nuclear option", also known as the "constitutional option." This would have effectively eliminated filibustering by reverting back to originalists' intentions of returning to the Senate the power of self-government with a simple majority rule. No longer would 60 votes be needed to confirm a nominee, 51 were sufficient.[129] Given that the GOP had

---

[127] Robert Novak. "Ted Kennedy's grand design" *CNN.com*
http://www.cnn.com/2003/ALLPOLITICS/02/27/column.novak.opini on.kennedy/
[128] Ibid.
[129] Ed Whelan. "The Halligan Filibuster and the New 'Gang of 14' Mythology—Part 1" *NationalReview.com* (Dec. 7, 2011)

a 55-45 majority, there was no doubt they were in a position of power to do just that.

Instead, a few of the panicked Dems coerced a few naïve Republicans (e.g., John McCain and Lindsay Graham) to form a caucus, the Gang of 14, which consisted of seven senators from each party. The seven Dems agreed to refuse to filibuster, effectively ending the practice; and, the seven Republicans would vote against the "nuclear option". But, the Gang of 14 agreement was weak and full of holes.

Republicans had the Dems by the balls and, once again, refused to squeeze.

While the agreement promised three judicial nominees a guaranteed vote on confirmation, it stated that all others during that 109th Congress "should be filibustered only under 'extraordinary circumstances'. The term 'extraordinary circumstances' was not defined."[130] That left the final decision to chance.

The agreement "expressly related *only* [emphasis his] 'to pending and future judicial nominations in the 109th Congress'...[2005 and 2006]."[131]

"Senator Schumer, then-Senator Obama, and other Democrats who were not signatories to the Gang of 14 agreement never regarded that agreement as somehow limiting their freedom to filibuster judicial nominees. That explains how ... Schumer and 32 other Democrats (not including Obama, as it happens) voted against, or

---

https://www.nationalreview.com/bench-memos/halligan-filibuster-and-new-gang-14-mythology-part-1-ed-whelan/.
[130] Ibid.
[131] Ibid.

failed to support, cloture on the nomination of Brett Kavanaugh to the D.C. Circuit."[132]

Kavanaugh had been nominated to the D.C. Circuit Court of Appeals in 2003. Finally, in '06, cloture was invoked; but, not until after a grueling confirmation process wherein several Dems (including Harry Reid, Patrick Leahy, Dianne Feinstein, and Ted Kennedy) expressed opposition via the "extreme circumstances" clause.

"In the 110th Congress, the Democrats had a 51-49 majority in the Senate, and no longer needed to filibuster nominees. Thus the purpose of the Gang of 14 disappeared."[133]

To the Republicans' credit, that year they, too, began filibustering then-President Barack Obama's judicial nominees. Then, the unthinkable happened.

"On November 22, 2013, at the direction of leader Harry Reid, Senate Democrats used the 'nuclear option' to revise Senate rules and eliminate filibusters of Presidential nominees, leaving the possibility of filibusters of nominees for the Supreme Court intact ... nominees can no longer be filibustered."[134] The Dems have been playing dirty for a very long time.

The Republicans felt betrayed and angry after their earlier compromise. Sen. McConnell stood on the Senate floor and issued the following warning to the ruling majority Democrats: "I say to my friends on the other

---

[132] Ibid.
[133] Wikipedia. "Gang of 14" (Last Updated Nov. 28, 2018) https://en.wikipedia.org/wiki/Gang_of_14
[134] Ibid.

side of the aisle, you'll regret this. And you may regret it a lot sooner than you think."[135] And, so they did.

In 2017, Democratic Minority Leader Chuck Schumer openly criticized Reid's move. The Senate make-up, under President Donald J. Trump was 51–49 with a Republican majority. The difference could not have been more striking, given the vacant Supreme Court of the United States (SCOTUS) seat still open.

To his credit, Senate Majority Leader Mitch McConnell had no hesitation expanding the "nuclear option" to include nominees to the SCOTUS. Republicans hardly needed an excuse for McConnell's action.

For his part, Reid defended his "nuclear option" decision saying that, because the Dems won confirmation of three D.C. Circuit Court of Appeals judges, the decision was worth it. I don't think too many Democrats today would agree.

Trump's first SCOTUS nominee in 2017, Neil Gorsuch, faced the usual obstruction from Democrats. But, nothing could have prepared the President and Republicans, or our nation, for what was coming next. It may well divide our country for generations to come.

In the summer of 2018, Justice Anthony Kennedy unexpectedly announced his retirement. Trump was less than two years into his presidency, and already facing his second SCOTUS nomination. His supporters were ecstatic. With the current Court at a 4-4, liberal vs. conservative bench, this next pick would be critical to the future of our country. It would boil down to whether we'd continue to be a constitutionally-originalist nation, or one of constitutionally-evolving laws. Most Trump

---

[135] Ibid.

supporters believed it amounted to a choice between the rule of law or chaos. To Deplorables, this was a moment for the survival, or death, of our nation.

True to his word, on July 9, 2018, Trump nominated a judge straight from his campaign-promised, prepared list of candidates. The name is one a lot of senators remembered well: Brett M. Kavanaugh.

Trump admittedly chose Kavanaugh for his impeccable credentials, his adherence to Constitutional principles, and his overwhelming support from peers for his even-keeled temperament.

Richard Land, president of Southern Evangelical Seminary remembers Kavanaugh's lengthy confirmation battle to the D.C. Circuit Court: "'It was a bruising confirmation then, mainly because of Democratic animus toward George W. Bush,'" Land told *The Daily Signal* the day after Kavanaugh was appointed by Trump. "'They will throw everything that sticks at him this time. They will attack him for being a Catholic, for being a white male, for working for George W. Bush and for Ken Starr.'"[136]

That would have been a breeze considering what was about to happen to Kavanaugh during his Supreme Court confirmation process. It's enough to make a grown man cry...and, he literally did.

The Democrats didn't try to conceal their plot to sabotage the SCOTUS nomination process. "In June, before President Trump even nominated Judge Kavanaugh, Sen. Minority Whip Dick Durbin (D-IL) said

---

[136] Fred Lucas. "Here's What Happened the Last Time Democrats Tried to Deny Brett Kavanaugh a Court Seat" *The Daily Signal* https://www.dailysignal.com/2018/07/10/heres-what-happened-the-last-time-democrats-tried-to-deny-kavanaugh-a-court-seat/.

that the Senate must 'consider the President's nominee once the new Congress is seated in January.'"[137]

On July 9th, the same day Kavanaugh was named, 2020 presidential hopeful, Sen. Kamala Harris, issued a press release even before the hearings began. It stated that: "Whether or a [sic] not the Supreme Court enforces the spirit of those words, 'Equal Justice Under Law,' is determined by the individuals who sit on that Court. ... Judge Brett Kavanaugh represents a direct and fundamental threat to that promise of equality and so I will oppose his nomination to the Supreme Court."[138]

Other Dems showed their biases, too: "'I will oppose him with everything I've got,' the New York Democrat" (Senate Minority Leader Chuck Schumer) told *CBS This Morning*, the day after the announcement was made. He explained his opposition this way: "'At a time when we have the Mueller investigation, Judge Kavanaugh is way at the extremes ... He believes a president shouldn't even be investigated ... with the overreach of presidential power, we shouldn't put him on the bench. And then, on gun rights, on LGBTQ rights, on environmental rights, he's way to the right of the American people.'"[139]

---

[137] White House. "Delay, Obstruct, and Resist Has Been Their Plan All Along" *GOP.com* (Sept. 27, 2018) https://www.gop.com/delay-obstruct-and-resist-has-been-their-plan-all-along-rsr?.

[138] Kamala D. Harris. "Senator Harris Statement Opposing Nomination of Judge Kavanaugh to the Supreme Court" *Kamala D. Harris, US Senator for California* (July 9,2018)
https://www.harris.senate.gov/news/press-releases/senator-harris-statement-opposing-nomination-of-judge-kavanaugh-to-the-supreme-court.

[139] Sandy Fitzgerald. "Schumer Blasts Kavanaugh: 'I Will Oppose Him With Everything I've Got'" *Newsmax* (July 10, 2018)
https://www.newsmax.com/politics/chuck-schumer-trump-brett-kavanaugh-supreme-court/2018/07/10/id/870838/.

Sen. Corey Booker, another 2020 presidential hopeful, added: "'In a moral moment, there is [sic] no bystanders. You are either complicit in the evil, you are either contributing to the wrong or you are fighting against it.'"[140] And, there was more.

Just one day after Trump nominated Kavanaugh, Sen. Hirono "said she would only vote for him if he turned 'miraculously into a Sotomayor [current female SCOTUS ultra-liberal justice].' ... In August, Sen. Richard Blumenthal (D-CT) claimed the confirmation process should be put on hold so the Senate can 'continue vital investigation of Trump campaign criminality & obstruction of justice.' ... and, Sen. Harris claimed 'Kavanaugh's hearings should be delayed until these investigations are completed.' ... In early September, Sen. Pat Leahy (D-VT) stated Judge Kavanaugh's hearings should be delayed because of 'partisan and incomplete vetting.'"[141] Do you see a pattern here? Based on recent history, this delay tactic was surely planned long before the nomination.

Judge Kavanaugh's confirmation process began unremarkably enough, given the Dem's animus. Soon, however, it became evident that they couldn't argue against him on policy. He ably avoided positioning himself on any legal issue one way or the other (a format also followed by his predecessors). So, the Dems resorted to their tactic of delay. For this, they needed to create enough doubt in the public's mind to hold the cloture vote off until after the midterms. If they got

---

[140] Rusty. "Cory Booker Calls Americans Who Support Judge Kavanaugh 'Complicit in Evil'" *The Political Insider* (July 25, 2018) https://thepoliticalinsider.com/cory-booker-judge-kavanaugh/.
[141] White House. Ibid.

control of the Senate, they could avenge the Merrick Garland coup by delaying a second Trump SCOTUS nominee until after the 2020 presidential election. It was a brazen plan.

Tensions heated up as Dems hammered their requests for more documents based on Kavanaugh's past rulings, even requesting all emails and texts...far more documents than ever demanded of any other.

In his request for the "release of classified documents written by nominee Brett Kavanaugh about the use of 'racial profiling' at airports in the aftermath of the 9/11 attacks", New Jersey Democratic Sen. Cory Booker turned a Supreme Court confirmation hearing into a starring film role for himself Thursday — bizarrely claiming, 'this is the closest I'll get to an 'I am Spartacus' moment.'"[142] In a baffling reference to the 1960 movie "Spartacus", he "made a point of saying he was willing to get expelled from the Senate by releasing emails the committee had deemed classified",[143] a move clearly against Senate rules. The emails, it was later discovered, had already been turned over that very morning and Booker knew it.

The Dems used most of their time grandstanding for political points. The Republicans finally had enough of the delay tactics. Time was running out to get the judge on the bench prior to the October 1st session so Republicans started to wind the process down.

After the fourth day of the hearings, on September 7th, at least two Democratic senators, including ranking

[142] Bob Fredericks. "How Cory Booker's 'Spartacus' moment fizzled out" *New York Post.* https://nypost.com/2018/09/06/how-cory-bookers-spartacus-moment-fizzled-out/.
[143] Ibid.

member Dianne Feinstein, called Kavanaugh a liar and besmirched his good name on multiple other issues. White House spokesman, Raj Shah, felt compelled to say: "'We should put these Democratic senators under oath, because they are the ones deliberately misleading the public. They've violated Senate rules, leaked confidential information and trafficked in conspiracy theories — all in a desperate attempt to smear Judge Kavanaugh's stellar reputation. The good news for the country is that it has been a resounding failure.'"[144]

Uh, not so fast Mr. Shah. The biggest bombshell of all was yet to drop.

"The fifth rule of ethics of means and ends," according to Alinsky *"is that concern with ethics increases with the number of means available and vice versa."*[145] In other words, as options to fight a battle decrease, the less ethical the attack should be. He writes that, "[t]o me, dragging a person's private life into this muck is loathsome and nauseous...*but,* if I had been convinced that the only way we could win was to use it, then without any reservations I would have used it."[146]

After Kavanaugh publicly answered the Senate Judiciary Committee's (SJC) questions in over 32 hours of hearings, replied to 1,278 written interrogatories from senators on both sides, met one-on-one privately with them, and after the government provided over a million documents demanded by the Dems in one more

---

[144] Charlie Savage and Sheryl Gay Stolberg. "As Hearings End, Democrats Accuse Supreme Court Nominee of Dissembling" *The New York Times* (Sept. 7, 2018) https://www.nytimes.com/2018/09/07/us/politics/brett-kavanaugh-confirmation-hearings.html.

[145] Ibid. Alinsky, pg. 32.

[146] Ibid, pg. 33.

futile attempt to delay, the worst character assassination attempt ever on a judicial nominee was launched.

On September 13th, mere days before the cloture vote, ranking member Sen. Feinstein announced that she was in possession of explosive news. "'I have received information from an individual concerning the nomination of Brett Kavanaugh. ... That individual strongly requested confidentiality, declined to come forward or press the matter further, and I have honored that decision. I have, however, referred the matter to federal investigative authorities,' she said".[147] Republicans around the country could hear the wheels of justice grinding to a halt. Democrats rejoiced.

On September 16th, "the woman's identity was revealed. Dr. Christine Blasey Ford [a California-based, liberal professor] came forward as the author of [a] letter, charging Kavanaugh with sexual assault."[148] The contents of that letter ended up, mysteriously, in the hands of *The Washington Post*.

What followed was a gripping he said/she said tale of two Americas. The Republicans attempted to handle the uproar by rule of law. They treated the accuser with kid gloves most necessary in the midst of a #MeToo movement started by sexual abuse victims of a well-known movie mogul. The Dems chose chaos, as usual.

Salacious headlines bombarded the public daily, dragging Judge Kavanaugh and his family's good name

---

[147] Ryan Grim. "Dianne Feinstein Withholding Brett Kavanaugh Document From Fellow Judiciary Committee Democrats" *The Intercept*. (Last Updated Sept. 16, 2018)
https://theintercept.com/2018/09/12/brett-kavanaugh-confirmation-dianne-feinstein/.
[148] Ibid.

through the mud. Much of the slinging was done before any facts were known.

While Senator Hirono told all men in America to "shut up", she was only one of the Dems sitting on the SJC, and in the Senate, who abased Judge Kavanaugh. Some even called for waving due process of the law!

"Ford has to be believed because, in the words of ABC Chief Political Analyst Matthew Dowd, 'For 250 years we have believed the he in these scenarios. Enough is enough.'" Joy Behar of *The View* "called Kavanaugh a 'coward' and 'probably guilty.'" *New York Times* columnist Paul Krugman called out the judge as "smarmy, smirking, entitled and mercenary."[149]

"The Atlantic turned the whole history of American jurisprudence on its head and dumped responsibility on the accused. 'Kavanaugh Bears the Burden of Proof,' though innocent until proven guilty is the American legal standard. ABC merely ignored the death threats Kavanaugh and his family have received."[150]

"'Women deserve to be angry...,' said talk show host Andy Richter. 'This country's government is an abuser. We live in the most shameful times.' ... Now armed leftists, some with funding from George Soros [far-left billionaire who funds anti-capitalist causes], are calling for mass violence if Kavanaugh is confirmed."[151]

---

[149] Dan Gainor. "Ford's accusations against Kavanaugh reveal big problems in media" *foxnews.com* (Sept. 23, 2018) https://www.foxnews.com/opinion/dan-gainor-fords-accusations-against-kavanaugh-reveal-big-problem-in-media.
[150] Ibid.
[151] Frank Hawkins." Obama's America on Display at Kavanaugh Hearings" *American Thinker* (Oct. 4, 2018) https://www.americanthinker.com/articles/2018/10/obamas_america_on_display_at_kavanaugh_hearings.html

The unequal justice was palpable.

America has seen this movie before. The white Duke University lacrosse players falsely accused of raping a black woman. A white prosecutor wrongly charged with raping black teenager Tawana Brawley, as the Reverend Al Sharpton defends her in the spotlight of public opinion. The University of Virginia violent gang rape as reported in a totally made-up story by the *Rolling Stone* magazine in 2014. These are just the most famous cases of men falsely accused. When rape accusations are later proven false, it derails the lives of the accused, ruins reputations, and causes irreparable damage for years to come. For those reasons, the presumption of innocence is vital in every single case. In fact, the Dems have been using that argument against the death penalty for decades.

While the country anxiously awaited the upcoming hearing at which Dr. Ford agreed to testify, additional accusers stepped forward with stories of their own. Every day seemed to bring more bad news for Kavanaugh and his supporters. One woman, named Deborah Ramirez, relayed how the judge had exposed himself to her at a Yale college. Another accused him of gang rape over the course of high school.

Other damaging stories about his "alcoholism" and "temperament" became public, one more salacious than the last, until the most absurd began to make the previous story less believable.

"On a side note, I have the unique experience of being both the victim of physical abuse, with stalking, and, in a separate case, the victim of an *accuser* who later recanted about the alleged harassment by me. But, the damage to my reputation was done. He claimed he did it because he believed I, his boss, was about to fire him. I was not. Both situations were incredibly stressful and life-altering. I wouldn't wish either on anybody. So, watching this spectacle and knowing the tricks of the left, I couldn't help but be skeptical.)

From the moment Ford began testifying, I was uncomfortable. I had even more doubts when I learned of her choice of lawyers who were recommended by Feinstein. One of them is a known anti-Trump activist. The other also represents Andrew McCabe, disgraced fired former FBI Deputy Director and anti-Trumper.

An experienced sexual abuse interrogator, Rachel Mitchell, was hired by Republicans so a panel of "old, white men" couldn't "intimidate" Ford during the hearings. When asked unexpected questions, Dr. Ford looked like a deer in headlights. At the end of the hearing, she received back pats and hi-fives from supporters, and all were smiling as though they had just won the lottery. It seemed inappropriate behavior given the gravity of the situation. Certainly not how I would have behaved having gone through far worse abuse than she was claiming. Even so, I gave her the benefit of the doubt, as did most Americans. Immediately following Ford's testimony, many people believed the judge's chances for a seat on the Supreme Court were over.

When it was time for the judge to testify, his opening statement was riveting and wholly believable to me, as was his testimony. He was defending his very existence. The Dems complained that his testimony was too angry and not befitting a judge for the Supreme Court. Most on the right believed that anyone accused of such outrageous acts would, and should, have behaved exactly as Kavanaugh did.

When the hearings ended, the Dems successfully garnered support from one never-Trumper Republican Senator, Jeff Flake, to withhold his vote on cloture until an FBI investigation into the allegations could take place. Republicans were furious. This aided the Dems in delaying the nomination yet again. That Feinstein unethically withheld the "confidential" letter from the SJC for a month seemed intentional. Besides, Kavanaugh had undergone no fewer than five background checks for his high security clearances over the years.

Chairman Chuck Grassley was in a tight spot. To not allow the FBI investigation would forever taint Kavanaugh. To allow it held the risk of delaying cloture until after midterm elections should the FBI hit a snag. To the Republicans' credit, they allowed the probe, but limited it to one week. The Dem's delay tactic worked.

Experts believe that two events were the nominee's saving grace: his own testimony; and, a Trump rally in Mississippi on September 25th at which Trump called out the inconsistencies in Dr. Ford's testimony...something the "fake news" media refused to do.

"I had one beer. Well, do you think it was -- nope, it was one beer," Trump told the crowd, mocking Ford's testimony. "How did you get home? I don't remember. How'd you get there? I don't remember. Where is the place? I don't remember. How many years ago was it? I don't know...I don't know. I don't know," the President continued. "What neighborhood was it in? I don't know. Where's the house? I don't know. Upstairs, downstairs –

– where was it? I don't know –– but I had one beer. That's the only thing I remember."[152] It was classic Trump.

The "fake news" media, in unison, reported that the President had denigrated Dr. Ford. His supporters said he was simply exposing her testimony and ensuring the American people were given the facts.

The FBI turned up nothing new. The judge became the newest Supreme Court Justice after a narrow 51-49 vote on October 6th. The leftists could not have been more unhinged. Their complete lack of ethics in this desperate attempt to derail Kavanaugh's confirmation backfired. The American people did not approve.

The aftermath of the confirmation process was full of angry mob scenes all over the country. A writer for Comedy Central tweeted out what so many leftists were thinking: he was glad "they" had ruined Kavanaugh's life. A professor at Georgetown University also spoke for her comrades when she tweeted that white Republican senators should die miserable deaths. A Democrat staffer released private contact information on Republican senators via the internet as vengeance. Republican Senator Cory Gardner's wife received a video depicting a beheading after he voted for Kavanaugh.

America is headed for very troubled times if this behavior is left unchecked. The good news is that this issue may have been the single most important reason voter turnout exploded for the midterms. While the Dems won the House, the Republicans maintained a

---

[152] Allie Malloy, Kate Sullivan and Jeff Zeleny. "Trump mocks Christine Blasey Ford's testimony, tells people to 'think of your son'". *CNN* (updated Oct. 3, 2018)
https://www.cnn.com/2018/10/02/politics/trump-mocks-christine-blasey-ford-kavanaugh-supreme-court/index.html.

majority in the Senate, which is almost unprecedented during an incumbent president's first term.

In their overzealousness to "*make the enemy live up to their own book of rules*," the Dems failed at ruining Justice Kavanaugh's life.

Cloward-Piven, in their previously mentioned strategy paper, hailed Alinsky's fourth tactic saying that, "[t]he system's failure to 'live up' to its rule book can then be used to discredit it altogether, and to replace the capitalist 'rule book' with a socialist one."[153] That should leave no doubt in anyone's mind just what was at stake in this disturbing plot.

One of the left's favorite tactics is to ridicule the enemy. In chapter five, "Sticks and Stones", you'll learn just how powerful that weapon is. Fortunately, we have a president who ridicules better than most on the left and, it's working. So, if you're a never-Trumper, get on board. Your dislike of the man's behavior needs to come second to what he is achieving for Conservatives. *He needs you!* And, so does your country.

---

[153] "Cloward Piven Strategy (CPS)" *Discover the Networks* https://www.discoverthenetworks.org/organizations/clowardpiven-strategy-cps/. (Last Updated Oct. 17, 2018)

STICKS AND STONES

TACTIC #5: *"Ridicule is man's most potent weapon."*[154]

"'DO ME A FAVOR, can you say 'senator' instead of 'ma'am?' Mrs. Boxer pointedly asked the general. *'It's just a thing. I worked so hard to get that title, so I'd appreciate it. Thank you.'"*[155]

"He obliged. *'Yes, senator,'* he dutifully responded."[156]

"Some feminists consider the term 'ma'am' patronizing."[157] In the United States military, referring to a senior officer or senator as "sir" or "ma'am" is a sign of respect and a long-standing tradition. Yet during that Environment and Public Works Committee hearing on June 16, 2009, California Democratic Senator Barbara Boxer felt offended. *Or did she?*

It's worth noting that "Brig. General Michael Walsh of the Army Corps of Engineers ... [a] retired Army veteran...participated in Operation Praying Mantis to destroy the Iranian Navy in April 1988 by designing the

---

154 Ibid. Alinsky, pg. 128.
155 Amanda Carpenter. "Sen. Boxer to officer: Don't call me ma'am." *Washington Times*, (June 19, 2009)
https://www.washingtontimes.com/news/2009/jun/19/no-maam-for-boxer/
156 Ibid.
157 Ibid.

strategic concept of it as a Reagan appointee Army officer at the Pentagon."[158]

"Ma'am" Boxer is a well-known liberal feminist from California who played no small part during her twenty years in Congress stoking the cultural wars that have been so instrumental in dividing our country today. Watching the exchange between Boxer and Brig. Gen. Walsh, I couldn't help but feel embarrassed for our country. Here was a United States senator so concerned about her image that she was willing to humiliate a high ranking military officer on live TV for the world to see. It was despicable and, in my opinion, debased our military in the eyes of our enemies, especially those who regard women as second-rate citizens.

As disappointing was the weak response the incident got from Republicans. Our country has become so politically correct that substance has taken a back seat to appearance. It's pathetic; and, it's succeeding at transforming our once-proud American heritage.

Alinsky's fifth rule, *"Ridicule is man's most potent weapon"*, is one of the most utilized of them all, especially with Trump in the White House. Trump is the first president in my lifetime who totally understands this tactic and uses it himself against his opponents successfully on an almost daily basis. According to Alinsky, "[I]t is almost impossible to counterattack ridicule. Also it infuriates the opposition, who then react to your advantage."[159] So, the next time Trump tweets something that makes you cringe, *leave him alone!*

---

[158] Ibid.
[159] Ibid. Alinsky, pg. 128.

A 10-year-old North Carolina boy came home to his mother recently, unusually upset. When his mom asked why, he hesitantly told her that his teacher got very mad, even threatening to throw something at him. Instead, she ordered him to write the four-letter word he had called her on a piece of paper multiple times and get his mom to sign it. When the mom looked at the paper, she grew confused. On it, the boy wrote the word, "ma'am" over and over again, filling up the page. Having brought her son up to be respectful to all people, she visited the teacher to ask what the boy did wrong. The teacher responded by saying that her son "'was getting on her nerve when he called her ma'am.' but 'couldn't give [her] a reason of [sic] why that was bad.'"[160] Kudos to the mom for taking an active role. Shame on the school for moving the boy to a different class. That teacher should have been fired.

Alinsky called the silent majority, "Do-Nothings...These Do-Nothings appear publicly as good men, humanitarian, concerned with justice and dignity. In practice they are invidious. They are the ones Edmund Burke referred to when he said, acidly: 'The only thing necessary for the triumph of evil is for good men to do nothing.'"[161]

Republicans had better learn that lesson soon if they want to remain relevant. Americans are tired of the GOP cowering under threat of merely being called bad names by the left. The GOP has given up so much

[160] Madeline Farber. "North Carolina mom in 'disbelief' after son, 10, punished for calling teacher 'ma'am'" *FOX News* (Aug. 25, 2018) https://www.foxnews.com/us/north-carolina-mom-in-disbelief-after-son-10-punished-for-calling-teacher-maam.
[161] Ibid. Alinsky, pg. 20.

power over the years by buckling to the left's insane politically-correct demands. We finally have a man in the White House who fights for us and Deplorables love him for it.

When Alinsky wrote his list of tactics for the left to use against the "haves", he created the beginning of today's division in America. Throughout his book, the reader can find references Alinsky makes about the "enemy". His enemy is the government, corporations, banks, and the wealthy.

The present day division between our citizens isn't a disagreement between white or black, rich or poor, left or right, religious or atheist, haves or have-nots. It is a culture of war propagated by the left who, as Alinsky intended, have been playing a game with words meant to turn one against another.

Alinsky wrote that, "[A]ny revolutionary change must be preceded by a passive, affirmative, non-challenging attitude toward change among the mass of our people. They must feel so frustrated, so defeated, so lost, so futureless in the prevailing system that they are willing to let go of the past and chance the future."[162] That future, to the left, is socialism; and, they are using every ridicule trick in Alinsky's book to get us there.

Recently, the most famous rapper in the world visited the White House wearing the Make America Great Again (MAGA) hat. The African-American male, longtime friends with the president, went to speak with Trump about prison reform and gang violence in inter-cities, especially in his home city of Chicago. Kanye

---

[162] Ibid. Alinsky, Pg. xix.

West's visit to the Oval Office infuriated the left-wing "fake news" media to no end.

Trump's popularity among minorities is growing. A recent poll showed Trump's black vote nearly doubled in his first two years in office. "...Democrats, already in panic mode over the phony Russia collusion probe evaporating in futility as true Democratic collusion and corruption are revealed, and as the Trump agenda ... is succeeding, are terrified that blacks are peeling away.... Food stamp usage is in decline, as is black unemployment. Wages are rising, as is black home ownership. Congressional blacks like to insist that this is just a continuation of trends begun under Obama, but Obama did not cut regulations, cut taxes, boost domestic energy, rein in the EPA, and unleash entrepreneurs, black and white, freeing them to pursue their dreams unrestrained by government chains...we saw a 400% increase in the number of African American owned small businesses [under the Trump Administration].

"Crime (particularly gang crime), drugs, and poverty are concentrated now in urban areas run by Democratic socialists and progressives. What answer would the typical black Chicago resident give if asked if he was better off after eight years of Obama? What answer would he give now, after two years of the Trump boom?"[163] Trump's shout-out to blacks to join him, *"what have you got to lose?"*, along with his many accomplishments, is working.

---

[163] Daniel John Sobieski. "Blacks Like Trump? Don't Blame Kanye" *americanthinker.com* (October 14, 2018) https://www.americanthinker.com/articles/2018/10/blacks_like_trump_dont_blame_kanye.html.

The treatment of Kanye West by "fake news" media leftists was appalling. *CNN* led the apoplectic protestations against West's White House visit. On *CNN Tonight with Don Lemon*, the host, along with two other African-American political commentators, went on a rampage against the rapper. The only panelist who didn't was Scott Jennings, who happens to be white. Bakari Sellers, a frequent *CNN* guest, stated that: "'Anti-intellectualism simply isn't cool,' Sellers said. 'Kanye West is what happens when Negros don't read.'"[164]

Not to be outdone, fellow commentator Tara Setmayer remarked: "This is not the Kanye West of 2004...Now all of the sudden because he's put on a MAGA hat and he's an attention whore like the president, he's...the model spokesperson. He's the token negro of the Trump administration."[165]

Unable to know when to quit, Setmayer further drew the ire of viewers by "calling the situation 'ridiculous' and declar[ing] that 'no one should be taking Kanye West seriously' because he 'clearly has issues.'"[166] That was in reference to mental health problems, which West had recently made public.

Many famous African-Americans attacked *CNN* fiercely for their disgusting tactics, including football legend Herschel Walker and *Turning Point USA's* Candace Owens. That's exactly the kind of

---

[164] Brian Flood. "Kanye West segment on CNN labeled 'racist' for calling singer 'token negro of the Trump administration'" *FOX News* (Oct. 11, 2018) https://www.foxnews.com/entertainment/kanye-west-segment-on-cnn-labeled-racist-for-calling-singer-token-negro-of-the-trump-administration.
[165] Ibid.
[166] Ibid.

reaction such behavior should get. When we don't call people out, our children mimic bad behavior.

In July 2017, five girls in Pittsburg accused a fellow male high school student of sexual misbehavior. "The boy was charged with indecent assault and two counts of harassment. He pleaded not guilty, but was put on probation."[167] According to a lawsuit filed by his parents, the charges "led to the firing of their son from his job at a swimming pool and he was then 'forced to endure multiple court appearances, detention in a juvenile facility, detention at home, the loss of his liberty and other damages.'"[168]

A few months after the original charge, the first accuser "allegedly told her fellow classmates that she would 'do anything to get [the boy] expelled.' This led to a bullying campaign by other students against him. In one example provided by the lawsuit, someone taped a word "PREDATOR" on the student's back during a choir practice..."[169]

There is only one problem with this story: the girls made it all up. Upon questioning after her recantation, the first accuser "allegedly justified her decision to fabricate the allegations during a recorded interview with school officials," saying, "'I just don't like to hear him talk...I don't like to look at him...I just don't like him.'"[170] All girls involved, including several "witnesses"

[167] Lukas Midelionis. "'Mean girls': How to help your daughter from becoming one" *foxnews.com* (Oct. 10, 2018) https://www.foxnews.com/us/five-high-school-mean-girls-targeted-boy-with-false-accusations-of-sexual-assault-lawsuit-claims
[168] Ibid.
[169] Ibid.
[170] Ibid.

who also later recanted, were given special treatment and received no punishment. That is outrageous and only serves to condone more of the same behavior.

The "boy is now being homeschooled and suffers mental health problems,"[171] according to his parents. The girls have been dubbed "mean girls." *Big deal.*

"The only thing necessary for the triumph of evil is for good men to do nothing." In America, we are pretty good at that. But the consequences can be horrific. We need to start holding people accountable.

The award for the politician most adept at ridiculing "enemies", would have to go to Hillary Clinton, who was the inspiration for the title of this book, *Rules for* Deplorables. Nearing the final stretch of her presidential run against Trump, she made the unforgiveable mistake of alienating half of all Americans by insulting us.

Speaking at the "LGBT for Hillary" fundraising gala, she said, "'You know, to just be grossly generalistic [sic], you could put half of Trump's supporters into what I call the basket of Deplorables. Right? The racist, sexist, homophobic, xenophobic, Islamaphobic—you name it. And unfortunately there are people like that....'"[172] That speech was Alinsky's fifth tactic on steroids; and, it cost her dearly.

It is well-known that Hillary wrote her Wellesley College thesis on Alinsky so she, of all people, must know his tactics well. That paper was placed under lock and key at the college when she started her rise in the

---

[171] Ibid.
[172] Katie Reilly. "Read Hillary Clinton's 'Basket of Deplorables' Remarks About Donald Trump Supporters" *Time Magazine* http://time.com/4486502/hillary-clinton-basket-of-Deplorables-transcript/. (Sept. 10, 2016)

106

public arena. After the Clintons left the White House, however, it was made available for public viewing. Visitors can only view it on-site and can't make copies. Investigative reporter Bill Dedman has been there and wrote this: "[Hillary] closed her thesis by emphasizing that she reserved a place for Alinsky in the pantheon of social action — seated next to Martin Luther King, the poet-humanist Walt Whitman, and Eugene Debs, the labor leader now best remembered as the five-time Socialist Party candidate for president."[173] Eugene Debs was not only highly critical of capitalism, he helped establish the Socialist Party of America in 1897.

Kathy Shelton knows all about being trashed by Hillary. In 1975, with her first big case as an attorney, Hillary defended the then-12 year-old's accused rapist. Hillary stated, in an affidavit, that Kathy was "'emotionally unstable with a tendency to seek out older men and engage in fantasizing'. ... Years later, Shelton said that Hillary was 'gonna win her first case whatever it takes, whether she needs to lie, cheat or steal.'"[174] Alinsky's tactic to ridicule was Hillary's weapon even back then, by whatever means necessary.

In 1998, if you recall, Hillary was forced to come to her husband's defense yet again. With leaks about his

---

[173] Bill Dedman. "Reading Hillary Rodham's Hidden Thesis" *msnbc.com* (May 9, 2007)
http://www.nbcnews.com/id/17388372/ns/politics-decision_08/t/reading-hillary-rodhams-hidden-thesis/.
[174] Ariel Zilber and Gareth Davies. "Former Arkansas state employee who accused Bill Clinton of sexual harassment says she fears for her life if Hillary Clinton is elected president". *Dailymail.com* and *Mailonline* (Oct. 15, 2016)
https://www.dailymail.co.uk/news/article-3839570/Former-Arkansas-state-employee-accused-Bill-Clinton-sexual-harassment-says-fears-life-Hillary-Clinton-elected-president.html.

affair with Lewinsky becoming public, Hillary looked straight into the camera and told the American people that the entire story was a "vast right-wing conspiracy."

When asked in 2018 on *CBS's Sunday Morning* whether her husband should have stepped down as president over the affair in light of today's #MeToo movement, Hillary answered an emphatic, "'Absolutely not.' ... her husband's presidential affair with Monica Lewinsky wasn't an abuse of power — because the then-22-year-old White House intern 'was an adult'".[175]

During the Lewinsky controversy, Democrat "Charles Rangel questioned whether [Lewinski] 'played with a full deck.'"[176] But, he wasn't the only uncompassionate Democrat to come to Clinton's defense. "[A]n 'alert' posted on the feminist Women Leaders Online Web site, defend[ed] their favorite president of all time this way: 'Men acting like pigs is not against the law.'"[177] That's proof-positive that the left wasn't really concerned about women, even in the 90's. In fact, they were quite critical of Bill's "mistresses." It's no wonder men have experienced decades of confusion.

"Judy Mann, *The Washington Post's* feminist columnist...chided the press for not giving sufficient

---

[175] Marisa Schultz. "Hillary: Bill didn't abuse his power because Lewinsky 'was an adult'" *New York Post* (Oct. 14, 2018) https://nypost.com/2018/10/14/hillary-bill-didnt-abuse-his-power-because-lewinsky-was-an-adult/.

[176]. Michael Kruse. "The TV Interview That Haunts Hillary Clinton". *Politico*. (Sept. 23, 2016) https://www.politico.com/magazine/story/2016/09/hillary-clinton-2016-60-minutes-1992-214275.

[177] Marjorie Williams. "Lowering the Bar: Clinton and Women". *Vanity Fair* (Jan. 1, 2007) https://www.vanityfair.com/magazine/1998/05/williams199805

weight to the possibility that Lewinsky was embellishing her relationship with a celebrity just for attention—'a standard device for dingbats of all ages.'"[178]

Ridiculing the "enemy" is a tactic that has been used by the left for decades. Law professor Susan Estrich, who still appears on cable news shows today, wrote in her America Online column at the time that, "Lewinsky at least appears to have flirted her way to a job at Revlon, ... a $2 million modeling offer and the status of the most-sought after woman in the world. Not bad, some might say, for someone who can't type."[179] Estrich is a "spokeswoman" for women even today.

No one makes the hypocrisy on the left more apparent than a little-known woman named Karen Monahan. Having once dated Democratic Minnesota Representative, Keith Ellison, she accused him of sexual and physical abuse since late 2017. While the Dems railed against Kavanaugh's supposed sexual abuse, hardly a word was spoken about Ellison, even during his tight race to become the state's next Attorney General.

Ms. Monahan hasn't minced words about her treatment from the DNC: "'I've been smeared, threatened, isolated from my own party. I provided medical records from 2017, stating on two different Dr. [V]isits, I told them about the abuse and who did it. My therapist released records stating I have been dealing and healing from the abuse,' she wrote on social media. 'Four people, including my supervisor at the time, stated that I came to them after and shared the exact story I shared publicly, I shared multiple text [sic] between me

---

[178] Ibid.
[179] Ibid.

and Keith, where I discuss the abuse with him and much more. As I said before, I knew I wouldn't be believed.'"[180] She claims that the DNC ignored her claims. Ellison went on to win his race without a serious investigation.

"Stormy" Daniels came out of the woodwork just prior to the presidential general election. The porn-star demanded "hush" money to keep quiet about an alleged affair with Trump, about which she was threatening to go public. The "affair" supposedly took place over a decade prior. She received $130,000 from Trump's attorney in exchange for a confidentiality agreement. Whether Trump had an affair with "Stormy" or not, is not the issue. It would have been consensual and prior to his becoming president, not while he was in the Oval Office. The fact that "Stormy" made a deal and then later broke it by going public, tells me it was all about the money to begin with.

The amount of ridicule this president has been subjected to since taking office is unparalleled. The real shame of it is that our country, and the world, need our president's undivided attention for things that really matter. But, he's not the only target of the left's despicable tactics.

"NBC News Political Director Chuck Todd slammed Republicans for deploying 'a heavy dose of a bit of fear-mongering, conspiracy theories and even some mob-style antics. ... CNN's Chris Cuomo bashed the GOP for

---

[180] Daniel Moritz-Rabson. "Keith Ellison's Accuser Reiterates Claims Against Deputy DNC Chair Amid Kavanaugh Debate" *Newsweek* https://www.newsweek.com/accuser-reiterates-abuse-claims-against-keith-ellison-1129202 (Sept. 19, 2018).

promoting 'fear and loathing.' The term "scare tactics" was plastered on the TV screen as he spoke.'"[181]

NBC even lowered themselves to report on a disrespectful video showing a rapper getting a lap dance from a Melania Trump look-alike-stripper. No support groups for women were featured in that story.[182]

MSNBC's Joe Scarborough, a fierce anti-Trumper, told his viewers that Trump would not run in 2020, instead he'd "cash out". A ridiculous notion to any serious followers of the truth. Joe's wife, co-host and fellow Trump-hater, Mika Brzezinski, called Trump "base, animalistic and disgusting."[183] She wasn't referring to the video of our first lady depicted as a stripper, mind you. She was referring to our Commander-in-Chief. The left's tactics keep getting more transparent and crazy every day.

Calling Texas Democratic U.S. Senate hopeful Beto O'Rourke a "rock star" and the "Bobby Kennedy of millennials", ignored his prior drunk driving, hit-and-run charge. No Republican would have escaped such a lack of scrutiny.

The good news is that President Trump has Alinsky's fifth tactic mastered, as evidenced by his use of nicknames for his opponents, both domestic and foreign. Recall those he gave his Republican contenders during the presidential primary campaign. Some of the more memorable ones were: "Low Energy Jeb" (Bush), "Lyin' Ted" (Cruz), and "Little Marco" (Rubio). Bush never

---

[181] Dan Gainor. "Media embrace 'fear and loathing' of Trump and GOP as midterms near" *FOX News* (Oct. 21, 2018)
https://www.foxnews.com/opinion/media-embrace-fear-and-loathing-of-trump-and-gop-as-midterms-near.
[182] Ibid.
[183] Ibid.

recovered. Cruz, still in the Senate, has since joined Trump's agenda and just won another term. Rubio, remains in the Senate, but appears to still harbor ill-will towards Trump earning him the ire of his early Tea Party supporters, like me, as a result. He'd be smart to get on the Trump train while he still can.

The president has effectively used the art of ridicule to brand his Democratic foes, as well, starting with "Crooked Hillary". The name stuck so well throughout the campaign that his supporters chanted "lock her up, lock her up" at almost every rally. We're still waiting.

After becoming president, Trump has ridiculed never-Trumpers, Democrats, members of the "fake news" media and even foreign leaders with whom he wishes to negotiate. His strategy, arguably, has reaped untold success.

Never-Trump Republican Senators Bob Corker ("Liddle Bob Corker") and Jeff Flake (Jeff Flakey) have been relegated to the dustbins of history after making the unforgivable mistake of publicly denouncing our president on numerous occasions. They had no choice but to retire due to losing popularity at home.

Democratic Senator Richard Blumenthal was given the dishonorable nickname by Trump of "Da Nang Blumenthal" as a result of his hypocritical accusations calling then-Judge Kavanaugh dishonest when he himself lied for decades to the American people about being a war hero dodging bullets in Da Nang, Vietnam.

Another Democratic senator, and 2020 aspirant, Elizabeth Warren earned the nickname "Pocahontas", after years of lying about her so-called Cherokee Indian heritage to gain special minority status as a college student first, then a tenured professor. After Trump's constant dares for her to take a DNA test and come clean (as she is pasty white), she finally did. Incredibly, she made the results public, which showed her to have only 1/1024th percent of Indian blood, making her the laughing stock of the left and drawing the ire of the Cherokee nation. To earn their forgiveness, Warren is now campaigning for reparations for Native Americans from the American taxpayers!

Trump has even given the liars in mainstream media the memorable moniker, "fake news", as a group. "Psycho Joe" is Joe Scarborough. "Dumb as a Rock" Is reserved for his wife and co-host, Mika Brzezinski. "Sour Lemon" is *CNN's* Don Lemon. And, to name a few news organizations: "Failing *New York Times*", "Clinton News Network (*CNN*)", "Deface the Nation", and "Enemy of the American People." It absolutely drives the media crazy and Deplorables love it because we've known for years that the phony news outlets are no more than a propaganda arm of the Democratic Party.

The most inspiring spectacle to watch, though, is how the president uses the "art of ridicule" to negotiate with foreign leaders, allies or not. He loves to put them on the defensive, before he goes in for the close. The best example is "Little Rocket Man", nickname for North Korean (NOKO) leader Kim Jong-un. The left, and never-Trumpers, went absolutely nuts when Trump first used the term. They were convinced that he was stoking WWIII. Deplorables knew differently. While NOKO's leader has not yet started to dismantle his nuclear warheads, after the summit between Kim and Trump in June 2018, no new missiles have been deployed (the first time that has happened in years). Also, three American hostages have been released (without any ransom being paid), numerous meetings between NOKO and South Korea have occurred, and the dialogues between our Secretary of State Mike Pompeo continue. The "fake news" media may criticize the negotiations as being too little and too slow but, as President Trump said recently at one of his midterm campaign rallies: prior presidents over decades did nothing...Trump began historic negotiations only months ago and "fake news" claims he has failed.

I've never seen anyone make use of Alinsky's fifth tactic, *"ridicule is man's most potent weapon"*, so successfully. Trump gets it. Even better, as so many Democrats and Republican never-Trumpers deride him for the practice, he's not backing down. We can all be thankful for that, because it's working.

When Trump calls "Stormy", "Horseface", just cringe and let it go. We've been praying for a leader that would make good on campaign promises for at least as long as I've been alive. Let's back off and let him do his job. What Trump has accomplished in his first two years in office, with all those lined up against him, has been short of amazing. His gains are far more important than the silly nicknames he gives those he must combat every single day. It is who he is. It's what we voted for.

In the next chapter, "Stupid is as Stupid Does", find out how Alinsky's sixth tactic has actually worked to dumb down millennials; and, why that is now coming back to haunt the left. It spells good news for Trump and you're about to learn why.

STUPID IS AS
STUPID DOES

TACTIC #6: *"A good tactic is one your people enjoy."*[184]

"MY FEAR IS THAT THE whole island will become so overly populated that it will tip over and capsize," fretted Rep. Hank Johnson (D-Ga.) during a House Armed Services Committee hearing in 2010 about whether to send Marines to the U.S. territory of Guam. To which an amazingly composed, and generously kind, Adm. Robert Willard, head of the U.S. Pacific fleet paused and replied, *"We don't anticipate that."*[185]

Incredibly, Rep. Johnson continues to get re-elected. In 2016, he was still a member on the House Armed Services Committee! He currently serves on the Judiciary Committee and on the Transportation and Infrastructure Committee. *Infrastructure?* That alone should concern all Americans.

While speaking at an event in 2016, sponsored by the U.S. Campaign to End the Israeli Occupation, an anti-Israel organization that galvanizes supporters of the Boycott, Divestment, and Sanctions [BDS] movement, [Johnson] made news again by "comparing

---

[184] Ibid. Alinsky, pg. 128.
[185] Stephanie Condon. "Hank Johnson Worries Guam Could 'Capsize' After Marine Buildup", *CBS News* (April 1, 2010) https://www.cbsnews.com/news/hank-johnson-worries-guam-could-capsize-after-marine-buildup/.

Jewish people who live in disputed territories to 'termites' that destroy homes".[186] That's what virulently anti-Semitic Louis Farrakhan has said. Predictably, Rep. Johnson received rounds of applause for his comment.

It doesn't take much to turn Alinsky's sixth tactic for radicals against the left when their base has a level of understanding so elementary. Yet, during my lifetime, never has a single Republican turned this tactic against them, until Donald J. Trump.

By understanding that *"a good tactic is one your people enjoy"*, the Dems have been incredibly successful for decades at keeping their colleagues and constituents loyal and complicit. They've achieved this through indoctrination by staffing our educational systems and media with extreme leftists. As a result, they've been able to hold on to power with shockingly ignorant representatives such as dumb-dumb Hank Johnson, pompous Barbara Boxer, and naïve Alexandria Ocasio-Cortez. But, that is also a direct result of complacency by Republicans. Today, Americans are paying dearly for that apathy. Donald J. Trump has marked the end of that era.

President Trump is that rare individual who is able to face challenges as though they are 3-dimensional chess games. He is so far ahead of his opponents that they really believe he's either delusional, a liar, or even a traitor (he's been called all three), simply because they are far below his level of understanding. This is true for

---

[186] Adam Kredo. "Congressman who once feared Guam could capsize compares Jewish settlers to 'termites'" *Fox News Politics* (July, 25, 2016) http://www.foxnews.com/politics/congressman-who-once-feared-guam-could-capsize-compares-jewish-settlers-to-termites.

almost every topic he speaks or tweets about. To him, it's an intellectual and logical game, with high stakes.

Moderate Democrats, many Independents, and all never-Trumpers, are either unable to see the big picture, or don't believe our country is really in trouble. It shows in their virulent, anti-Trump sentiment. They think they are smarter than him. They're wrong.

Deplorables, on the other hand, understand him because we think like him; so, his words and actions make total sense. We "get it", his haters don't. While it may be frustrating for us to witness this level of animosity against our president, it may help to realize that it stems from the complete lack of comprehension of multi-dimensional, complex issues. The left hopes their "useful idiot" constituents stay stupid enough to believe Guam will tip over if too many Marines land. That's a form of enslavement. Minorities, especially, are waking up to that realization. We are not idiots.

Trump doesn't show his hand in many situations because it could compromise sensitive negotiations. He's far ahead of his opponents and keeps his intentions unknown until it benefits him (aka, US). It's that uncertainty that drives his opponents, especially the "fake news" media, crazy. The mere term "fake news" is enough to send them off a cliff, and Trump knows it. That's why he does it. He *enjoys* it.

If the media was fair and balanced, Trump would have a favorability rating way above today's 47%. A "wide-ranging study of broadcast news coverage of Trump in the first four months of [2018] reveals that it was 90 percent negative — just as it was throughout

2017".[187] Even so, Trump's ratings have gone up.[188] That's because more and more Americans are recognizing the blatant bias and are no longer willing to be dumbed down. *Thank God.*

There is no difference between the "fake news" media of today, and that of Joseph Goebbels' (the Nazi propagandist) time. Yet, the left has the audacity to call Trump and his supporters the fascists. Unfortunately, lots of people believe it. That's why Trump has called "fake news", the "enemy of the people". Many disagree with that concept, including his own daughter, Ivanka. But, many of us do not. We truly believe there is great danger in "fake news".

The left, the Dems and never-Trumpers blame Trump for dividing the country. Yet, they are the ones responsible. Trump calls them out on it, unlike any president before him. Deplorables love him for it.

When news outlets lie about, omit, or bury news, they prevent their audiences from objectively understanding facts. This enables the "fake news" media to shape their audience's thinking to align with the left's narrative. That is propaganda, pure and simple.

As important as the lies propagated by the "fake news" media, is the rewriting of our history in our children's schoolbooks. We are teaching our kids to hate America based on falsehoods. The younger generation today has been irretrievably brainwashed. That's both sad and scary.

---

[187] Jennifer Harper. "Media get trumped: President's polls improve despite 90% negative coverage" *Washington Times* https://www.washingtontimes.com/news/2018/may/8/donald-trumps-polls-improve-despite-90-negative-co/.
[188] Ibid.

As far back as at least the sixties, Saul Alinsky's tactics were being used as the basis for the transformation of our educational systems. Vladimir Lenin once famously said, "Give me just one generation of youth, and I'll transform the whole world." We are way past that point in America. Today's youth are the proof, and our future dilemma.

"The National Education Association [NEA] has made a glowing assessment of radical socialist community organizer Saul Alinsky and is enthusiastically recommending American public school teachers read two of his books, including one dedicated to Satan."[189]

The NEA is the largest labor union in the United States. It represents public school teachers, most of whom have no idea that a staggering amount of their dues goes towards the leadership's bloated salaries and leftist political causes that work to undermine our capitalist system and replace it with socialism.

According to World Net Daily (WND), "[o]n its website, the NEA dubs Alinsky 'an inspiration to anyone contemplating action in their community! And to every organizer!' ... It recommends Alinsky's 'Rules for Radicals,' ... a socialist strategy for gaining political power to redistribute wealth from the 'haves' to the 'have-nots.'"[190]

It's not hard to grasp how the NEA's rapid growth in leftist causes became possible. A 1972 document, called "Alinsky for Teacher Organizers", intended to create organizational structures within the school

---

[189] "NEA raves to teachers about Alinsky 'guidebook'" *WND* (Nov.3, 2009) https://www.wnd.com/2009/11/114881/.
[190] Ibid.

systems. In it, you'll find proof that some of our most influential Democratic leaders were directly involved early on. The tentacles run deep; and, it's a pretty safe bet that most Americans have absolutely no idea.

For instance, "when Bill Clinton was governor of Arkansas, he brought Marc Tucker into the state to redesign or transform their education system around the system[']s governance philosophy. Tucker would later pay Mrs. Clinton over $100,000 to promote America's Choice: High Skills or Low Wages! [a school program]. ... The strategies, tactics and beliefs of Saul Alinsky [that would be incorporated into the program] find basis in the Hegelian Dialectic developed by Georg Wilhelm Im Friedrich Hegel. [In essence: create a conflict and mold the opposing reactions to a pre-determined solution.] His philosophy would be furthered by Karl Marx."[191] Marc Tucker, it should be noted, has been the president of the nonprofit, National Center on Education and the Economy (NCEE), from 1988 to present. Americans should be outraged.

"In an 18-page 'Dear Hillary' letter," after Bill Clinton became president, "he [Tucker] told the incoming first lady, who many at the time viewed as a co-president [of the NCEE], ... the time had come 'to remold the entire American system' into a 'seamless web that extends literally from cradle to grave and is the same system for everyone.' Via national standards, the system would be all-controlling: curriculum, pedagogy, testing, teacher training and licensure, and virtually everything else. Workforce boards would tweak curricula

191 J. Michael Arisman, Midwest Training Consultant. "Alinsky for Teacher Organizers" *National Education Association* (1972) http://www.mikemcmahon.info/unionorganize.pdf.

to meet state-determined labor needs."[192] In other words, bye-bye to local control of schools, hello to federal control (i.e., socialism). That's one more reason to be thanking our lucky stars that Donald J. Trump won the election.

Is it already too late? With most Americans asleep at the wheel over the past several decades, giving the NEA and the NCEE a thirty-year head start, it's hard to say. But, to do nothing ensures that our children's education will bring our country one step closer to living under socialist rule. It's our choice. You can bet the left hopes we keep sleeping.

One of the "core values" listed on the NEA's website is: "Collective Action. We believe individuals are strengthened when they work together for the common good. As education professionals, we improve both our professional status and the quality of public education when we unite and advocate collectively."[193] Beware socialist keywords, such as, "collective bargaining", "common good", "common core", and "social justice".

Don't expect the NEA and other leftist groups to slow down. They've got other plans for our children, as they promise on their website: "Fortunately, another generation of NEA members and leaders are stepping up to become social justice activists. They are defending

---

[192] Robert Holland. "Awaiting a second 'Dear Hillary' letter: An educator determined to push Soviet-style education for the masses holds sway" *The Washington Times* https://www.washingtontimes.com/news/2016/aug/21/hillary-clinton-and-soviet-style-education/.
[193] "Putting our Values to Work: A Resource for Association Social Justice Activists and Organizers" *National Education Association* https://www.nea.org/assets/docs/14695-Putng_R_Values_to_Wrk_11.pdf.

the democracy that gave birth to public schools. They are rallying for the civil rights which the social justice activists of the past sacrificed so much to achieve."[194]

As it is, our colleges have become so dumbed down they are churning out what has become a new urban dictionary noun: "snowflakes". They are even demanding the installation of "safe rooms" on campuses to avoid "unpleasantries".

Unlike the 18-year-olds of the "Greatest Generation" who fought in WWII, today's kids are living at home well into their 20s and 30s, have college debt up to their eyeballs, think socialism is the next best thing to sexting, and hate America and everything we stand for. Their heroes are Che Guevara, Mao Zedong, Colin Kaepernick, the Castro brothers, and Alexandria Ocasio-Cortez. It's no wonder socialism is on the rise!

Recently, the newly-installed president of San Francisco's school board "broke with protocol...by deciding to skip the Pledge of Allegiance before a meeting, *The San Francisco Chronicle* reported. In its place, Steven Cook recited a quote from the poet Maya Angelou: "*When you learn, teach. When you get, give.*"[195] Spare me. Today, it's in a meeting, tomorrow it's in classrooms. This is just one more way to dumb our kids down by preventing them from learning the true history of our great nation. They are being taught to hate our country and everything in it.

---

[194] Ibid.
[195] Bradford Betz. "San Francisco school board president drops Pledge of Allegiance" *FOX News* (Oct. 11, 2018) https://www.foxnews.com/us/san-francisco-school-board-president-drops-pledge-of-allegiance.

For the successful transformation of America from capitalism to socialism, it is necessary to rewrite history and erase the patriotism that is the glue that keeps our citizens united. That takes time, patience and drive by the socialist activists, and a willingness of the majority to do nothing. It's only going to get much worse, unless we take a stand now.

Most Americans today don't realize that the Nazi official party name was the "National Socialist German Workers' Party". It began as a "movement known as National Socialism. Under the leadership of Adolf Hitler, the party came to power in Germany in 1933 and governed by totalitarian methods until 1945."[196] From the very beginning, Hitler's stated goals were to use socialist ideologies to garner mass appeal, then expand territory and create a master Aryan race.[197] Which he did, of course, by exterminating millions of Jews and other "undesirables".

Today in America, the Democratic Socialists of America (DSA) love to compare our president to a totalitarian or a fascist, even calling him a "Hitler" and his supporters "Nazis". Hence, the Antifascist movement they've created.

Young people's minds are being twisted by the left's false definitions of words like "totalitarianism", "fascism", "nationalism" and even "socialism" itself. The Antifa thugs and young DSA members are, in fact, being used by the left to do the exact same bidding for the Democrats that Hitler achieved with "Brownshirts" [aggressive mob-like youth similar to today's Antifa

---

[196] "Nazi Party" *Encyclopaedia Britannica* (Last Updated Sept. 26, 2018) https://www.britannica.com/topic/Nazi-Party.
[197] Ibid.

movement] and Nazi youth in Germany eighty-five years ago. Our history is being rewritten as we sleep.

A hundred years prior to the Nazis, the German-Jewish poet, Heinrich Heine, had declared that, "[W]herever books are burned, human beings are destined to be burned too."[198] Education is the food for life and freedom. If you can rewrite history, you can transform a country and divide the people in it.

In 1933, with the help of students and "Brownshirts", Hitler and Goebbels began book burnings on a mass scale in order to erase their history of all things "un-German". That enabled the Nazis to mold the students' minds into believing the party's political agenda.

Our current-day kids have no idea what socialism even is, because they aren't being taught history at all, or they are being taught a much skewed version of it.

Social media giants are practicing a modern-day book burning by manipulating search engines under the guise of banning "hate" speech. What they are really doing is silencing alternative viewpoints. That is way more dangerous than book burning because it is on a global scale.

"Before Hitler, German university towns had been counted among the world's great centers of scientific innovation and literary scholarship. Under Hitler, Germany's intellectual vitality quickly began to diminish. Truth, rational thinking and objective knowledge, the foundation stones of Western Civilization, were denounced by Nazified students and professors in favor

---

[198] "The Triumph of Hitler: The Burning of Books" *The History Place* (2001) http://www.historyplace.com/worldwar2/triumph/tr-bookburn.htm.

of mysticism, speculation and collective thinking toward a common goal – the pursuit of a glorious future for Germany."[199] The familiarities are frightening. It only took Hitler twelve years to destroy his country.

Our institutions of higher learning have suffered a similar fate. Because of a coordinated effort by the left, our colleges are packed by leftist, tenured professors anxious to fundamentally transform America.

According to radio talk show host Michael Knowles, a recent 11-page flyer distributed by Young Democratic Socialists of America [YDSA], pushes millennials to "'take jobs as teachers' as a way to move teachers unions 'in a more militant and democratic direction.' Knowles said that according to numerous surveys, 'the blood-soaked history' of socialism is unknown by millennials, leading them to identify as supporters of the movement.

"Campus Reform [a conservative watchdog group on liberal campuses] reported that the ... pamphlet notes teachers are able to use their relationships with students to discuss 'campaigns around police brutality, immigrant rights, and environmental justice.'"[200] Given the aforementioned NEA's core values, one shudders to think of the next generation of students about to emerge.

Millennials who haven't gone to college aren't immune from propaganda. With Democrats keeping

---

[199] Ibid.
[200] "Knowles: Dem Socialists Pushing to Infiltrate Schools Because 'They Can't Win in the Battle of Ideas' *FOXNews Insider* http://insider.foxnews.com/2018/08/25/young-democratic-socialists-america-releases-pamphlet-targeting-teachers-unions-michael.

poverty at all-time highs in once-thriving American cities, crime is rampant and anger is out-of-control.

Recently, "[S]upporters of U.S. Senator [sic: Representative] Maxine Waters (D-Calif.) gathered outside her West Coast office to protest a patriotic group that was scheduled to rally later in the day. Waters has gained national attention of late by voicing her hatred for Trump and whipping up her constituents. At the rally, the supporters were able to grab an American flag off the back of a passing pickup truck. The flag was then stepped on and set ablaze as someone stoked the flames. A few people cheered and someone yelled, 'This is not the American flag, this is their flag.'"[201] Our nation is totally divided.

We need real solutions soon to reverse the takeover of our educational systems. The left loves Alinsky's sixth rule, *"A good tactic is one your people enjoy."* They've gained enormous financial security in tenured professorships where they can't be fired, on that tactic alone. They're able to work on transforming our country into what they believe will be a socialist utopia while doing exactly what they enjoy, and getting paid mighty well for it. What the left doesn't understand is that eventually the very mob rule they so carefully crafted over the years, will someday come back to bite them.

Just as Hitler's "Brownshirts" bullied dissenters on the streets, today's left shuts free speech down on the internet.

---

[201] Paulina Dedaj. "Maxine Waters supporters burn American flag outside California rep's office" *FOX News* (July 19, 2018) https://www.foxnews.com/politics/maxine-waters-supporters-burn-american-flag-outside-california-reps-office

Netflix actor Israel Broussard, for example, made the unforgiveable mistake of "liking tweets from Daily Wire [E]ditor-in-chief Ben Shapiro, Donald Trump, and Senator Marco Rubio."[202] After an onslaught of hate-filled tweets from left-wing critics, Broussard didn't only acquiesce, he groveled for forgiveness. "I am deeply sorry for my inappropriate and insensitive words and likes on social media," he wrote. "I take full responsibility for my actions and I sincerely apologize. This has been a pivotal life lesson for me. I am dedicated to becoming a more informed and educated version of myself."[203] Broussard was publicly "re-educated" and didn't even know it. Who needs "re-education camps" when it can be done online? But, before we judge this young man's response, let's remember that he's financially dependent on his "Hollyweird" connections and probably not yet politically matured. Still, it gives us an idea of just how intolerant the "party of tolerance" really is.

The better thing to remind ourselves of is how truly stupid so many in the Democratic Party are. That gives us the advantage and we should use it.

The good news is when these dumb-as-rocks students get into the real world, they'll become part of the Democratic Party. They'll start turning on their own. DSA already has. They are using the same tactics the Dems have taught for decades, only they are even more radical. In 2019 we are witnessing, for the first time, a

---

[202] James Barrett. "Netflix Star Apologizes After Being Outed For Liking Shapiro, Rubio, Trump" *The Daily Wire* (Aug. 23, 2018) https://www.dailywire.com/news/34944/netflix-star-apologizes-after-being-outed-liking-james-barrett
[203] Ibid.

serious division in the Democratic Party. We should do everything we can to encourage that split. We are the logical ones. They are, as Trump likes to say, about mobs, caravans, open borders and abolishing ICE. That's all Americans should need to know.

There are many actions Deplorables can take to counter the indoctrination of our kids. Stop sending money to your alma mater, unless you know their agenda. Send your kids to responsible schools that won't turn them into "Snowflakes", like Hillsdale College, Biola University and College of the Ozarks. They are fast-becoming the responsible and respected universities, with unbiased professors who have a heavy emphasis on America's true history, Constitutional laws, and the values our country's Founding Fathers envisioned. Private, conservative learning centers like Prager University (a non-profit organization for continuing education) are great options, too.

If you grew up in the baby-boomer generation, as did I, you'd think Purdue University is a safe bet. You'd be wrong. They now send "admitted undergraduate students a survey where they have the option of identifying their sexual identity (choices: asexual, bisexual, gay, straight/heterosexual, lesbian, pansexual, queer, questioning, same-gender loving, two spirit, prefer not to disclose, and not listed) and their gender identity (choices: woman, man, FTM/transgender man/trans man, MTF/transgender-woman/trans woman, gender queer, prefer not to disclose, and not listed)."[204] To the left, it's all a game. They laugh at the stuff the American people let them get away with. It's another way to create chaos in an otherwise orderly-structured world.

Alinsky's *"a good tactic is one that your people enjoy"* describes exactly these types of programs. Envision the snowflaky administrators of these colleges "one-upping" their competitors, seeing who can add the most gender-/sexual-identifying adjectives to their applications. To Deplorables, it's breaking down the fabric of our country. But, they don't stop there. If you checked some of the curriculum these institutions are adding, you'd be shocked.

I recently watched Pete Hegseth on *FOX & Friends* when he visited College of the Ozarks in Missouri. What originally caught my attention was when one of the students he interviewed mentioned that the college had boycotted NIKE products after the "I Can Do It" campaign was launched, with flag-kneeling Colin Kaepernick as its spokesman. The students in the background cheered the boycott. I was impressed upon learning that the school's nickname is "Hard Work U" because every single student works on campus throughout their college years and graduates debt-free. I guarantee you those students won't become "Snowflakes"!

That's the kind of out-of-the-box thinking Deplorables must support in order to play catch up with the left. While it seems they are just ignorant enough to

---

[204] "Colleges and Universities with LGBTQ Identity Questions as an Option on Admission Applications & Enrollment Forms" *Campus Pride* (Last Updated Fall 2018)
https://www.campuspride.org/tpc/identity-questions-as-an-option/.

fail, it's too important for our country to not take them seriously.

What I love about President Trump is that he understands he's dealing with an opponent that has purposefully dumbed down its own constituents. And, he calls them out on it. No matter how much flak he gets, he never backs down. That's because he really *enjoys* the game, too. He's got guts and it filters down to the people around him: to his administration, to Congress, and yes, even to never-Trumpers. As long as he can hang in there, we must, too.

The next time a Democrat says something really dumb as Rep. Hank Johnson said about an island tipping over, we cannot feel embarrassed for him and sweep it under the rug. We must humiliate him publicly ad nauseam, just like the Dems do to Republicans. It's the only way to teach the youth that "stupid" is not a quality to be admired.

The Dems have already told us what they are planning to do next. In the following chapter, "Impeach 45", find out how dangerous the next two years will be as the newly-empowered, House Majority Dems start their long-promised, eighty-five new investigations of our president.

But, fret not. President Trump still has cards in his back pocket. And, he plans to use every single one.

IMPEACH 45

TACTIC #7: *"A tactic that drags on too long becomes a drag."*[205]

"THERE'S A DIFFERENCE IN HOW some of our leadership talk about how we should handle all of this," complained California Congresswoman Maxine Waters, while accepting an award from the Stonewall Young Democrats recently. *"They say, Maxine, please don't say impeachment anymore. And when they say that, I say 'impeachment, impeachment, impeachment, impeachment, impeachment, impeachment, impeachment.'"*[206]

"While many in party leadership have shied away from those demands, Waters and her allies are emboldened by the prospect of Democrats retaking the House in the midterms and, potentially, using a majority to launch impeachment proceedings."[207]

Many Democrats had remained quiet about their impeachment plans for our 45th President of the United States. But it's not because they don't agree with Waters. They just didn't want to alienate the more moderate voters in the midterm elections. But, you can bet

---

[205] Ibid. Alinsky. pg. 128.
[206] Andrew O'Reilly. "Maxine Waters goes on Trump 'impeachment' tear, vows to 'get him'" *foxnews.com* (Sept. 10, 2018) https://www.foxnews.com/politics/maxine-waters-goes-on-trump-impeachment-tear-vows-to-get-him.
[207] Ibid.

that is exactly what the Dems plan to do. Moderate Dems are well aware of Saul Alinsky's seventh rule: "*A tactic that drags on too long becomes a drag.*" They want to be sure the "I-word" doesn't get stale. Alinsky warned that "man can sustain militant interest in any issue for only a limited time."[208]

Before Trump even took his oath of office on January 21, 2017, there were calls from the left, anti-Trumpers and never-Trumpers that our President should be impeached. That is unprecedented. Check out what the "fake news" media was saying back in 2016, *before Trump was even the Republican nominee.*

According to Darren Samuelsohn of *Politico* in April, 2016: "'Impeachment' is already on the lips of pundits, newspaper editorials, constitutional scholars, and even a few members of Congress. From the right, Washington attorney Bruce Fein puts the odds at 50/50 that a President Trump commits impeachable offenses as president. Democratic Rep. Alan Grayson says Trump's insistence on building a wall at the U.S.-Mexico border, if concrete was poured despite Congress's opposition, could lead down a path toward impeachment. Even the mainstream Republican head of the U.S. Chamber of Commerce recently tossed out the "I-word" when discussing the civilian backlash if Trump's trade war with China led to higher prices on everyday items sold at Walmart and Target.

"On his radio show last month, Rush Limbaugh even put a very brisk timeline on it: 'They'll be talking

---

[208]Ibid. Alinsky, pg. 128.

impeachment on day two, after the first Trump executive order,' he said."[209] As usual, Rush was right.

So let's not pretend this vendetta against Trump is something new. Whether he did all things right or wrong from the beginning wouldn't have changed a thing.

Samuelsohn's article warns what types of Trump's actions, were he to become president, could justify impeachment deserves full copy in this chapter. Given 20/20 hindsight, it's downright laughable, yet worrisome that this is really how the left thinks. Samuelsohn wants us to imagine the following: "...travel on the *Politico* time machine to the summer of 2017: President Trump, survivor of a Republican civil war and Hillary Clinton's Democratic machine, is making good on his promise to 'Make America Great Again'"[210].

Samuelsohn portends that: "[T]rump has ordered federal contractors to start building the wall between the United States and Mexico, though neither Mexico nor the U.S. Congress will pay for it. Trump has directed the National Guard to patrol Detroit, Chicago, New York and other neighborhoods with large Muslim populations, and accusations are swirling that he is illegally rounding up suspected Islamic extremists and shipping them off to special detention centers, including the recently reopened Alcatraz Island and to several of the World War II-era internment camps the U.S. government used for Japanese-Americans. Despite the counsel of his foreign policy and military advisers,

---

[209] Darren Samuelsohn. "Could Trump Be Impeached Shortly After He Takes Office?" *Politico* (April 17, 2016)
https://www.politico.com/magazine/story/2016/04/donald-trump-2016-impeachment-213817.
[210] Ibid.

Trump has commanded the CIA to resume waterboarding and other forms of torture to obtain information about imminent attacks. Inside the intelligence and defense communities, a full-blown internal war has broken out as some interrogators and high-ranking officials follow Trump's orders, while others refuse to cooperate. Some resign their posts and begin leaking details to the media and Congress. Trump has also ordered airstrikes on the family members of known terrorists from Afghanistan to Libya. CNN airs live coverage of the bombings and protests sweep across the Middle East, North Africa and Europe as the death toll rises for the parents, siblings, spouses and children of ISIL and Al Qaeda fighters. At the United Nations, a resolution is passed, calling for Trump to be tried for war crimes.

"On talk radio and cable news, the #NeverTrump movement has morphed into #DumpTrump: Limbaugh thunders from the right that it's time to hand the keys to Vice President Jeff Sessions, while Rachel Maddow and Lawrence O'Donnell dedicate their nightly MSNBC broadcasts to tallying lists of alleged high crimes and misdemeanors.

"Most importantly, the polls have turned against Trump. He still has his most passionate supporters, but the honeymoon in the Oval Office is clearly over. Enough of the American public had voted to hire Trump—he'd captured the Electoral College in November 2016 without winning either the popular vote or a plurality— hoping he'd make America great again. But now the country is clearly dissatisfied with how he's going about doing it. And as the bad headlines keep piling up,

Trump's once-vaunted poll numbers are anything but *yuuuuge.*"[211]

That's exactly what the naysayers believed would happen if Trump were to become president. Is it any wonder they were in a tizzy the moment he won?

Deplorables knew better. We knew that the main threat President Trump would present would be to clean house. We knew he wanted to build the wall, protect our Constitution, and recalibrate the SCOTUS to ensure our constitutional rights would be secure for generations to come. We also knew he wanted to deregulate businesses, get government out of our lives, and go after Hillary Clinton and her cronies (don't worry, he still has time). We knew, too, that he was going to make our trade deals fairer, keep us safer, and get us out of climate change deals that are based more on global redistribution of wealth than science. Most of all, we knew he was the only man who could do all these things.

What we didn't know (at least I didn't) was the extent to which the "swamp" would fight back. I didn't know the level of hatred that was buried deep within our government agencies against our constitutional protections. I didn't know how widespread the RINO (Republican-In-Name-Only) elites had become and how many of them would oppose all things conservative. I, and I think most, just didn't know. Now that we do, our fight has become ever more urgent.

Alinsky's first rule of means and ends states that, *"the ethics of means and ends is that generally success or failure is a mighty determinant of ethics."*[212] He

---

[211] Ibid.
[212] Alinsky. pg. 34.

explains that, "The judgment of history leans heavily on the outcome of success or failure; it spells the difference between the traitor and the patriotic hero. *There can be no such thing as a successful traitor, for if one succeeds he becomes a founding father.* [emphasis his]"[213]

That, friends, is what this fight is all about. If the left wins this fight, they will become the new founding fathers of a socialist America.

There's a lot riding on who succeeds in this battle between the left, the establishment, and never–Trumpers versus President Donald J. Trump and Deplorables. Our country is at a crossroads. Either the left wins with its values, or we do with ours.

We know what our values are. But what, exactly, are the values of the left?

Luckily, we don't have to search far to find out. They have shown us, especially over these past two years. I boil it down to two men in this country: President Trump and a guy named George Soros, the face of the left.

We know the left wants open borders, stands for higher taxes, aims to abolish ICE, will enforce single-payer health care for all (including illegal immigrants), wants to bankrupt our country by embroiling us in a war on climate that we'll never win, and believes our Constitution is a living, breathing document meant to change with the times. They've also repeatedly said they want free college educations and guaranteed incomes for all, and to replace 100% of our fossil fuels with solar and wind power. In other words, we know their overall goal is to replace our democracy and all its freedoms, with a socialist state aimed at total government control.

---

[213] Ibid.

If you don't know all that, and you would be abhorred to learn it is true, you owe it to the future of our country to start doing your research.

The reason people are on the fence about Trump is because they don't understand the urgency of losing our country. Nor did the Venezuelans, until it was too late.

Trump is the first politician I've known in my lifetime who understands the truth. Without him, we can kiss the America we once knew goodbye forever.

Is it possible this great man who is forsaking his salary to work tirelessly for us could get Impeached? Let's examine that question in more detail.

Less than a year into Trump's first term, six "House Democrats introduced five articles of impeachment against [him]...from obstruction of justice for interfering in the Russia investigation to bully pulpit."[214]

In support of their argument, Democratic Rep. Al Green (D-Texas) reported that "'Article II Section IV of the Constitution of the United States of America was drafted for a time such as this and a president such as Trump.'"[215]

"The five articles of impeachment the lawmakers introduced ... are: 1. Obstruction of justice regarding the Russia investigation and firing of FBI Director James Comey 2. Violation of Article I, Section 9 of the U.S. Constitution - Foreign Emoluments 3. Violation of Article II, Section 1 of the U.S. Constitution - Domestic Emoluments 4. Undermining the Independence of the

[214] Aaron P. Bernstein/Reuters. "6 Democrats introduce 5 Articles of Impeachment against President Trump" *ABC News* (Nov. 15, 2017) https://abcnews.go.com/Politics/democrats-introduce-articles-impeachment-president-trump/story?id=51167864
[215] Ibid.

Federal Judiciary and the Rule of Law 5. Undermining Freedom of the Press."[216]

Minority Leader Nancy Pelosi and Whip Steny Hoyer disagreed with the far-left Dems. "'We've made the judgment that the facts aren't there yet,' Hoyer, D-Maryland, told ... reporters ... citing a 'number of investigations' that 'should run out' before pursuing impeachment."[217]

As far as the first article of impeachment put forth by the Dems, we know, from the "Collusion Delusion" chapter, that the Russia investigation is not going as the Dems had planned. There has not been one scintilla of evidence that Trump either colluded with Russia, or obstructed justice by firing Comey. In fact, we now know that Assistant Attorney General Rod Rosenstein actually recommended the firing of Comey in a letter to the president. That has been made public. So, obstruction of justice for firing Comey is easy for Trump to defend. But, he doesn't have to even do that. A president has full right to fire whomever he wishes.

The second and third articles of impeachment the Dems say bolster their claims, regard foreign and domestic emoluments, or profit, salary, or fees from office or employment. That is ridiculous. While those who hate Trump love to spread the rumor that he's making money off his presidency, i.e., from Saudi Arabia real estate, no such proof has ever been presented to support that claim. Nevertheless, House Democrats are pushing to get Trump's tax returns made public so they can, again, go in search of a crime.

---

[216] Ibid.
[217] Ibid.

The fourth article has to do with undermining the rule of law and the judiciary. This is the most laughable of all given how much the left disrespects the rule of law in so many cases, e.g., their recent call for the abolishment of ICE and their flagrant waiving of Kavanaugh's due process. I've seen no evidence that Trump has in any way interfered with the DOJ or Mueller in their investigations.

The Dem's final claim for impeachment is the most ridiculous: "Undermining Freedom of the Press". I have never witnessed a president give more press conferences or allow so much access to him than this one. Never once have I seen this president restrict the press's freedoms other than one *CNN's* bully reporter who totally disrespected the privilege of attending a press conference in the White House time after time.

The left's real strategy for impeaching President Trump is to lay the groundwork in support of why he is unfit for duty. Remember the fifth tactic of Alinsky's is "*ridicule is man's most potent weapon*," and, that the "people" would even come up with their own ways to do this. Several important recent events come to mind.

A "D.C. Advisory Neighborhood Commission...is backing a petition...to pull the Trump International Hotel's liquor license -- citing D.C. law that only individuals of 'good character' qualify for a liquor license."[218] The left knows that, if it keeps chipping away at Trump's character, the insults will eventually be accepted as truth.

---

[218] Adam Shaw. "DC commissioners fight to revoke Trump Hotel liquor license" *foxnews.com* (July 20, 2018)
https://www.foxnews.com/politics/dc-commissioners-fight-to-revoke-trump-hotel-liquor-license

According to *National Review*, "Joe Scarborough Says Trump Is More of a Threat Than Terrorist Attacks."[219] The host of "Morning Joe " on *MSNBC* wrote an op-ed insulting our president by writing that he "has done more damage to the dream of America than any foreign adversary ever could."[220] Scarborough had backed Trump early in his candidacy. Whatever happened to turn the two against each other later is anybody's guess. His attack on Trump, stupidly, was published on the 17th anniversary of the 9/11 terrorist attacks on the World Trade Centers, killing almost 3,000 Americans. It backfired completely.

The left is so full of rage for Trump (and all Conservatives) that they make irrational mistakes and lose the high ground. That will be their undoing.

Fortunately, the American people are finally paying attention to bias from the "fake news" media and we're gaining in numbers. It's important to ensure that truth prevails so our values remain. Only then will we win the war between the left's socialist dream and our Constitutional experiment.

A Democratic newcomer challenged long-held Texas Republican Senator Ted Cruz's seat during the midterms. Early in the contest, Beto O'Rourke led by a wide margin. Following the SCOTUS issue, his lead began to narrow. Conservatives and moderates alike were appalled by the treatment Kavanaugh received, by the mob-like violent protests afterwards, and by the

---

[219] Alexandra DeSanctis. "Joe Scarborough Says Trump Is More of a Threat Than Terrorist Attacks" National Review (Sept. 11, 2018) https://www.nationalreview.com/corner/joe-scarborough-says-donald-trump-more-threatening-than-terrorist-attacks/
[220] Ibid.

surprise attacks on GOP politicians in public places. In addition, a caravan began marching north from Central America through Mexico towards our southern border.

What hurt Beto O'Rourke the most, though, was how he miscalculated his voters less than three weeks before the midterms. According to *Time* magazine, O'Rourke "told a national television audience Thursday night that he'd vote to impeach President Donald Trump and believes Texas can lead the way to a national embracing of relaxed immigration policies and gun control — unapologetically liberal positions that may be hard for some in his deep-red state to stomach."[221]

Most shocking is how acceptable it is for Dems to support impeachment without our president having committed even one provable offense. Even more alarming is how the once-deep-red state of Texas is becoming normalized to liberal ideas that would have been unthinkable a decade ago. Moderate Texans, as well as all Americans, need to wake up.

The biggest proponent of the impeachment of President Trump isn't even on the ballot, yet. An ultra-left group, called "Need to Impeach", is quietly forming and waiting to strike. It has been funded by billionaire Tom Steyer, who is eyeing the presidency in 2020. He has invested $50-$120 million dollars of his own money to ready his powerful political machine to spring into action when the time is right. The group has reached a staggering six million members in its first year, all of whom are Americans who want to see President Donald J. Trump impeached.

---

[221]Will Weissert, "Beto O'Rourke Doubles Down on Claim He'd Support President Trump's Impeachment" *Time* (Oct. 18, 2018) http://time.com/5429191/beto-orourke-trump-impeachment/.

Prior to the midterms, *The Atlantic* claimed that, "[I]f Democrats win the House, Need to Impeach will immediately move to the next phase, with a plan that includes activating its list to immediately pressure new members to sign on with... Trump's impeachment, flooding them long before they have staff set up in Washington. A group of constitutional lawyers is already under contract drafting specific articles of impeachment against Trump."[222]

If the "Need to Impeach" campaign is unsuccessful in its stated goal, no matter. Steyer has succeeded in building the "biggest voter list in politics – bigger than the NRA".[223] This positions him perfectly when he makes his run to replace Trump in 2020, an idea many Democratic strategists predict is the real aim behind the move. "For every 1 million people who've signed up with Need to Impeach, 85 percent are registered [voters], 95 percent support Democrats and 34 percent reliably show up".[224] Impressive machine for an anti–Trumper.

We know that Republicans were blinded by their zeal to impeach former President Clinton in the 90's. A majority of Americans weren't on board, causing the GOP to lose the majority in the midterms. Will the same thing happen to the Dems in 2020? According to *The New Yorker*, it very well could. The House rejected Democratic Rep. Al Green's amended initiative to impeach Trump by a vote of 355–66.

---

[222] Mike Blake/Reuters, "How Tom Steyer Built the Biggest Political Machine You've Never Heard Of", *theatlantic.com* (Oct. 18, 2018) https://www.theatlantic.com/politics/archive/2018/10/tom-steyers-plan-impeach-trump/573382/
[223] Ibid.
[224] Ibid.

Green "began contemplating Trump's removal when the President fired James Comey [upon Deputy Attorney General Rod Rosenstein's suggestion] ... when Trump was [wrongly accused of] equating white-supremacist protesters in Charlottesville with those who had rallied against them, Green decided to take formal action: 'That's when I realized he was unfit to be President.'"[225] You don't say. Actually what Trump said was that there were good and bad people intermixed with both groups. That was true. Antifa was present on one side, and skinheads on the other. Many others were decent and non-violent people expressing their opinions.

After a bit of digging, I found some interesting news about Congressman Al Green's animus towards Trump, even before he became our president. Andrew Schneider, who "reports on major policy issues before the Texas delegations in the U.S. House and Senate, as well as the Texas governorship, the state legislature, and county and city governments,"[226] wrote this: "Houston's Green is the first Texan to join the boycott [of Trump's inauguration]...Green cited Trump's language during the campaign as one of the main reasons he'll be staying away from the Capitol on Friday, when Trump takes the oath of office...Green also echoed Atlanta Congressman John Lewis, who is boycotting the

[225] Jeffrey Toobin. "Will the Fervor to Impeach Donald Trump Start a Democratic Civil War?" *The New Yorker* (May 28, 2018) https://www.newyorker.com/magazine/2018/05/28/will-the-fervor-for-impeachment-start-a-democratic-civil-war
[226] Andrew Schneider. "Congressman Al Green Boycott Trump Inauguration" *Houston Public Media* https://www.houstonpublicmedia.org/articles/news/2017/01/17/184015/congressman-al-green-to-boycott-trump-inauguration/.

event as well, by saying Trump will not be a legitimate president."[227]

To recap: A U.S. Congressman boycotts the inauguration of a United States President, duly elected, because he believes that *"Trump will not be a legitimate president."* Five months later, that same Congressman claims a different reason for impeachment: "that's when I realized he was unfit to be President". Which is it Rep. Green? Is he an illegitimate president, or unfit? It's all hogwash. The Democrats don't need a reason to impeach 45. They simply hate him. Deplorables couldn't stand Obama either. But, being lovers of the rule of law, we allowed him to serve out his terms, relatively un-impinged, because we knew that is what the majority of the voters wanted. Democrats don't care about the rule of law and they prove that day after day.

Presumably, the Democrats are split on the action of impeachment. *The New Yorker* and I agree on one thing: if little else, this division could well lead to a civil war in the Democrat Party. And, that's good news.

While Rep. Al Green is busy drafting impeachment initiatives, Minority House Leader, Nancy Pelosi, is trying to tamp down the whole matter. She says that "[I]mpeachment is not a political tool. It has to be based on just the law and the facts. ... When we are in the majority, we are going to try to be unifying, and there is no way to do impeachment in a bipartisan way right now."[228] She's right. Of course, now that the Dems won control of the House in the midterms, impeachment will go forward. You can bet on it.

---

[227] Ibid.
[228] Ibid.

"According to a Quinnipiac University poll taken in April [2018], fifty-two percent of American voters oppose impeachment. Another poll ... reported that forty-seven percent would definitely vote against a candidate who wanted to remove Trump from office. ... [S]eventy-one per cent of Democrats already favor impeachment."[229] For those reasons, Democratic candidates during the midterms claimed they were against impeachment. They were lying. And, undercover videos from a watchdog group called Veritas proved it.

By the Dems winning majority of the House in the 2018 midterms, President Trump's agenda and much of what he has accomplished in his first two years, will come to a grinding stop as our next two years will be filled with investigation after investigation.

Rep. Elija Cummings (D-Md.) is among the few outspoken Democratic leaders, along with Pelosi, who are downplaying impeachment proceedings. As the new chairman of the House Oversight and Government Reform Committee, he says he is placing a majority of the legitimacy for impeachment on the outcome of the Trump-Russia investigation. In talking to a conservative audience prior to the midterms, he said: "I want to get the facts in ... You look at the indictments [of the Mueller investigation], you look at the convictions, and he seems to be methodically and carefully looking at the entire situation. So we want to see what he's doing".[230]

---

[229] Ibid.
[230] Julia Manchester. "Cummings throws cold water on impeaching Trump" *The Hill* (Oct. 1, 2018) https://thehill.com/hilltv/rising/409220-cummings-throws-cold-water-on-impeachment.

While Cummings sounds logical in saying he wants to wait for Mueller's investigation to be wrapped up, you can be sure that even if Trump is exonerated fully for obstruction and collusion, as is appearing to be the case, the Dems intend to begin their own expensive, taxpayer-funded, long-reaching witch hunts.

We know, unfortunately, that many Democrats have already called for additional impeachment proceedings once they are done with Trump. Next, they'll go after newly-confirmed Justice Kavanaugh. Then it will be Vice President Pence. They've told us that is their plan. It will become a movement not unlike the one led by Senator Joseph McCarthy and the House Committee on Un-American Activities in its zeal to find and prosecute those believed to be in the Communist Party.

Within hours of being sworn in to Congress, freshman Democratic "Rep. Rashida Tlaib, D-Mich., told a cheering crowd of supporters on Thursday that the Democrats 'are gonna impeach the motherf---er' in a video posted online."[231]

The good news is that both the incessant impeachment threats and the never-ending Mueller investigation follow the caution of Alinsky's fifth rule: *"A tactic that drags on too long becomes a drag".* While the special counsel's investigation is losing the interest of the American public, impeachment is not, yet.

The left has been both active and successful in coming up with new accusations against our President

---

[231] Jane C. Timm, "New Democratic Rep. Rashida Tlaib uses expletive while calling for Trump impeachment" NBC News (Jan. 4, 2019) https://www.nbcnews.com/politics/politics-news/new-democratic-congresswoman-appears-use-expletive-while-calling-impeachment-n954616.

based so far on his character style alone. One such complaint focuses on his heavy use of daily tweets. The left has been trying to convince Americans that his tweeting alone should justify Trump's impeachment, claiming it proves he is "unfit" for office.

Deplorables, on the other hand, love Trump's tweets. Those who wish that he'd tweets less, or that his tweets are better filtered, don't understand how powerful his tweets really are. The following chapter, *"Trick or Tweet"*, will help the reader understand why the president should continue his tweets, warts and all.

TRICK OR TWEET

TACTIC #8: *"Keep the pressure on."*[232]

"OBAMA JUST ENDORSED CROOKED Hillary. He wants four more years of Obama—but nobody else does!"[233] Republican Presidential nominee @realDonaldTrump tweeted that message to his millions of twitter followers on June 9, 2016, after former President Obama endorsed Hillary, hoping she would become his successor. The response was swift and pointed.

"DELETE YOUR ACCOUNT,"[234] responded Trump's rival, Democratic contender Hillary Clinton. It became the most retweeted tweet of the entire election cycle. Who would have guessed that conversations between politicians, normally reserved for debates, would be reduced to a 140-characters-or-less message board available for all voters to see? Politics sure have changed since I voted in my first election.

While many people feel that Trump shouldn't tweet as much, or at all, Deplorables disagree. I feel, for the first time in my life, that my president is communicating directly with *me*. Yes, sometimes he makes me wince

---

[232] Ibid. Alinsky. pg. 128.
[233] Brooke Seipel. "The most retweeted tweet of campaign? Clinton telling Trump to 'delete your account'" *The Hill* (Nov. 17, 2016) https://thehill.com/blogs/ballot-box/presidential-races/304770-the-most-retweeted-tweet-of-the-campaign-clinton-telling.
[234] Ibid.

like when he called his former aid, Omarosa, a "dog" after she released secret tapes of conversations between them from inside the White House. But, who could blame him? He was betrayed and wanted his followers to know it. I knew his reasons were justified. I like it that he fights back. Of course, his naysayers accused him of being a racist because Omarosa is black. Give me a break. He would have ridiculed anybody who betrayed him the same way.

Unlike past politicians, who are afraid the "fake news" media will pounce on them, Trump confronts the criticism. It gives him a chance to expose his enemies and set the record straight. He tweets precisely because he knows that the oh-so predictable anti-Trump media will try to deflect the public's attention from his accomplishments. He is a genius at playing the media and *keeping the pressure on!*

Other than *FOX News*, Trump gets very little positive media coverage for his side of any story. That makes his tweets the only means for him to ensure that the American people get the truth directly from him. Anyone who tries to get the President to stop tweeting shouldn't be giving him advice on anything.

"Alinsky's ninth rule of the ethics of means and ends is that any effective means is automatically judged by the opposition as being unethical." [235] As an example, Alinsky refers to revolutionary hero, Francis Marion of South Carolina, otherwise known as "the Swamp Fox". How apropos!

According to Alinsky, "Marion was an outright revolutionary guerrilla. He and his men operated

---

[235] Ibid. Alinsky. pg. 35.

according to the traditions and with all of the tactics commonly associated with the present-day guerrillas [as does Trump and his Deplorables]. Cornwallis and the regular British Army [as does the left, 'fake news' media, and the establishment] found their plans and operations harried and disorganized by Marion's guerrilla tactics. Infuriated by the effectiveness of his operations, and incapable of coping with them, the British denounced him as a criminal and charged that he did not engage in warfare 'like a gentleman' or 'a Christian.' He was subjected to an unremitting denunciation about his lack of ethics and morality for his use of guerrilla means to the end of winning the Revolution."[236]

While many, including Trump's own daughter Invanka, disagree with him about the effect of the media on the direction of our country, I couldn't agree more with Trump that the "fake news" media *is* the enemy of the people. They are no longer fair watchdogs over our government as our Founding Fathers had hoped.

The media was biased against former Presidents Ronald Reagan and George W. Bush, as well. Reagan called them out for it, but Bush failed to do so, and it drove a lot of us crazy. What Bush did not understand about "fake news", and what Trump absolutely does, is that "the stakes here are astronomically high, with democracy itself under attack."[237] It's that misunderstanding that gets both Conservatives and all Americans in

---

[236] Ibid. pp. 35–36.
[237] Brian Resnick "The science behind why fake news is so hard to wipe out" *VOX* (Last Oct 31, 2017) https://www.vox.com/science-and-health/2017/10/5/16410912/illusory-truth-fake-news-las-vegas-google-facebook.

trouble. It emboldens the left and ensures that they are able to take us one step closer to socialism.

It's up to all of us to know the truth and share it with our family and friends via every social media possible. President Trump needs us to be his eyes, ears and voices. We can't be that if we are listening to "fake news".

Brian Resnick, writing for *VOX*, a liberal media source, makes a good case how easily people are swayed by "fake news". He says that, "[E]ach time a reader encounters [a fake story] on Facebook, Google, or really anywhere, it makes a subtle impression... Each time, the story grows more familiar. And that familiarity casts the illusion of truth. The more we hear a piece of information repeated, the more we're likely to believe it. 'Even things that people have reason not to believe, they believe them more' if the claims are repeated, Gord Pennycock, a psychologist who studies the spread of misinformation at Yale University, says.

"And recent research shows the illusory truth effect is in play when we hear or read fake news claims repeated, regardless of how ridiculous or illogical they sound." [238]

Pennycock details the sheer number of people that just one bit of "fake news" can impact. He believes that, "[I]f a group of participants hadn't seen [the "fake news" story] before, about 5 percent said it was accurate. If the group of participants had seen it before in an earlier stage of the experiment, around 10 percent said it was accurate. That's twice as many people agreeing an outlandish headline is truthful. ... And while the change

---

[238] Ibid.

is small, think about this: Facebook and Google reach just about every person in the United States. A 5 percent increase in the number of people saying a fake news headline is true represents millions of people. [That doesn't even consider the global audience.]

"In one arm of his experiment, Pennycook even put a warning around the fake news headlines when participants first read them. 'Disputed by 3rd Party Fact-Checkers,' the note read (which is Facebook's exact wording for how it labels dubious stories). The warning made no difference.

"Increasingly there's evidence that the Russian government used Facebook to target Americans with misinformation and messaging to sow unrest during the 2016 election. Facebook made it easy.

"'These companies are the most powerful information gatekeepers that the world has ever known, and yet they refuse to take responsibility for their active role in damaging the quality of information reaching the public,' Alexis Madrigal writes in the Atlantic." [239]

Resnick sums up by saying that, "Facebook, Google, Twitter, and other forms of social media are the newspapers of today. They need to take the spread of misinformation on their platforms more seriously. They need to step up in their role as near-ubiquitous news publisher."[240] He could not be more right. But, who will oversee social media? They have been outed recently as extreme leftists from the top down.

That's why it's so important, as Ronald Reagan so famously said, "trust, but verify". We bear huge

---

[239] Ibid.
[240] Ibid.

responsibility in ensuring that we are getting the truth before we form opinions of our leaders.

Had patriots like Sean Hannity *(FOX News)*, Tom Fitton *(Judicial Watch)*, John Solomon *(The Hill)*, Sara Carter *(Circa News)*, and others, not searched so diligently for the truth on behalf of the American people over the past two years, President Donald J. Trump may not have survived even his first year in office. What I learn from them doesn't even make it to the mainstream media for three months to a year later. But, their information is always proven out, eventually. Unfortunately, damage is already done to our country.

According to *Politico*, when Trump first began tweeting back in 2005, he did so for marketing purposes, specifically to promote his reality show, *The Apprentice*, and a new book. Initially, his tweets were done in the third person, leading most to believe they were written by staff. "That changed in the summer of 2011, during the formative stages of the 2012 presidential race. Mulling a run, Trump made a concerted effort to lift his public profile. Rather than engage in policy debates, he focused on stirring controversy by attacking President Barack Obama and congressional leaders...."[241]

In January of 2012, the slogan "Make America Great Again" was tweeted out for the first time by @realdonaldtrump. But, "[I]t wasn't until 2015, when he announced his presidential bid, that his Twitter audience exploded. By early 2016, ... according to a POLITICO analysis at the time ... his follower count had

---

[241] Nicholas Carr. "Why Trump Tweets (And Why We Listen)" *Politico* https://www.politico.com/magazine/story/2018/01/26/donald-trump-twitter-addiction-216530.

154

shot ahead of those of other politicians, including his soon-to-be rival, Hillary Clinton. ... Twitter had for the first time become a primary outlet for the views of a major American politician. With Trump's election, the transformation was complete: The social network had become the new public square."[242]

During one of his campaign rallies, Trump announced that, once elected, he would no longer tweet. This brought boos from his supporters and, undoubtedly, relief to his opposition. Yet, when he won and found himself with fewer outlets for his opinion-sharing than he had while campaigning, he couldn't contain himself. I'm glad for that.

"Because his tweets command the authority of the presidency, they're guaranteed to get noticed and discussed. Trump's tweets don't just amass thousands of likes and retweets. They appear, sometimes within minutes of being posted, in high-definition blowups on "Fox & Friends" and "Morning Joe" and "Good Morning America." They're read, verbatim, by TV and radio anchors. They're embedded in stories in newspapers.... They're praised, attacked and parsed by Washington's myriad talking heads. When Trump tweets—often while literally watching the TV network that will cover the tweet—the jackpot of attention is almost guaranteed.

"Because Trump, by all accounts, spends an inordinate amount of time monitoring the media, the outsized coverage becomes all the more magnified in his mind. And as the signals flow back to him from the press, he is able to fine-tune his tweets to sustain or amplify the coverage. For Trump, in other words,

---

[242] Ibid.

tweeting isn't just a game of chance. It's a tool of manipulation."[243]

The *Politico* article quoted from above, is intent on calling Trump an "addict" of tweeting, driven by what the writer says is a scientifically-proven release of brain chemicals like dopamine. While that is a possible theory, other biased statements in the article, against Trump, make one view the writer's analysis of an addicted-to-tweets-Trump with skepticism.

For example, the author says that, "Twitter feeds Trump's craving for power as well as his craving for attention, and that's a dangerously combustible blend."[244] Why does the writer assume that Trump's craving for power and attention is dangerous? Probably 100% of Trump's Deplorables believed that Obama's craving for power and attention was the "dangerous combustible blend". What the two men have done, and are doing, with their power and attention are vastly different. Obama wanted to fundamentally transform America into a socialist state. Trump wants to restore it to greatness. If Trump is addicted to tweeting, that's just fine with me. We should judge him by his accomplishments. If tweeting is one vehicle by which he achieves those, what's the problem?

Another example of the writer's bias is exposed when he ridicules Trump's "branding" of his opposition. He claims Trump's name-calling, e.g., "Pocahontas" (presidential 2020 contender, Elizabeth Warren), "Little Rocket Man" (North Korea's Kim Jung Un), and "Crooked Hillary" (Clinton), "reveals a trait fundamental to his

---

[243] Ibid.
[244] Ibid.

character. Name-calling is a tactic common to bullies. It's symptomatic of a pathological desire to magnify one's power and status by diminishing other people, draining them not only of importance but of complexity."[245] I couldn't agree more. Every one of the people listed above needed diminishing in order for Trump to succeed with his agenda against them.

No other conservative politician in my lifetime has ever fought back with the same tactics the left has been using for years to weaken Republicans. Finally, we have someone in the White House who recognizes the dangers and power of the left's tactics. Trump will use whatever means necessary to weaken his enemies, foreign and domestic. That is successful strategy on which we should all back him.

The writer's bias does, however, give us a window into why the left hates Trump so much. It can't be that they really hate *how* he fights. They've been using the same tactics for decades. It can't be *him*, personally, that they hate so much. They loved him pre-presidency. Rather, it's his agenda. He uses any means necessary precisely because he understands that, *this is war!*

The author of the article does make a revealing observation, though, as he analyzes Trump's tweeting routine. "He has learned, as candidate and even more so as president, that certain types of tweets (the abrasive, taunting ones, usually) at certain times of day (the crack of dawn, if you want to set the daily news agenda) tend to produce the biggest, longest-lasting media buzz. And so those are the tweets he routinely delivers...."[246]

---

[245] Ibid.
[246] Ibid.

The writer, at least, acknowledges that Trump's tweets have a measure of success with Congress. "Trump is anything but a 'very stable genius' (as he described himself in a now-famous tweet on January 6), but there is a genius to his use of Twitter. His manipulations work. Sometimes his tweets have actually pushed his policy agenda forward. When, in a November 13 tweet about the drafting of the tax-overhaul bill, he declared, 'We're getting close! Now, how about ending the unfair & highly unpopular Indiv Mandate in OCare & reducing taxes even further.' Republicans rushed to incorporate a repeal of the insurance mandate into the legislation."[247] Kudos to Trump. And, to set the record straight, Trump *is* a "very stable genius". The left's bias just won't allow them to see it.

Politico isn't the only media outlet to confuse Trump and his tweeting habits with that of a deranged man. Take an article by *MarketWatch*, for example, that interviewed several "leading political scientists" for their opinions about the subject. Not one of the interviewees, all professors at once-highly-respected universities, held a positive view of Trump's tweets. The article's headline was a dead give-away on what tone they were going to take.

Entitled, "He is a Big and Dangerous Child", the article includes comments by the professors like this: "they are the expressions of rage and frustration, like a child who can't get his way. The only difference is that he is a big and dangerous child." And, this: "The tweets have been disruptive to regular order on Capitol Hill. I have over 140 former students who now work on the

---

[247] Ibid.

Hill, and they say it is harder to pursue policy goals. The primary goal is to keep being the most important story out of Washington every day. It's all about him." And, finally, this: "Trump and Twitter are the two biggest disrupters in our political system. He's very similar in tactics to those used by Joseph McCarthy. He's always changing the subject and making so many claims they are hard to run down."[248] Bravo, President Trump. You are succeeding as the Great Disrupter. Exactly what Deplorables were hoping for when we voted for you! Bear in mind that none of the three professors are psychologists. They are *political scientists*, who aren't as smart as Trump. *Keep the pressure on, Mr. President!*

Then there are the really "out-there" loons who have no clue that there is a method of madness to Trump's genius tweets. Everything he tweets, says, or does in public has its purpose, whether the left and the establishment want to believe it, or not.

Here's a headline by a reporter at the *Chicago Tribune*, for example: "*Trump posts 11 nutty tweets by noon — if this was your relative, you'd be worried.*"[249] The writer describes Trump as "rage-tweeting and spouting conspiracy theories."[250] He tells the reader that, even if we are Trump supporters, we should read a tizzy of tweets the president posted one typical

---

[248] Greg Robb. "He is a big and dangerous child': What political scientists think of Trump's tweets" *MarketWatch* https://www.marketwatch.com/story/he-is-a-big-and-dangerous-child-what-political-scientists-think-of-trumps-tweets-2018-08-30.

[249] Rex Huppke. "Trump posts 11 nutty tweets by noon — if this was your relative, you'd be worried" *Chicago Tribune* (Aug. 30, 2018) http://www.chicagotribune.com/news/opinion/huppke/ct-met-trump-tweets-huppke-20180830-story.html.

[250] Ibid.

Thursday morning so we can see just how dangerous and nutty he is. Let's humor him then, shall we?

"5:50 a.m.: 'The hatred and extreme bias of me by @CNN has clouded their thinking and made them unable to function. But actually, as I have always said, this has been going on for a long time. Little Jeff Z [Jeff Zucker, President of CNN Worldwide] has done a terrible job, his ratings suck, & AT&T should fire him to save credibility!' *[I rate this one, TRUE.]*

"6:02 a.m.: 'What's going on at @CNN is happening, to different degrees, at other networks – with @NBCNews being the worst. The good news is that Andy Lack(y) [NBC News Chairman] is about to be fired for incompetence, and much worse. When Lester Holt got caught fudging my tape on Russia, they were hurt badly!' *[I rate this one, TRUE.]*

"6:11 a.m.: 'I just cannot state strongly enough how totally dishonest much of the Media is. Truth doesn't matter to them, they only have their hatred & agenda. This includes fake books, which come out about me all the time, always anonymous sources, and are pure fiction. Enemy of the People!' *[I rate this one, TRUE.]*

"6:20 a.m.: 'The news from the Financial Markets is even better than anticipated. For all of you that have made a fortune in the markets, or seen your 401k's rise beyond your wildest expectations, more good news is coming!' *[I rate this one, TRUE.]*

"6:44 a.m.: 'Ivanka Trump & Jared Kushner had NOTHING to do with the so called "pushing out" of Don McGahn. The Fake News Media has it, purposely, so wrong! They love to portray chaos in the White House when they know that chaos doesn't exist–just a "smooth running machine" with changing parts!' *[I rate this one, PROBABLY TRUE.]*

"6:56 a.m.: 'The only thing James Comey ever got right was when he said that President Trump was not under investigation!' *[I rate this one, PROBABLY TRUE.]*

"7:54 a.m.: 'Wow, Nellie Ohr, Bruce Ohr's wife, is a Russia expert who is fluent in Russian. She worked for Fusion GPS where she was paid a lot. Collusion! Bruce was a boss at the Department of Justice and is, unbelievably, still there!' *[I rate this one, TRUE.]*

"8:17 a.m.: 'The Rigged Russia Witch Hunt did not come into play, even a little bit, with respect to my decision on Don McGahn!' *[I rate this one, PROBABLY TRUE.]*

"8:39 a.m.: 'I am very excited about the person who will be taking the place of Don McGahn as White House Counsel! I liked Don, but he was NOT responsible for me not firing Bob Mueller or Jeff Sessions. So much Fake Reporting and Fake News!' *[I rate this one, PROBABLY TRUE.]*

"8:49 a.m.: 'Will be going to Evansville, Indiana, tonight for a big crowd rally with Mike Braun, a very successful businessman who is campaigning to be Indiana's next U.S. Senator. He is strong on Crime & Borders, the 2nd Amendment, and loves our Military & Vets. Will be a big night!' *[I rate this one, TRUE.]*

"11:54 a.m.: 'CNN is working frantically to find their 'source.' Look hard because it doesn't exist. Whatever was left of CNN's credibility is now gone!'"[251] *[I rate this one, TRUE.]*

---

[251] Ibid.

The reporter makes the assumption that, "[I]f you or I spent every morning writing like that, we'd be rightfully fired and escorted off to the Illinois Home for the Tragically Unhinged."[252] *[I rate this one, PANTS-ON-FIRE, FALSE.]* That kind of reporting is exactly why Trump, and Deplorables, distrust the "fake news" media. Their hatred of all things President Trump says or does requires strong condemnation. Trump is stirring things up. But, Deplorables knew our country, and all its corruptness, needed stirring up. Trump plays the Alinsky game better than anyone on the left could ever hope to do. I'll say it again, *"keep the pressure on"*, Mr. President!

Even *NPR* (*National Public Radio*) joined the fray in condemning the president over his tweets. In one article, the African-American author, Ayesha Rascoe, tries to make the case that Trump's tweets are racist.

On the one hand, Rascoe points out that Trump's "summer was marked by tweeting insults about black Americans who criticize him and praise for black celebrities who back him."[253] That's a strange statement to make, given that she later reveals, "Trump tweeted almost 900 times about everything from tariffs to North Korea. Nearly 50 tweets were focused on a black person or black Americans in general, with 20 of those tweets negative in tone."[254]

Rascoe quotes a UC Berkeley law professor who said "'Trump is intentionally engaging in racially provocative

---

[252] Ibid.
[253] Ayesha Rascoe. "'Low IQ,' 'SPECTACULAR,' 'Dog': How Trump Tweets About African-Americans" *NPR* https://www.npr.org/2018/09/10/645594393/low-iq-spectacular-dog-how-trump-tweets-about-african-americans.
[254] Ibid.

language...[a]nd if he wants to suggest that he's not, the burden of proof should be on him and his administration."[255] Say, what? This from a "law" professor? That's reminiscent of the left saying Justice Kavanaugh had no right to the presumption of innocence during his hearings (even though there was no corroborating evidence to support any of the accusers' claims).

Let's break Rascoe's assertions down. She says that Trump mentioned African-Americans 50 times out of his 900 summertime tweets. That's 0.055%. Wow, he must be a racist. Twenty of those tweets about blacks were negative. That's 0.022%. That proves it. C'mon, Ms. Rascoe, you should hold yourself to a higher standard than that.

Rascoe also says that, according to the chair of the political science department of Howard University, "ubiquitous talk of black unemployment is a way to shield Trump from accusations of racism."[256] According to him, "'[T]he target is really white voters who are going to be uncomfortable with thinking that they're voting for an overtly racist president. When Trump talks about black unemployment he is not talking to black people. He's talking to the white voters that they don't want to scare away as they head into the 2020 election.'"[257]

That's the kind of talk that angers most white people and divides races. For Rascoe to quote such "experts" exposes her racism, not only towards Trump, but towards all white people, as well.

---

[255] Ibid.
[256] Ibid.
[257] Ibid.

In March of 2017, Trump tweeted out a series of postings calling attention to the possible wiretapping of Trump Tower prior to the presidential election. He laid the blame squarely on Obama and his administration. At the time he was ridiculed as being paranoid. Those of us who believe in him, knew there must be something behind his claims. It's looking more and more as though he was right.

In September 2017, *CNN* reported that, "US investigators wiretapped former Trump campaign chairman Paul Manafort under secret court orders before and after the election, sources tell CNN, an extraordinary step involving a high-ranking campaign official now at the center of the Russia meddling probe."[258] *FactCheck* and *CNN* claimed that the wiretapping was only done on Paul Manafort and Carter Page, not the president. That's laughable.

Given the facts laid out in "Collusion Delusion", there should be little doubt as to what the investigation is really about. Manafort has not been convicted of one charge that involved Russians, to-date. But, he was the easiest target for the FBI to justify wiretapping Trump.

Most experts agree that normal FBI and DOJ protocols would have been to alert an important political figure, if a suspected spy was in their midst. Much like they alerted Dianne Feinstein recently when it was discovered she had a Chinese spy as her driver for more than twenty years! They didn't wiretap the driver. They

---

[258] Evan Perez, Shimon Prokupecz and Pamela Brown. "Exclusive: US government wiretapped former Trump campaign chairman" *CNN* (Updated Sept. 19, 2017)
https://www.cnn.com/2017/09/18/politics/paul-manafort-government-wiretapped-fisa-russians/index.html.

alerted Feinstein and arrested him before he could do further damage.

There are many people who believe that Trump's tweets are bad for our democracy. They believe his tweets are full of lies and distort the truth. While not always thrilled with everything the president tweets, Deplorables do not want him to stop.

President Trump *"keeps the pressure on"* with his tweets, so much so that he makes his opponents dizzy. They can't keep up; and, that frustrates them. The "fake news" media is easy to confuse. As the media arm of the left, it has been "conditioned" to report propaganda, instead of critically and subjectively, as reporters are trained to do. Every time Trump does something to better our country, "fake news" attacks him using the exact same talking points as the left commands.

For example, as Trump is currently trying to solve the border problem once and for all, the government has been shut down because the Democrats refuse to fund a wall. Thankfully, Trump is not bowing to pressure. The left's newest attack is to claim that Trump is "manufacturing a crisis" at the border.

A comical, blatantly coordinated, and calculative barrage of attacks against Trump and his border wall solutions, came from Pelosi and almost all Dems, CNN and all of the other "fake news" cable outlets, and even Democratic pundits. They all shared two words in common: "manufactured crisis". Sean Hannity, Tucker Carlson, and other "real news" media folks are to be commended for the montages they created, exposing the left's coordinated talking point.

Rush Limbaugh, the father of talk news radio, brought to my attention, in the midst of the chaos the left is creating regarding our much-needed wall funding, that our president tweeted, "'President Obama, thank you for your great support - I have been saying this all along!' — Donald J. Trump (@realDonaldTrump) January 10, 2019."[259] Trump included a video of Obama, from 2014, in which the then-president says, "'[w]e now have an actual humanitarian crisis on the border that only underscores the need to drop the politics and fix our immigration system once and for all.'"[260] Rush takes the video one step further, wherein the rest of Obama's proclamation can be heard that, "[I]n recent weeks we've seen a surge of unaccompanied children arrive at the border brought here and to other countries by smugglers and traffickers. The journey is unbelievably dangerous for these kids.'"[261] Rush points out that, even then, it was well-known that unaccompanied children were in danger due to open borders. It is this courageous news reporting that all Americans need to stay tuned into in order to get the real facts.

Coordinated, and fake, reporting by the left has been *"keeping the pressure on"* Trump since his election. He has just proven to be better at employing Alinsky's tactic than they could ever dream to be.

The fact that Trump's tweets keep so many on the left steaming mad, should delight us all. It's why they hate him so much. Keep tweeting, President Trump. We love you for it.

---

[259] Rush Limbaugh. "Trump Thanks Obama for His Support on Border Crisis That Left Says Is 'Manufactured'". *The Rush Limbaugh Show* https://www.rushlimbaugh.com/daily/2019/01/10/trump-thanks-obama-for-his-support-on-border-crisis/.
[260] Ibid.
[261] Ibid.

The next chapter, "Unmask the Boogeymen", addresses who Trump's real enemies are, in and out of government. More importantly, you'll learn why they hate him so much. Trump is on a tear to drain the swamp. While it may not be happening as quickly as Deplorables would like, Trump will not let us down.

UNMASK THE BOOGEYMEN

TACTIC #9: *"The threat is usually more terrifying than the thing itself."* [262]

"DONALD TRUMP'S PRESS CONFERENCE performance in Helsinki rises to & exceeds the threshold of 'high crimes & misdemeanors'", tweeted former CIA director John Brennan on July 16, 2018, following a historic summit between our President and Russia's Putin. *"'It was nothing short of treasonous. Not only were Trump's comments imbecilic, he is wholly in the pocket of Putin. Republican Patriots: Where are you???'"* [263]

Wisely, "[t]he Founding Fathers crafted a very narrow definition of treason because they were sensitive to the possibility it would be used to destroy political opponents." [264]

The U.S. Constitution ensures that a charge of treason is incredibly difficult to prosecute. Article III, Section 3 reads: *"Treason against the United States, shall consist only in levying War against them, or in adhering to their Enemies, giving them Aid and Comfort."* [265]

---

[262] Ibid. Alinsky. pg. 129.

[263] Jeffry Bartash. "Is Trump treasonous? Here's the legal and historical answer to that charge" *MarketWatch* https://www.marketwatch.com/story/is-trump-treasonous-heres-the-legal-and-historical-answer-to-that-charge-2018-07-17.

[264] Ibid.

[265] Ibid.

The penalty is death.

Alinsky's ninth tactic, *"the threat is usually more terrifying than the thing itself,"* is used effectively by the left to cause paralyzing results. Reality for the one threatened can be in perception alone. Merely defending such attacks requires time and energy. The end goal of the left is to demonize and demoralize its target.

That the most powerful man in the world must defend himself against being called "imbecilic" and "treasonous" in public by a former CIA director, is indefensible. To say it following the president's summit with a foreign leader, especially a foe such as Putin, could itself be traitorous.

What Alinsky says about traitors versus patriots has everything to do with who wins in the end. *"The seventh rule of the ethics of means and ends"*, he claims, *"is a mighty determinant of ethics.* The judgment of history leans heavily on the outcome of success or failure; it spells the difference between the traitor and the patriotic hero. *There can be no such thing as a successful traitor, for if one succeeds he becomes a founding father."*[266]

Trump spent his first day as president at CIA headquarters in Langley, Virginia, addressing hundreds of agency personnel. *"'I am so behind you'"*, he assured them. *"'There is nobody that feels stronger about the intelligence community and CIA than Donald Trump,'* blaming any suggestion of a 'feud' on the media."[267]

---

[266] Ibid. Alinsky, p. 34.
[267] Associated Press and TOI Staff. "Ex-CIA director blasts Trump for carping about media during agency visit" *Times of Israel* (Jan. 22, 2017) https://www.timesofisrael.com/ex-cia-director-blasts-trump-for-carping-about-media-during-agency-visit/.

The "fake news" media, and others aligned against him, had been relentlessly accusing Trump of colluding with the Russians to influence the election. The speech at Langley was his "attempt at a fresh start with the intelligence agencies he will now rely on for guidance as he makes weighty national security decisions."[268]

While high-level CIA officials stood mostly stone-faced, many of the "400 other officers in attendance cheered on the president during his remarks."[269]

John Brennan fired back at Trump the very next day saying he was "deeply saddened and angered at Donald Trump's despicable display of self-aggrandizement in front of CIA's Memorial Wall of Agency heroes," and that the president "should be ashamed of himself."[270]

Why would a former CIA director try to divide President Trump and the CIA from the outset? A little background into who Brennan is, and the rest of the "deep state", will soon make that crystal clear.

In 2016, while addressing a "panel discussion regarding diversity in the intelligence community during the Congressional Black Caucus Foundation's annual conference," Brennan remarked: "'So if back in 1980, [I] was allowed to say, 'I voted for the Communist Party' ... and still got through, rest assured that your rights and your expressions and your freedom of speech as Americans is something that's not going to be disqualifying of you as you pursue a career in government.'"[271] Isn't that reassuring?

---

[268] Ibid.
[269] Ibid.
[270] Ibid.
[271] Natalie Johnson. "CIA Director Once Voted for Communist Presidential Candidate" *The Washington Free Beacon* (Sept. 21, 2016)

Trevor Timm of *The Guardian* believed, in 2014, that then-CIA Director Brennan should have been fired for lying to the American people and to the Senate. "[A]n internal investigation by the Central Intelligence Agency's inspector general found that the CIA 'improperly' spied on US Senate staffers..., it was hard to conclude anything but the obvious: John Brennan blatantly lied to the American public. Again."[272]

Paul Sperry wrote an article in 2016 that includes evidence Brennan also lied about 28-pages of the 2002, 9/11 report that he refused to declassify despite bipartisan pressure. They expose Saudi involvement in the terrorist attack and would enable the relatives of victims to sue. Sperry, former Washington bureau chief of Investor's Business Daily, says that even Brennan's boss, then-President Obama, "despite repeated promises to 9/11 families, refuses to make [the 28 pages] public."[273]

A 2017 article written by investigative journalist, George Neumayr entitled, "Confirmed: John Brennan Colluded With Foreign Spies to Defeat Trump", was prophetic for its time. In it, he says that "Brennan teamed up with British spies and Estonian spies to cripple Trump's candidacy. He used their phony intelligence as a pretext for a multi-agency

---

https://freebeacon.com/politics/cia-director-once-voted-for-communist-presidential-candidate/.

[272] Trevor Timm. "CIA director John Brennan lied to you and to the Senate. Fire him" *The Guardian* https://www.theguardian.com/commentisfree/2014/jul/31/cia-director-john-brennan-lied-senate.

[273] Paul Sperry. "The establishment is lying about the 9/11 report" *New York Post.* https://nypost.com/2016/05/02/the-establishment-is-lying-about-the-911-report/.

investigation into Trump, which led the FBI to probe a computer server connected to Trump Tower and gave cover to Susan Rice, among other Hillary supporters, to spy on Trump and his people ... leaking out mentions of this bogus investigation to the press in the hopes of inflicting maximum political damage on Trump."[274] Releasing American's names that get caught up in such surveillance is a process called "unmasking". Neumayr's research led him to believe Brennan stacked the CIA with leftists for just such a president as Trump.

When Trump's National Security Advisor, Michael Flynn, a retired Lieutenant General in the Army, wanted to redo many of the Obama-era Middle-East policies, "Brennan and other Obama aides couldn't resist the temptation to take him out after rifling through transcripts of his calls with the Russian ambassador [Kislyak]. They caught him in a lie to [Vice President] Mike Pence and made sure the press knew about it."[275] After sacrificing 33 years of his life honorably serving our country, Flynn was charged by Special Counsel Mueller with lying to the FBI. He pled guilty only to spare his son from also being investigated and after having spent most of his life's savings on his own defense.

Known top Obama officials responsible for the leaks and unmasking of Trump and his staff included "Susan Rice, Obama's national security adviser; former U.N. Ambassador Samantha Power...'";[276] and, Ben

---

[274] George Neumayr. "Confirmed: John Brennan Colluded With Foreign Spies to Defeat Trump" *The American Spectator* (April 19, 2017) https://spectator.org/confirmed-john-brennan-colluded-with-foreign-spies-to-defeat-trump/
[275] Ibid.
[276] Richard Pollock. "New Calls for Criminal Investigation of Obama Aides in 'Unmasking' Scandal" *The Daily Signal*

Rhodes, former deputy national security adviser for strategic communications. All of whom should have known better.

Emmy award-winning, senior investigative reporter for the Daily Caller News Foundation, Richard Pollock says that, "[U]nmasking or identifying U.S. citizens who are communicating with foreign governments ... or principals for genuine intelligence purposes is legal, but obtaining the identity of U.S. citizens for partisan political purposes is not permitted under any circumstances. The leaking of 'unmasked' U.S. citizens to the ... media is unlawful."[277]

According to Retired Col. James Williamson, who served in the Army Special Forces for 32 years in the intelligence field, even "James Clapper [former NSA Director under Obama] ... has been complicit and probably should be investigated as a co-conspirator.... He knew what the constraints were. These hundreds of unmasking requests came after the election."[278]

Retired Air Force Col. James Waurishuk, a 30-year senior intelligence officer who served on the National Security Council and was also deputy director for intelligence at U.S. Central Command said that "[w]hen you're dealing with the political use of intelligence methods and capabilities with regards to unmasking, you have suspected criminal activity."[279] How, then, was this illegal unmasking and leaking allowed to occur?

---

https://www.dailysignal.com/2017/08/03/new-calls-criminal-investigation-obama-aides-unmasking-scandal/.
[277] Ibid.
[278] Ibid.
[279] Ibid.

Days before Obama handed the White House keys to Trump, he pulled a fast one. On December 15, 2016, Obama directed Clapper to sign changes that "permitted all 17 intelligence agencies to share raw intelligence that the NSA once exclusively held, including unmasking information, for the first time."[280] This allowed for the sharing of highly-classified data to all of the agencies, not only making unmasking easier, but also making the leaker's identity more difficult to trace. On January 3, 2017, Obama's then-AG, Loretta Lynch, gave the changes her final approval, setting the rule into action.

Obama's supporters justified this policy change by saying it was long overdue. If so, why did he wait until just days before his eight-year term ended when Trump was entering the White House?

After FBI Deputy Director McCabe was fired (by the FBI, not Trump) for lying to his own agency, John Brennan blamed President Trump in this tweet: "When the full extent of your venality, moral turpitude, and political corruption becomes known, you will take your rightful place as a disgraced demagogue in the dustbin of history."[281] By ridiculing and demonizing the president, a la Alinsky tactic #5, could Brennan have been trying to divert attention from his own past corrupt actions?

Upon seeing the tweet, Rudy Giuliani (former Mayor of New York City during 9/11 and current legal counsel to Trump) criticized Brennan for leaking the Steele

---

[280] Ibid.

[281] Edmond DeMarche. "Ex-CIA director John Brennan should face grand jury over Russia probe handling: Giuliani" *FOX News* (Aug. 14, 2018)
https://www.foxnews.com/politics/ex-cia-director-john-brennan-should-face-grand-jury-over-russia-probe-handling-giuliani.

dossier. He believes Brennan "should face a grand jury for his role in peddling the salacious Trump dossier that kicked off the 'phony' Russia investigation."[282] Unconvincingly, "Brennan told NBC's *Meet the Press'* in February [2018] that the dossier played no role in the intelligence community's assessment that was presented to both President Obama and Trump. Brennan said there were items in the dossier that raised his suspicions on whether it was accurate."[283] Hard to believe this man once ran our CIA.

One of the more reasoned voices in media is Victor Davis Hanson, a senior fellow at the Hoover Institution. In an article posted in June of 2018, he makes no secret what kind of dishonest broker he believes John Brennan to be. Hanson lists a series of lies propagated by Brennan over many years and describes him this way: "If there is such a thing as a dangerous 'deep state' of elite but unelected federal officials who feel that they are untouchable and unaccountable, then John Brennan is the poster boy."[284]

In May 2017 according to Hanson, Brennan "almost certainly did not tell the truth to Congress when he testified in answer to ... questions that he neither knew who had commissioned the Steele dossier nor had the CIA relied on its contents for any action. Yet There [sic] are also numerous reports that, despite his denials about knowledge of the dossier, Brennan served as a

---

[282] Ibid.
[283] Ibid.
[284] Victor Davis Hanson. "A Reply to Ronald Radosh's Smear" *National Review* (June 4, 2018) https://www.nationalreview.com/corner/john-brennan-dishonesty-long-record/.

stealthy conduit to ensure that it was disseminated widely."[285]

Even "retired National Security Agency Director, Michael Rogers, and...Clapper, have conceded that the Steele dossier — along with the knowledge that it was a Clinton campaign-funded product — most certainly *did* help shape the Obama's intelligence communality interagency assessments and actions, often under the urging of Brennan himself."[286]

Hanson opines that, "[w]e are currently witnessing two parallel Investigations: ...Robert Mueller's, who is mandated to explore whether ... Trump colluded with the Russians to warp the 2016 election leading to Hillary['s] defeat, ... another by federal agencies and congressional committees into whether members of the Obama administration's intelligence and national-security teams improperly used their powers to surveille (and unmask and leak the names of) U.S. citizens, including misleading a U.S. FISA court on the basis of an opposition-researched and unverified dossier, to monitor improperly a political campaign by the insertion of an "informant"..., and to leak damaging but unproven information to alter a presidential election and transition. That numerous FBI and DOJ officials have already been reassigned, resigned, fired, or retired has nothing to do with a conspiracy theory. The facts will eventually come out about both lines of inquiry, but we already know ... about the proven lack of veracity of one John Brennan and his various iterations."[287]

---

[285] Ibid.
[286] Ibid.
[287] Ibid.

While Brennan has been verbally assaulting Trump since his candidacy, the attacks ratcheted up just after the president met with Russian President Vladamir Putin at the Helsinky Conference in the summer of 2018. At the press conference, following their private meeting (a controversial practice Trump has adopted undoubtedly to prevent unfair media coverage and leaks), Trump made an unforced error that got blown way out of proportion.

Trump was already on record agreeing with the intelligence community that Russia meddled with our 2016 election. One *ABC News* article in 2017 could not have been clearer: "Trump says he agrees with US intelligence community that Russia meddled in election". It went on to report that, "[W]hile President Donald Trump says he believes Russian President Vladimir Putin is sincere when he denies that Russia sought to interfere in the 2016 U.S. election, the president said he personally believes the conclusion of the U.S. intelligence community -- and not Putin -- that Russia did in fact meddle in the election."[288] What else should our leader do while attempting to rework relationships around the world? Does the left expect Trump to call foreign leaders "liars" to their face?

According to the Associated Press, at a news conference in Hanoi, Vietnam, six months prior to the Helsinki Summit, "Trump has suggested that the ongoing probe into contacts between his campaign and the Russians was hurting the U.S. relationship with

---

[288] Jordyn Phelps. "Trump says he agrees with US intelligence community that Russia meddled in election" *ABC News* (11/12/17) https://abcnews.go.com/Politics/trump-agrees-us-intelligence-community-russia-meddled-election/story?id=51091798.

Moscow and could hinder efforts to solve crises like Syria and North Korea. ... The day before, Trump had told reporters that Russia President Vladimir Putin has again denied meddling in the 2016 election. Trump did not make clear whether he believed Putin but did make clear that he did not want to revisit the issue. ... President Donald Trump says he believes in the U.S. intelligence agencies despite his past skepticism about Russian meddling in the 2016 election. ... The president says during a joint news conference with Vietnam President Tran Dai Quang that the U.S. Intelligence agencies are 'currently led by fine people.' He adds, 'I believe very much in our intelligence agencies.' ... Trump says he believes 'having Russia in a friendly posture as opposed to always fighting them is an asset.' ... [He] accused Democrats of trying to sabotage relations between the two countries."[289] That is the real reason political hacks like John Brennan are tirelessly working to demonize Trump publicly. His actions and words are outrageous and destabilize an already unstable world that Trump is desperately trying to right.

As Trump stood at the dais, with Putin beside him, the president was asked a question by a reporter as to whether or not he believed Putin meddled in the presidential election. His exact answer was that he "had no reason to think Russia would have interfered"[290].

---

[289] "The Latest: Vietnam wants peaceful end to sea disputes" *Associated Press* (Nov. 12, 2017)
https://apnews.com/9be0ac5d4cff46439f3e811ad90fcec3.
[290] Kathryn Watson. "Trump claims he misspoke about Russian meddling in Putin press conference" *CBS News*
https://www.cbsnews.com/news/trump-meets-with-members-of-congress-today-after-helsinki-putin-meeting-live-updates-2018-07-17/

Trump's supporters believed either he misspoke or he was playing 3-D chess again. But, his haters saw yet another reason to pounce.

Trump corrected himself as soon as he returned home, explaining that the word "would" should have been "wouldn't". He took the time to read the scripted answer to the American people on live TV remarking that he had misread the word. It was painful to watch him defending himself, on the world stage, as though being forced to say, "I am not a crook".

The press attacked Trump for days. Even conservative newscasters, like Neil Cavuto, piled on. With so much at stake in world relations, the bunch of them should be ashamed. "Only a handful of Republicans, like Sen. Rand Paul, R. Kentucky, have defended Trump's performance at the press conference."[291]

Forced to expose his hand in sensitive negotiations with Putin or any world leader, just to silence his detractors at home, is tragic and dangerous. Trump alluded to that when he said, "'it's very important to get along with Russia, as well as China, especially as it relates to confronting North Korea. What I believe is that we have to get to work. And I think everybody understood this that heard the answer,' he said. 'We have to get to work to solve Syria, to solve North Korea, to solve Ukraine, to solve terrorism.'"[292]

Our president, undeterred as always, just moved on to his next campaign promise. In the end, he will beat his opponents, I've no doubt. He has already shut

---

[291] Ibid.
[292] Ibid.

Brennan up for the time being by revoking his security clearance. It's long past due. There are plenty more to lose theirs, as well.

Since being fired by Trump in May 2017, more information about former FBI Director James Comey, and his "deep state" connections, has emerged. Around the same time the first FISA warrant was issued to spy on Trump's campaign, Comey was dealing with yet another Hillary-induced-fire-in-the-hull crisis.

Huma Abedin, long-time close aide to Hillary, was married to a disgraced, Democratic congressman. The pervert, Anthony Weiner, had been convicted of sexting pictures of Weiner's "weiner" to a minor. He was sentenced to 21 months in a federal prison. During the investigation of him, authorities uncovered over 700,000 of Hillary's missing emails on his laptop. The American public had been told that her emails were no longer accessible, that they had been purposely destroyed by her then-I.T. guy, presumably to erase any evidence.

Comey's original "statement closing out [Hillary's] email case accused ... [her] of having been 'grossly negligent' in handling classified information. ... The tough language was changed to the much softer...'extremely careless' ... when Comey announced in July 2016, there would be no charges against her. The change is significant, since federal law states that gross negligence in handling the nation's intelligence can be punished criminally with prison time or fines."[293] The change was made in Comey's own handwriting.

---

[293] John Solomon. "Early Comey draft accused Clinton of gross negligence on emails" *The Hill* (Nov. 6, 2017)

Now Comey had a problem. He had already stated that he received the Weiner laptop tip on October 27th, less than two weeks before the election. FBI and DOJ protocol is to avoid making public announcements that could affect a candidate within sixty days of an election. *Newsweek* downplayed the newly-discovered emails reporting that, "[f]rom the information obtained ... it was ... clear that, because of the accounts involved, almost all of the documents were going to be duplicates or personal emails."[294] Comey and the "fake news" media tried to convince the American people that the FBI was in possession of some new, technologically-advanced software that would sift through the emails on Weiner's laptop at warp speed, kicking out all duplicates and leaving just a small number for agents to examine manually. Supposedly, they did just that in a record twelve hours. *Nothing to see here*, they tried to convince us, *just move along*. Many people took the FBI director at his word. Deplorables did not.

We now know that there was no special software program. Comey outright lied. "Despite claims from ... Comey to the opposite ... [o]nly 3,077 of the nearly 700,000 emails discovered ... were, in fact, reviewed. ... The search ... uncovered additional instances of Clinton transmitting and receiving classified information via her private, unauthorized email account, according to one U.S. law enforcement official. 'President Trump tweeted about the findings on Saturday,

---

https://thehill.com/homenews/senate/358982-early-comey-memo-accused-clinton-of-gross-negligence-on-emails.
[294] Kurt Eichenwald. "Here's What the FBI Found in the Emails on Anthony Weiner's Laptop" *Newsweek* (NOV. 6, 2016) https://www.newsweek.com/what-fbi-found-emails-anthony-weiner-laptop-517652.

threatening to interject himself into an investigation into corruption at the FBI.'"[295] It's coming.

According to what Sydney Powell, former federal prosecutor and senior fellow at the London Center for Policy Research had to say, he should. She makes the case that not only was Comey first alerted by the field agent in New York on September 28th about the laptop (a full month before he claimed), that tip was ignored. "The Weiner laptop almost certainly contains the answers to the public's questions about all things Clinton – her scandals, the Clinton Foundation pay-to-play, obstruction of justice and also possible espionage act violations."[296] Comey's handling of Hillary's destroyed emails was a cover-up, plain and simple.

On November 6th, just days before the election, Comey "confidently" alerted the public that Hillary was innocent of any wrongdoing. It was unconscionable.

There are plenty of other corrupt deep state actors who have been hell-bent on destroying President Trump before, during, and after his election.

Former FBI General Counsel James Baker testified to Congress that DOJ Deputy AG Rod Rosenstein had "discussed secretly recording President Trump and invoking the 25th Amendment to remove him from

---

[295] Joe Williams. "FBI failed to review hundreds of thousands of emails on Anthony Weiner's laptop: Report" *Washington Examiner.* (Aug. 26, 2018) https://www.washingtonexaminer.com/news/fbi-failed-to-review-hundreds-of-thousands-of-emails-on-anthony-weiners-laptop-report.

[296] Sydney Powell, "The FBI Deliberately Ignored 'Golden Emails,' Crucial Abedin Messages And More" *The Daily Caller.* https://dailycaller.com/2018/06/22/fbi-ignored-golden-emails-and-abedin-messages/.

office...."[297] It is widely believed that Trump is well aware of that and is leveraging the explosive information to gain Rosenstein's cooperation with important matters. If so, Trump has mastered Alinsky's ninth tactic, "the threat is usually more terrifying than the thing itself", and he should be commended for it.

Chris Swecker, who served 24 years in the FBI as Special Agent, and retired as Assistant Director with responsibility over all FBI Criminal Investigations, believes that, "fired FBI Director James Comey and fired Deputy Director Andrew McCabe have done more damage to America's premier law enforcement agency than anyone in its storied 110-year history."[298] He also referenced fired FBI Agent Peter Strzok in his assessment and claimed that many current and former FBI employees share his views.

Former FBI lawyer, Lisa Page, known for her anti-Trump text exchanges with since-fired Agent Strzok, was also "a lead [prosecutor] on the Russia case when it started in summer 2016, and she helped it transition to Mueller through summer 2017."[299] According to *The Hill's* John Solomon, in closed-door hearings she testified that, "[A]fter nine months of using some of the

---

[297] Catherine Herridge. "FBI lawyer's testimony at odds with Rosenstein denial on 'wire' report" *FOX News* (Oct. 9, 2018) https://www.foxnews.com/politics/fbi-lawyers-testimony-at-odds-with-rosenstein-denial-on-wire-report.
[298] Chris Swecker. "Former FBI official: Firing Strzok was justified – he, Comey and McCabe disgraced the FBI" *FOX News* (Aug. 14, 2018) https://www.foxnews.com/opinion/former-fbi-official-firing-strzok-was-justified-he-comey-and-mccabe-disgraced-the-fbi.
[299] John Solomon, "Lisa Page bombshell: FBI couldn't prove Trump-Russia collusion before Mueller appointment" *The Hill* (Sept. 16, 2018) https://www.foxnews.com/politics/kavanaugh-accuser-referred-to-doj-for-false-statements-grassleys-office-announces.

most awesome surveillance powers afforded to U.S. intelligence, the FBI still had not made a case connecting Trump or his campaign to Russia's election meddling."[300] If true, on what basis was the special counsel investigation opened?

Special Counsel Robert Mueller, quite possibly the dirtiest "deep state" player of them all, has been investigating our president for over two years. A few of Trump's associates have been arrested (some convicted and sentenced), but none for involvement with Russia, Mueller's mandate.

Retired Special Agent and former Minneapolis Division legal counsel for the FBI, Coleen Crowley, once reported directly to Mueller. She claims that "Mueller was chosen for the job not because he has integrity, but because he will do what the powerful want him to do."[301] She states that under Mueller's FBI, the DOJ's IG found that the "FBI overstepped the law improperly serving hundreds of thousands of 'national security letters' to obtain private (and irrelevant) metadata on citizens, and for infiltrating nonviolent anti-war groups under the guise of investigating 'terrorism'".[302] Mueller is no stranger to using laws against our own citizens.

When it comes to Russia collusion, Mueller himself has much to answer for. He was directly responsible for, arguably, the most damaging scandal involving Russia to ever hit our country. And, it had nothing whatsoever to do with Donald Trump and his campaign.

---

[300] Ibid.
[301] Coleen Rowley. "No, Robert Mueller and James Comey Aren't Heroes". *The Huffington Post*. (June 6, 2017)
https://www.huffingtonpost.com/entry/conflicts-of-interest-and-ethics-robert-mueller-and_us_5936a148e4b033940169cdc8
[302] Ibid.

As reported by John Solomon and Alison Spann in *The Hill* on October 16, 2017, while Mueller was the FBI Director in 2009, "[F]ederal agents used a confidential U.S. witness working inside the Russian nuclear industry to gather extensive financial records, make secret recordings and intercept emails ... that showed Moscow had compromised an American uranium trucking firm with bribes and kickbacks in violation of the Foreign Corrupt Practices Act, FBI and court documents show. They also obtained an eyewitness account ... indicating Russian nuclear officials had routed millions of dollars to the U.S. designed to benefit former President Bill Clinton's charitable foundation during the time Secretary of State Hillary Clinton served on a government body that provided a favorable decision to Moscow,....[303]

"[C]onservative author Peter Schweitzer and The New York Times documented how Bill Clinton collected hundreds of thousands of dollars in Russian speaking fees and his charitable foundation collected millions in donations from parties interested in the deal while Hillary Clinton presided on the Committee on Foreign Investment in the United States. ... Others sat on the deciding committee, including, "[then–Attorney General] Eric Holder and other Obama administration officials."[304]

Instead of bringing the racketeering scheme down in 2010, as they should have for national security

---

[303] John Solomon and Alison Spann. "FBI uncovered Russian bribery plot before Obama administration approved controversial nuclear deal with Moscow" (Oct. 16, 2017) https://thehill.com/policy/national-security/355749-fbi-uncovered-russian-bribery-plot-before-obama-administration.
[304] Ibid.

reasons, the DOJ kept the investigation open for four more years. During that time, Hillary's "State Department and government agencies on the Committee on Foreign Investment in the United States unanimously approved the partial sale of Canadian mining company Uranium One to the Russian nuclear giant Rosatom, giving Moscow control of more than 20 percent of America's uranium supply."[305] The FBI's "confidential witness, an American businessman ... began making kickback payments ... with the permission of the FBI.

"[T]he main Russian overseeing Putin's nuclear expansion inside the United States ... supervised a "racketeering scheme" that involved extortion, bribery, money laundering and kickbacks that were both directed by and provided benefit to more senior officials back in Russia."[306]

The chair of the House Intelligence Committee, while the FBI probe was ongoing, claims he knew nothing about the investigation. According to him, "[N]ot providing information on a corruption scheme before the Russian uranium deal was approved by U.S. regulators ... has served to undermine U.S. national security interests by the very people charged with protecting them.... The Russian efforts to manipulate our American political enterprise is breathtaking."[307]

Incredibly, none other than then–U.S. Attorney Rod Rosenstein and then–Assistant FBI Director Andrew McCabe supervised the investigation. Their boss was Mueller when the investigation began, and later Comey,

---

[305] Ibid.
[306] Ibid.
[307] Ibid.

as the investigation ended in 2015.[308] Can anybody spell "motive" for the Trump-Russia collusion investigation?

Not only are those who were involved in the "Uranium One" scandal corrupt, they put our national security at risk. Readers can, and should, do further research on this scandal to fully understand the dangers these "boogeymen" have put our country in. Incredulously, not one of those involved have, to-date, been held accountable for selling twenty percent of America's much-needed uranium to the Russians. Yet, Mueller's witch hunt against Trump marches on.

Leaders in some of our most trusted government agencies are intent on a soft coup of our current administration. These aren't conspiracy theories. The evidence is overwhelming and provide the motive for the witch hunt against President Trump. We must wake up and help him clean out this "swamp" while we still have a president in office who is willing and able. To ignore these scandals is to expedite the end of our democracy.

Even some Republicans are complicit in doing just that. In March, 2018, the House Committee on Oversight and Government Reform and the House Judiciary Committee requested then-AG Sessions to appoint a special counsel to investigate the "FBI and DOJ decisions [relating to Crossfire] in 2016 and 2017."[309] Sessions,

---

308 Ibid.
309 Senators Jim Jordan, Mark Meadows and Doug Collins. https://republicans-oversight.house.gov/wp-content/uploads/2019/01/2019-01-07-JDJ-DC-MM-to-Huber-re-DOJ-investigation-due-1-21.pdf?utm_source=House+Judiciary+Committee+Press+Releases&utm_campaign=da271be239-EMAIL_CAMPAIGN_2019_01_07_04_54&utm_medium=email&utm_term=0_df41eba8fd-da271be239-135044217.

disappointingly, refused to do so. Instead, he appointed U.S. Attorney John W. Huber from Utah to review whether or not the law was followed during the MYE and Crossfire investigations, including the FISA warrant applications. Nine months later, there is still no word from Huber. When asked to appear before Congress in December, 2018, Huber declined. It's infuriating and leaves one wondering just how deep this swamp runs.

In a letter dated January 7, 2019, Republicans Jim Jordan, Mark Meadows and Doug Collins, some of the few representatives to have doggedly pursued the truth, asked why Huber had not yet interviewed "more than a dozen current and former DOJ and FBI personnel" pertinent to the investigation. The letter asked specific questions, the answers to which will prove whether Huber is part of the same systemic stall-and-deny tactics as is practiced by the DOJ, or if he is part of the cover-up.

It is imperative that we start holding people who break our laws accountable. No longer can we afford to let these corrupt officials off the hook. They will only get stronger and more entrenched, until we lose America to left-leaning socialists because we can't quit bickering amongst ourselves.

We can be paralyzed by fear and ignore the dangers, or we can keep reminding ourselves that *"the threat is usually more terrifying than the thing itself"*. The evil-doer swamp creatures could care less about our country. But, Trump cares and he has a plan. You can bet he is laser-focused with his 3-D chess game to checkmate the left in one final blow. The unmaskers have more to fear than just fear alone.

While the "boogeymen" are easy to unmask, the "resistance" is not. In the following chapter, "Resistance", find out who they are and how we can help Trump weaken their power. Some of the "resistance" may be leaders you respect and have admired for years. Some may even be misguided patriots. You may be shocked by their complicit attempts to take down our duly-elected president thereby leading our country ever-closer to becoming a banana republic. Don't be afraid. Remember that the threat is usually more terrifying than the thing itself. It's far better to know who are these "enemies of change" that keep us in multiple quagmires with war after war, in dumb policy after dumb policy, and in traditions that may have, at one time, been good for our country but are now leading us to destruction. Open your eyes. Trump was voted for by Deplorables for one main reason: to be our "Disrupter-in-Chief. It's time we let him disrupt.

RESISTANCE

TACTIC #10: *"The major premise for tactics is the development of operations that will maintain a constant pressure upon the opposition."*[310]

"'...OURS IS NOT THE popular 'resistance' of the left. We want the administration to succeed...But we believe our first duty is to this country...the president continues to act in a manner that is detrimental to the health of our republic. ... [His] erratic behavior would be more concerning if it weren't for unsung heroes in...the White House.... [I]n this chaotic era...Americans should know that there are adults in the room.... Given the instability...there were early whispers...of invoking the 25th Amendment, which would start a complex process for removing the president. But no one wanted to precipitate a constitutional crisis. So we will do what we can to steer the administration in the right direction until — one way or another — it's over."[311] – ANONYMOUS

Someone inside the White House purportedly wrote the above in a letter on September 5, 2018. It was sent to the *New York Times* Op-Ed whose editorial board made the decision to publish it anonymously because it was written by "a senior official in the

---

[310] Ibid. Alinsky. pg. 129.
[311] Anonymous. "I Am Part of the resistance Inside the Trump Administration" *New York Times*
https://www.nytimes.com/2018/09/05/opinion/trump-white-house-anonymous-resistance.html?module=inline.

Trump Administration whose identity is known to us and whose job would be jeopardized by its disclosure. We believe publishing this essay anonymously is the only way to deliver an important perspective to our readers."[312] *How big of you.*

Given the clear bias the *NYT* has exhibited against our president in the past, we may never know whether or not the letter is real. If it was drummed up by the editors to stoke further division between Trump and his inner circle, they succeeded. The damage such attacks do to our country is wide-reaching. In this chapter, the letter will be treated as authentic.

Alinsky's tenth tactic, *"[t]he major premise for tactics is the development of operations that will maintain a constant pressure upon the opposition"*, is one that the left and anti-Trumpers have mastered. They aren't satisfied with lobbing one attack at their enemy. Their attacks are multipronged.

That an unelected official would think Trump supporters agree with him shows how out-of-touch never-Trumpers are. Do not doubt for one second that "Anonymous" is not a never-Trumper. The letter reveals arrogance: *"'The dilemma - which [Trump] does not fully grasp - is that many of the senior officials in his own administration are working diligently from within to frustrate parts of his agenda and his worst inclinations. I would know. I am one of them.'"*[313]

"Anonymous" is the delusional one. Why he believes that the American people would feel safer knowing he is in control of the White House is hard to fathom.

---

[312] Ibid.
[313] Ibid.

Sounding very much like the "establishment", the letter's ideologies are old-school. How do I know? Because, they disagree with Trump's. The letter writer's way of thinking has been tried for decades, and has failed. We voted for Trump because he has fresh, straight-forward ideas that finally sound logical to us. Now this bozo (and others, apparently) is actively working to undermine the American electorate.

The letter states that Trump *"complained for weeks about senior staff members letting him get boxed into further confrontation with Russia, and he expressed frustration that the United States continued to impose sanctions on the country for its malign behavior. But his national security team knew better - such actions had to be taken, to hold Moscow accountable."*[314]

I have a message for our president: *GET RID OF THESE POMPOUS IDIOTS, NOW.*

Trump is so much more in touch with what's needed to bring Russia, China, North Korea and Iran to the negotiating table than is the "resistance". When he begins a negotiation, he first praises the leader of the country. No matter how evil that leader is, Trump has sense enough to build his ego up first. For that, the "resistance" gets unhinged because they don't understand Trump's strategies at all. When they are outspoken about it, especially publicly, they weaken him and all he is trying to do for our country.

If the foreign leader doesn't respond the way Trump wants, he denigrates him in front of the entire world (i.e., Little Rocket Man), for which the "resistance" goes even more ballistic. The good news is that, as confused

---

[314] Ibid.

as Trump's domestic opponents are, you can bet his foreign ones are even more so. Strangely, the "resistance" may, unintentionally, actually be helping our president in the global arena.

Trump studies his opponents inside and out before negotiations even begin. He sizes them up in a way that the "resistance" never could. Perhaps he may not read every daily report, which drives the establishment crazy; but, you can bet he understands exactly what motivates people. He likes to have fresh eyes, not those clouded by years of miscalculations. After learning the opponent's culture, style and personality, Trump treats the negotiations accordingly. He's brilliant. The "resistance", on the other hand (like John Brennan), are pompous, self-serving, linear-thinking and knee-jerk reactionaries. Trump is none of those, although they think he is.

Given "Anonymous'" letter, the left's reaction to the Helsinki summit with Putin makes a lot more sense. The "resistance" would keep us in a perpetual war. Trump wants none of that, and his actions prove it.

Chris Farrell, Director of Investigations & Research for *Judicial Watch* and former Military Intelligence officer, understands Trump. In an article for *FOX News*, he made a strong case for "Anonymous" to be hunted down and imprisoned. I agree. He says that punishment for offending 18 USC Section 2384 – Seditious Conspiracy is 20 years. Its definition is to "'conspire to overthrow, put down, or to destroy by force the Government of the United States,' and 'prevent, hinder, or delay the execution of any law of the United

States.'"[315] I say, *lock both "Anonymous" and Hillary up together and throw away the key.*

Avowed never-Trumper, and *NYT* columnist Bret Stephens, wrote a revealing article recently that should give Deplorables hope that at least some never-Trumpers may unite with us in the near future. His, "For Once I'm Grateful for Trump", piece addressed the shameful way in which the left treated now-Justice Kavanaugh and expressed Stephens' relief that Trump stood by the judge's side. In it, he says he's "grateful that, in Trump, at least one big bully was willing to stand up to others."[316] Yes, Bret, that's why Deplorables voted for him!

"The third rule of the ethics of means and ends is that in war the end justifies almost any means."[317] Alinsky draws on Abraham Lincoln's experience during the Civil War, explaining that, "when Lincoln was convinced that the use of military commissions to try civilians was necessary, he brushed aside the illegality of this action with the statement that it was 'indispensable to the public safety.' He believed that the civil courts were powerless to cope with the insurrectionist activities of civilians. 'Must I shoot a simple-minded soldier who deserts, while I must not touch a hair of a wily agitator who induces him to

[315] Chris Farrell. "NY Times anonymous anti-Trump op-ed writer is a criminal who belongs in prison" *FOX News* (Sept. 7, 2018) https://www.foxnews.com/opinion/ny-times-anonymous-anti-trump-op-ed-writer-is-a-criminal-who-belongs-in-prison.

[316] Bret Stephens. "For Once, I'm Grateful for Trump" *New York Times* https://www.nytimes.com/2018/10/04/opinion/trump-kavanaugh-ford-allegations.html.

[317] Ibid. Alinsky, pg. 29.

desert...'"[318] Like Lincoln, Trump thinks outside the box and he's not afraid to act, so long as it protects America.

Lincoln was facing the prospect of either winning a war that could unite our country, or continue the abominable practice of slavery. In a sense, Trump is facing similar challenges.

Today, we face a cultural war that is dividing our country. To the left, it is war and they will use any means necessary to win it. Fortunately, Trump feels the same way. Establishment Republicans just don't understand the lengths to which the Dems will go to win. Unless, and until, Republicans grow some balls and learn to fight back, we will continue to have divisions within our own party.

Everything our President is trying to accomplish, internationally and domestically, is being compromised by false accusations and dishonest reporting. Imagine how the world is viewing us through their prism. By all credible accounts, foreign leaders either respect Trump, or fear him. It's the will of the American people that's not trusted, as stoked by anti-Trump sentiment. This puts us in a dangerous position of weakness, and diminishes Trump's strengths.

Because the left has infiltrated the media, Hollywood, academia and the Democratic Party, they are able to keep pressure on Trump from multiple fronts at once, and constantly.

A revealing memo on the "resistance" was written by Rich Higgins, a former Pentagon official who served in Trump's NSC's strategic-planning office as director under then-NSC Director Michael Flynn. Higgins claims

---

[318] Ibid. Alinsky, pp. 29-30.

that Flynn was forced out of the White House, via the Mueller investigation, because John Brennan and others were against his intended reversals of Obama's Middle-East policies. Higgins was pressured to resign in July, 2017, by Flynn's replacement, retired Lt. General H.R. McMaster, an establishment man. That move came as a direct result of an email Higgins shared with others in the White House that is now known as "The Richard Higgins Memo". In it, he warned the president and others that the White House was infiltrated by Obama holdovers who were hell-bent on subverting Trump's policies. Once the memo was leaked, McMaster hunted down its author and ousted him, along with other Flynn loyalists. When Trump was made aware of Higgins' departure from the White House, he is said to have taken a personal interest in the memo, and was furious that Higgins et al, were gone. Disappointingly, Trump hung on to McMaster for a year, finally forcing him into retirement on March 22, 2018.

The entire memo is a must read in order to understand who the "resistance" is, and what their goals are. It's frightening. While many on the left have decried the memo as conspiratorial and loony, one ought to remember that when the left is being exposed is when their ridiculing begins.

Higgins explains that "[t]he Trump administration is suffering under withering information campaigns designed to first undermine, then delegitimize and ultimately remove the President. ... Attacks on President Trump are not just about destroying him, but also about *destroying the vision of America that lead [sic] to his election.*"[319] [Emphasis his]. He believes that "these campaigns run on multiple lines of effort, serve as the non-violent line ... of a wider movement, and execute political warfare agendas that reflect cultural Marxist outcomes. ... Because the hard left is aligned with Islamist organizations at local (ANTI FA working with Muslim Brotherhood doing business as MSA and CAIR), national (ACLU and BLM working with CAIR and MPAC) and international levels (OIC working with OSCE and the UN), recognition must [be] given to the fact that they seamlessly interoperate at the narrative level as well. In candidate Trump, the opposition saw a threat to the 'politically correct' enforcement narratives they've meticulously laid in over the past few decades. In President Trump, they see a latent threat to continue that effort to ruinous effect and their retaliatory response reflects this fear."[320]

If these theories sound crazy, you have a lot of waking up to do. The left hopes you don't. But, ask yourself this: if Higgins is right, would you feel concerned about America's future knowing that a purposely entrenched, decades-in-the-making plot is being cultivated to turn our country into a socialist state? If so, perhaps you now understand why Deplorables are so united behind Trump, even when we may sometimes disagree with him. We know that he is our only hope against this silent take-over of America.

Higgins maintains that Marxists aren't the only group working against our democratic system of

---

[319] Richard Higgins. "The Complete Richard Higgins Memo" *Free Republic* (May 2017) http://freerepublic.com/focus/f-news/3576249/posts.
[320] Ibid.

freedoms. "...'deep state' actors, globalists, bankers, Islamists, and establishment Republicans"[321] are also heavily invested. Additionally, it is the means by which these groups spread their tentacles that enable their goals to succeed. In order for that to happen, "...America, both as an ideal and as a national and political identity, must be destroyed."[322]

Groups assisting those wanting to transform America are fairly easy to identify. Higgins says they include the mainstream media (via disinformation), academia (via indoctrination), the "resistance" (via infiltration), global corporatists and bankers (via financial support), the left (via Alinsky's tactics), the Republican elitists (via caving to Alinsky's tactics), and Islamists (whose rallying cry, "'[b]y their own hands!' has been the declared strategy of the Muslim Brotherhood since 1991. This strategy seeks to divide American society against itself with the forced imposition of Islamist objectives on one half of American society by the other half.")[323]

By ridiculing Conservatives as "islamophobic", these groups have been dividing our nation, intentionally, for decades. They've been quietly creating a pathway for integrating all things Islam into our culture. No one today would dare object to allowing Muslim culture at a public school. Yet, all things white, Christian, or patriotic, are being systematically banned. You can bet by now Trump knows it. But, do you?

CNN's host, Don Lemon, made a racist statement that shocked even his most liberal followers. In

---

[321] Ibid.
[322] Ibid.
[323] Ibid.

discussing thousands of Central American immigrants marching to our borders demanding entry, he said, "[w]e have to stop demonizing people and realize the biggest terror threat in this country is white men, most of them radicalized to the right, and we have to start doing something about them."[324] Ok, Don, can we stop demonizing white people now?

Not to be outdone, his colleague, Jake Tapper, remained silent when one of his guests, *GQ Magazine* columnist Julia Ioffe said this: "I think this president, one of the things that he really launched his presidential run on is talking about Islamic radicalization and this president has radicalized so many more people than ISIS ever did."[325] Are you getting the picture yet?

Most people do not have time to research every major news story. They rely on mostly biased headlines. That's a mistake that may lead to our country's demise. At the very least, the issues that would shape a voter's mind should be researched for accuracy. Otherwise, the vote should not even be cast, as it negates another from a well-researched voter who makes an educated decision based on facts.

During the midterm election campaigns of 2018, Google censured a political ad from Tennessee's Republican candidate for Senate, Marsha Blackburn. Her

[324] Brian Flood. "CNN host: 'The biggest terror threat in this country is white men'" *FOX News* (Oct. 31, 2018) https://www.foxnews.com/entertainment/cnn-host-don-lemon-says-white-men-are-biggest-terror-threat-to-americans.
[325] Brian Flood. "CNN slammed as 'disgraceful' after Jake Tapper silent when guest says Trump radicalized more people than ISIS" *FOX News* (Oct. 31, 2018) https://www.foxnews.com/entertainment/cnn-slammed-as-disgraceful-after-jake-tapper-silent-when-guest-says-trump-radicalized-more-people-than-isis.

ad portrayed actual video clips of leftist mob violence. Google said it was too violent! In 2017, Twitter banned her ad opposing Planned Parenthood, which incredibly still receives taxpayer funding even after two years of Republican majorities in both the House and Senate.

It was revealed that, two years after Trump became president, Google was behind a "get out the Latino vote" program during the 2016 elections. An email "was written by the tech giant's former head of multicultural marketing and details a range of efforts to increase Latino turnout, including the support of a partner organization that helped to drive voters to the polls."[326] If Google and other social media monopolies aren't soon regulated, illegal immigrants will one day soon be choosing our politicians, and our borders will be wide open to all.

Hollywood is another propagandistic arm of the left. Jane Fonda, once known as "Hanoi Jane" because she gave aid and comfort to the North Vietnamese as our American soldiers were being tortured in nearby POW camps, is back at it again. Most Vietnam Vets still detest Fonda, understandably so, because she posed on top of a North Vietnamese military tank in a show of "friendship" with our enemy. So, it shouldn't surprise anybody that she recently compared Trump to Hitler. "'Attacking the media is the first step in the move towards fascism,' Fonda (now 80) said, according to Variety. 'The cornerstone to democracy is an

---

[326] Christopher Carbone. "Leaked Google employee's email reveals effort to boost Latino vote, surprise that some voted for Trump" *FOX News* (Sept. 12, 2018) https://www.foxnews.com/tech/leaked-google-employees-email-reveals-effort-to-boost-latino-vote-surprise-that-some-voted-for-trump

independent, democratic media. And it's under attack in a major way because bad guys are running it all. We have to make sure it doesn't continue.'"[327] Does she not realize that Trump calls the "fake news" the "enemy of the people" precisely because of false statements like hers? An "independent, Democratic media" *is* the cornerstone of democracy, Hanoi Jane, but the propaganda they spew out daily, is not. She spread propaganda in the 60s and 70s, and she's doing it again.

Academia, too, has been a major facilitator for the left's agenda for at least a generation. We must recognize it and ensure that the radical professors in our schools are balanced with more moderate and conservative educators if we are to turn this dangerous trend around. Indoctrination of our young is simply unacceptable.

Academia's resistance to all things great about America, and their teaching our students the same, has been astonishingly successful. They've managed to brainwash an entire generation of Americans. It may well be too late to save millennials. But, if we have a chance to save the generation after them, we must start reversing the left's tactics now. The steps we take today will determine whether the United States of America retains its structure, or becomes the "Un-United States of Socialism".

The level of dishonesty, hate, and resistance by the left has reached an all-time high. Consider a video that

---

[327] Judy Kurtz. "Jane Fonda compares Trump to Hitler while urging Americans to vote" *The Hill* (Nov. 2, 2018) https://thehill.com/blogs/in-the-know/in-the-know/414582-jane-fonda-compares-trump-to-hitler-while-urging-americans-to.

was purposely edited to depict Kavanaugh as anti-women. It was distributed by 2020 Democratic presidential hopeful, Kamala Harris, during his nomination proceedings. *"The Washington Post* gave the senator four Pinocchio's, its most egregious rating, saying the post omitted crucial facts such as that Kavanaugh was actually quoting the terminology used by the plaintiff in a 2013 court case rather than stating his actual views [on abortion]."[328] Harris was a prosecutor before becoming a state senator. She can't claim ignorance. Yet, she will probably get a lot of votes as a presidential candidate, because most people aren't paying attention.

Also exposed by the Trump phenomena, is the dark underbelly of our bloated, highly–infiltrated, federal government. In October, 2018, a D.C. federal judge accused career State Department officials of being "intentionally deceptive" in order "to derail a series of lawsuits seeking information about former Secretary of State Hillary Clinton's private email server and her handling of the 2012 terrorist attack on the U.S. Consulate in Benghazi, Libya."[329] We can thank the ever-vigilant *Judicial Watch* for relentlessly filing FOIA requests to expose government cover-ups in spite of the resistance by many in our own agencies.

---

[328] Lukas Mikelionis. "Kamala Harris' edited Kavanaugh video, 'made-for-TV' questions draw scrutiny" *FOX News* (Sept. 13, 2018) https://www.foxnews.com/politics/kamala-harris-edited-kavanaugh-video-made-for-tv-questions-draw-scrutiny.

[329] Gregg Re. "State Department provided 'clearly false' statements to derail requests for Clinton docs, 'shocked' federal judge says" *FOX News* (Oct. 17, 2018) https://www.foxnews.com/politics/state-department-provided-clearly-false-statements-to-derail-hillary-clinton-doc-requests-federal-judge-says.

A great article, written by James Simpson for *American Thinker,* reveals the harsh realities of government infiltration by the left. He credits *Project Veritas* (another commendable watch-dog organization) for exposing the level of disloyalty many federal employees harbor. One of their undercover videos "presents a portrait of a State Department bureaucrat committed to [the "resistance"]. The employee caught on tape, one Stuart Karaffa, says, 'Resist everything ... every level, f--- s--- up.' Karaffa is a self-identified member of Democratic Socialists of America, and uses work time to draft DSA-related political emails, a violation of the Hatch Act. What about getting caught? He says, 'I don't have anything to lose. It's impossible to fire federal employees....'"[330] That kind of attitude starts at the top. Such unethical behavior needs to be dealt with harshly, and stopped.

The Government Accountability Office estimates that it "takes on average from 170 to 370 days to fire a poor-performing employee."[331] That's ridiculous.

Project Veritas' Simpson adds that, "President Obama made matters worse, politicizing the hiring process under a 2010 executive order that circumvented many federal hiring rules. This made it easier for him to seed the bureaucracy with his people. We are witnessing the results. It's called the Deep State."[332] And, it's intentional.

---

[330] James Simpson. "Want to make federal employees easier to fire?" *American Thinker* (Sept. 20, 2018)
https://www.americanthinker.com/blog/2018/09/want_to_make_fe deral_employees_easier_to_fire.html.
[331] Ibid.
[332] Ibid.

Fortunately, "there is new legislation being considered in Congress...: the Merit Act (H.R. 559). ... [It] would greatly streamline the process for firing employees who are poor performers, insubordinate, or otherwise engaged in misconduct. ... The legislation shortens the appeals process and reduces the burden of proof required to fire a bad employee."[333] Let us pray it passes. If not, bureaucracy and the "deep state" will only get worse.

While organized groups of the "resistance" may be easy to identify, lone wolves are not. Take General James Mattis, for example. When Trump announced his decision for a troop withdrawal from Syria, Mattis vehemently opposed. In his resignation letter, Mattis wrote that, "[B]ecause you have the right to have a Secretary of Defense whose views are better aligned with yours on these and other subjects, I believe it is right for me to step down from my position."[334] As logical as that may sound, I was amazed at how many people were angry about it. They weren't mad at Mattis, they were furious with Trump.

I expected the usual hypocrites, like the self-described "dovish" Democrats, to lash out at Trump for wanting our troops home. Which, predictably, they did. It didn't matter that Obama had fired Mattis years before, via text message, apparently for failing to carry out the then-president's will.

---

[333] Ibid.

[334] Abbey Vesoulis. "Mattis Quit After Trump's Syria Pullout. Here Are All the Times He Publicly Split With the President" *Time* (Dec. 21, 2018) http://time.com/5486300/james-mattis-disagree-donald-trump/

What I was particularly taken aback by was the number of so-called Trump supporters who turned on Trump for acting on what was part of his campaign promise. Mattis understood the Syrian pull-out promise when he accepted the job, yet he resisted Trump on the issue time and again.

In his farewell letter, Mattis further stated, "[w]e are in Syria right now to defeat ISIS and destroy the geographic caliphate, and make sure it doesn't come back the moment we will turn our back. So there's going to be a little while that we've got to work with the locals." Trump tweeted his counter-argument: "Why are we fighting for our enemy, Syria, by staying & killing ISIS for them.... Time to focus on our Country."[335] I couldn't agree more. The "geographic caliphate" has been trying to organize for thousands of years and will never stop until, and unless, they are successful. ISIS is one of many militant enforcers of that ideology and will never be completely destroyed. It is the philosophy of military men like Mattis, though, that has led to seventeen years of nation-building in places like Afghanistan and Iraq. New schools get built and destroyed many times over in those backward countries, as our infrastructure has become third-world-like.

So, with all due respect to General Mattis, and those Trump "supporters" who have deserted Trump before his promised mission is accomplished, I say *shame on you*. It is you who are holding our president back. We have a bigger war to win right here at home against the left, who are doing their utmost to destroy America. To waste our resources on the Middle-East any longer is to

---

[335] Ibid.

abandon our own. The naysayers claim that as Mattis' commander, Trump should listen to his generals. Hogwash. Just because a soldier has reached the rank of general, does not make him right on all issues. Mattis was right to say that Trump deserved a Secretary of Defense who would obey his Commander-in-Chief. For the sake of our country, let's hope he finds the right one this time.

One such man is Gen. Anthony J. Tata. He completely agrees with the Syrian pull-out. More importantly, he is the type of out-of-the-box visionary our country needs and our president deserves. He believes we cannot continue to spill our precious blood and resources on a region whose own neighbors won't even enter the fight, like Saudi Arabia. Let them kill each other off and when ISIS resurges, we'll deal with it. Tata disagrees with Mattis' preference to stay because, he says, doing so "'would invite the potential of mission creep toward nation-building.'"[336]

Explaining the likely reason Trump felt now is the right time to leave, Tata said that "[o]n Dec. 14, the Syrian Democratic Forces – in conjunction with U.S. forces and air power – defeated ISIS in the town of Hajin near the Iraq border and along the Euphrates River. This significant defeat of a remnant of ISIS forces was most likely a trigger for President Trump to declare that the original purpose of U.S. troops in Syria is nearly accomplished."[337]

---

[336] Gen. Anthony J. Tata. "Trump is right to withdraw from Syria – He should replace US troops with private contractors" *FOX News* (Dec. 22, 2018)
https://www.foxnews.com/opinion/trump-is-right-to-withdraw-from-syria-he-should-replace-us-troops-with-private-contractors.
[337] Ibid.

Sensibly, Tata also recognizes that the region is important for our country's future self-interest. He says "[t]here has always been a balance between our troops staying too long and not staying long enough in their engagements abroad. Small pockets of ISIS fighters remain and there exists the potential threats of Russian, Iranian and Turkish hegemonic interests."[338]

Tata offers solutions that make more sense than anything I've heard in recent memory. "[R]ather than ending our on-the-ground involvement entirely in anti-ISIS operations in that country, the president should replace the U.S. troops with a comparably sized group of private military contractors. The private contractors would be an economy of force that assists our allies in the region in post-conflict operations, such as providing security for private investment that will allow the region to stabilize. Further, this force could assuage the fears that the Kurds will be left unprotected and that Iran and Russia will be free to roam the country. Likewise, it could be a pilot project of sorts that allows us to determine the effectiveness of privatizing post-conflict operations."[339] Bravo, General Tata. Let's hope you have our president's ear.

When Trump's announcements, like a Syrian pull-out, are hammered by resisters trying to thwart his efforts, damage is done to our country. Rather than being united behind the president and his agenda, naysayers and good men like Mattis are just not able to put our country before their own self-interests. Democrats are winning this war at home precisely

---

[338] Ibid.
[339] Ibid.

because they stay united, no matter what. While Republicans are right to voice concern when they believe Trump may be making a tactical error, they are wrong to persist simply because they have a difference of opinion about policy. Trump's campaign promises are not negotiable. Can you say, "Read my lips"? By Mattis declining to assist in fulfilling one of the president's campaign promises, he not only proved himself to be part of the "resistance", he bordered on insubordination, in my opinion. Mattis was right to step down, and Trump had every right to accept his resignation.

The first step in staying ahead of your opponents is to understand how they think. With that knowledge, it becomes easier to see why the "resistance" behaves the way they do. It's also why understanding Alinsky's tactics is so critical to knowing how to counter the opposition.

Considering that, Alinsky's tenth tactic, *"the development of operations that will maintain a constant pressure upon the opposition"* begins to make sense. Trump understands that well. He's been the subject of constant, targeted attacks from many groups desiring the same goal: to create total chaos in order to transform America as we know it. They want global socialism. That means all Americans, not just the rich, will be responsible for the poor around the world, not just in our country. Even America's poorest will not escape the effects of the drain of our wealth.

Most Americans have no idea how entrenched the left, the establishment, and the never-Trumpers are in our government agencies, educational systems, and "fake news" media outlets. While these groups are non-violent in nature, their militant sidekicks, e.g., Antifa,

Black Lives Matter and Occupy Wall Street, are not. Likewise, the Council on American–Islamic Relations (CAIR) and the Muslim Brotherhood are the business "suits" to their militant brothers, the PLO, Hamas, Hezbollah, ISIS et al.

That's why the left sympathizes with Islamic groups. The DSA, especially, finds much common ground with CAIR and the Muslim Brotherhood, including wiping Israel off the face of the earth. What the left doesn't realize is that once Islamists gain the upper hand, and they will if the current trend continues, the two groups will clash. It's hard to imagine an ISIS acceptance of "Snowflakes", given the Islamists' vile hatred of gay people, women's rights, freedoms, diversity and peace.

The following chapter, "Mobs vs. Jobs", exposes the complete dichotomy between the ideology shared by Trump and Deplorables versus that of the left. There is no longer any common ground because the left, supported by the "fake news" media, has brainwashed its supporters into believing a utopic version of socialism. There is, no longer, any compromise possible.

The mobs of today, who are attempting to force socialism onto Americans, are funded by leftist billionaires hell-bent on destroying our country. "Mobs vs. Jobs" will introduce you to the people behind these violent movements, and their sinister intentions. You are not going to believe what's coming in our future if we don't take corrective action now.

MOBS VS JOBS

TACTIC #11: *"If you push a negative hard and deep enough it will break through into its counterside."*[340]

"IF THEY BRING A KNIFE to the fight, we bring a gun. ... We need to punish our enemies." –OBAMA. *"...I'd take [Trump] behind the gym and beat the hell out of him."* – FORMER V.P. BIDEN. *"When they go low, we kick them."* – FORMER US ATTORNEY GENERAL ERIC HOLDER. *"...if we are fortunate enough to win back the House..., that's when civility can start again."* –HILLARY. *"I just don't even know why there aren't uprisings all over the country...maybe there will be..."* –NANCY PELOSI. *"Tell them they're not welcome...anywhere!"* –REP. MAXINE WATERS. *"I hope they leave their bodies to science. I would like to cut them open."* –SEN. ELIZABETH WARREN. *"...get up in the face of some congressman."* –SEN. CORY BOOKER. *"...we've got to...fight in the streets..."* –V.P. CANDIDATE TIM KAINE.[341]

It has been said that before Trump even entered the White House, his rhetoric caused division in our country. This chapter explores that claim.

---

340 Ibid. Alinsky. pg. 129.
341 *Breitbart.com*. Majority of references are from a compilation of threats to Trump, his supporters and Republicans (Last Updated Nov. 6, 2018) https://www.breitbart.com/the-media/2018/07/05/rap-sheet-cts-of-media-approved-violence-and-harassment-against-trump-supporters/.

First, I'd like to give a hat check to *Breitbart* for creating the "Rap Sheet" with most of the quotes above and throughout this chapter. (You can google them at: *Rap Sheet: ***639*** Acts of Media-Approved Violence - Breitbart.* It'll blow your mind.) With truth subject to deletion by revisionists of history, the *Breitbart* posting has ensured that won't happen.

Every quote above is attributed to a Democrat, aimed at Conservatives. While most were directed at Trump and his party since he took office, one in particular was not. It is all we need to prove that Trump is not the one to blame for divisions in America today.

Prior to his first presidential election, Obama fooled moderate voters with his promise of civility to unite the two parties. Americans were sick of all the fighting and welcomed his words. But, as *Politico* revealed in a June, 2008 article, "[I]n the last 24 hours, [Obama has] completely abandoned his campaign's call for 'new politics', equating the election to a 'brawl' and promising ... that if there's a political knife fight, he'd bring a gun."[342] Strange words for a gun-control activist. He threw the first punch. His Republican presidential opponent John McCain, and his staff, were stunned. They shouldn't have been. Regrettably, they never hit back.

Even the liberal *Politico* concedes that, "Obama never paid much of a price for his willingness to go negative. He also...promised to be tougher than past Democrats, and bragged of his Chicago training."[343]

---

[342] Ben Smith. "Obama brings a gun to a knife fight" *Politico* https://www.politico.com/blogs/ben-smith/2008/06/obama-brings-a-gun-to-a-knife-fight-009692 (June 14, 2018).
[343] Ibid.

Did that sink in? A full ten years prior to Trump's presidency, Obama and the Dems were divisive. Republicans had the naïve John McCain actually *defending* his opponent on more than one occasion. A supporter once asked him whether or not Obama is an Arab sympathizer. McCain emphatically said, "No." What did that gain us? You be the judge.

Alinsky advised left-wing activists to always refer to their opponents as "100 per cent devil." He called this the ultimate "polarization" of a target. The self-avowed atheist even quoted the Bible to prove his point: "He that is not with me is against me (Luke 11:23)".[344]

Does that mean Conservatives must stoop to the same dirty tricks as the left? No, lest we lose credibility, too, over time. However, McCain did not truly know whether or not Obama was an Arab sympathizer. Many people are now convinced that he is, based on his presidential actions (i.e., the nuclear deal with Iran, eliminating Islamist keywords from our intelligence training manuals, stacking the White House with known Muslim Brotherhood adherents, emptying Gitmo, trading Bowe Bergdahl for Taliban prisoners, etc.).

That's why never-Trumpers really anger me. They'd rather back a gentleman loser, lacking courage (like Mitt Romney), than an uncouth winner with balls (like Trump). If you are one of those who just can't handle Trump's style, get out of his way and let him do his job.

The eleventh tactic in Alinsky's "Rules for Radicals", *"if you push a negative hard and deep enough it will break through into its counterside* ... is based on the principle that every positive has its negative. ... In a fight

---

[344] Ibid. Alinsky, pp. 133-134.

almost anything goes. It almost reaches the point where you stop to apologize if a chance blow lands above the belt."[345] Don't apologize, he says. Eventually, it will be your positive advantage. You must keep that leverage. Obama understands that the Chicago way. Trump does, too, as a New Yorker. Never–Trumpers do not.

Dems have been literal slave owners of black votes for over a hundred years, but most blacks don't even know it. With support from African–Americans like Kanye West, Lawrence Jones and Candace Owens, Trump has asked the black community, "*What have you got to lose?*" Because they feel left behind by Obama, many are heeding his call.

Alinsky outlines why blacks never gained much in return for years of loyal voting. He says, "[t]he pressure that gave us our positive power was the negative of racism in white society. We exploited it for our own purposes."[346] That explains a lot.

Even more sinister, Alinsky *purposely* redesigned elements of his tactics so blacks could relate. He'd make sure the tactic "connected with their hatred of Whitey. The one thing that all oppressed people want to do to their oppressors is shit on them."[347] Imagine for a moment if blacks were aware that the left has been using them as pawns against Republicans, just so Dems could hang on to power? Will blacks heed Trump's call? One can only hope.

To the left, truth doesn't matter. What does matter is how they couch their reactions towards Trump's actions. Alinsky says that the left's reactions should be

---

[345] Ibid, pg. 129–130.
[346] Ibid, pg. 144.
[347] Ibid, pp. 140–141.

clothed in "shock, horror, and moral outrage."[348] They should always be public; and, the more dramatic, the better. Overblown reactions to Trump in everything he does, falsely comparing him to Hitler and the KKK, calling him homophobic, racist, and xenophobic, etc., are the "means" the left uses to achieve their goals.

As in the previous chapter, Alinsky's third rule of ethics of means and ends, *"in war the end justifies almost any means"*, applies to the left's unapologetic, unethical shaming of all things conservative. We cannot allow ourselves to be bullied, or to allow the left to divide us. We must fight back like Trump does every single day. Eventually, people will tire of hearing the name-calling, and the impact of the words will diminish.

Sadly, Dems aren't the only group using hate speech. They have plenty of company. Take the liberal celebrities, for example. While many may not even be aware of the damage they're inflicting upon our nation, their words still aid the left's cause. They have huge audiences...sometimes in the tens of millions. A few of their hateful comments follow below.

"Yes, I'm angry. Yes, I'm outraged. Yes, I have thought an awful lot about blowing up the White House..." -MADONNA. *"Stop Gestapo tactics of ICE"* -CHER. "[New hit single, "Framed"]...*aggressively plots the murder of Ivanka Trump"* -EMINEM. *"Push Trump off a cliff..."* -ROSIE O'DONNELL. "[First Lady Melania is a] ...*feckless complicit piece of shit. ...we have an administration that is...pro-Nazi."* -KATHY GRIFFIN. *"When was the last time an actor assassinated a president?"* -JOHNNY DEPP. *"...doing the work of Goebbels."* -ADAM

---

[348] Ibid. pg. 130.

SCOTT. *"Rip Barron* [Trump's 11-yo son]*...from his mother's arms...put him in a cage with pedophiles."* - PETER FONDA. *"I'd have to kill Trump...."* -ADAM PALLY. *"...punch Nazis. ...riot when your college invites a Nazi. ...set it...on fire."* -LEXI ALEXANDER. "[Anti-fascist riots are] *...just the beginning."* -JUDD APATOW. *"WAKE UP & JOIN THE RESISTANCE. ONCE THE MILITARY IS W US FASCISTS GET OVERTHROWN."* -SARAH SILVERMAN. *"...if you're voting for Trump, it's time for the urn."* -MICHAEL SHANNON. *"...there will be blood in the streets."* -JAMES CROMWELL.[349]

Many of the threats above were made within Trump's first of couple months in office. Madonna's was made on January 21, 2017, during the "Woman's March", just one day after his swearing in. How are comments like these condoned? Once you realize who their leaders are, you'll understand.

Unless Democratic leadership is willing to call out hate-speech, our country will face more violence and division in the future. But, they won't. Alinsky told them to never admit weakness.

It would help if the propaganda-spreading press, or what Trump calls the "fake news", did their jobs instead of following the left's lead. Where entertainers might be forgiven for their ignorant rhetoric, albeit incendiary, the "fake news" media has no such excuse. They went to school to become journalists. You'd think they would have learned the necessity for truth in a democracy. Instead, they compete for the most creative headlines to frame Trump as evil about everything. It's inexcusable and dangerous.

---

[349] Ibid. *Breitbart.com.*

Honorable journalists get upset when Trump calls out the "fake news" media. They shouldn't. They wish he'd differentiate between "fake news" and "real news". But, Trump knows who's who. As importantly, fans know (thus the drop in *CNN's* ratings as *FOX News'* ratings increase).

Following is a sampling of why the "fake news" media is losing ratings.

"These people should be made uncomfortable, and I think that's a life sentence." -WASHINGTON POST COLUMNIST JENNIFER RUBIN. *"...standing at the border like Nazis."* –*MSNBC* CONTRIBUTOR DONNY DEUTSCH. *"...erroneously implied that a tattoo ... [on an ICE agent] essentially labeled him a Nazi. ... [in actuality, it was] the symbol for his platoon while he fought in Afghanistan."* –*NEW YORKER* REPORTER TALIA LEVIN. *"[Trump's people do] ...not appear to be human beings."* –*MSNBC* NICOLLE WALLACE. *"[I]...would poison President Trump if given the opportunity to cook for him."* –*CNN* HOST AND CHEF ANTHONY BOURDAIN (R.I.P.). *"[Trump is] ...a batshit crazy crypto-fascist who destroyed the GOP".* –NEVER-TRUMPER, *DAILY BEAST* GOP COLUMNIST RICK WILSON. *"Trump must be prosecuted...executed."* –*HUFFINGTON POST* CONTRIBUTOR JASON FULLER. *"Every morning I wake up ... and hope that this is the day that he is going to have a massive stroke, and ... be carted out of the White House on a gurney."* – PULITZER PRIZE-WINNING NOVELIST, MICHAEL CHABON. "[Called for]...*the first ISIS suicide bombing of a Trump property."* –*MSNBC* COUNTER-TERRORISM ANALYST MALCOLM NANCE. *"[Trump's] assassination is taking such a long time."* –*THE TIMES* (UK) COLUMNIST INDIA KNIGHT. *"If Trump Dies, Obama Could Pick New President."* –*CNN* YOUTUBE. *"[Called for] ... Murder in the White House...."* –PUBLISHER

AND EDITOR OF GERMAN NEWSPAPER, *DIE ZEIT*, JOSEF JOFFE. *"…it's about time for a presidential assassination." -UK TELEGRAPH COLUMNIST MONESHA RAJESH.*[350]

I wish I could say the venom stops with the three leftist groups above. Unfortunately, educators are part of the vitriol, too. Knowing that over 90% of those who educate college students today are ultra-left, we should all be worried about the next generation.

"No Trump, no KKK, no fascist USA!" -ANTIFA PROTESTERS AT UC, SANTA CRUZ COLLEGE REPUBLICANS MEETING. *"White Supremacist … educational justice is racial justice."* -HARVARD STUDENTS PROTESTING EDUCATION SECRETARY BETSY DEVOSS. *"To save American democracy, Trump must hang. The sooner and the higher, the better. #Theresistance, #DeathToFascism."* -CAL STATE, FRESNO, SELF-DESCRIBED MARXIST PROFESSOR, LARS MAISCHAK. *"House Republicans should not be shot, they should be guillotined."* TWEET BY ATHENS DEMOCRATIC SOCIALISTS OF AMERICA, UNIVERSITY OF GEORGIA. *"DIE"* [shouts teacher in front of her class as she shoots toy pistol at video of Trump during inauguration]. -UNIDENTIFIED TEACHER, W.H. ADAMSON HIGH SCHOOL, DALLAS, TEXAS. "[In class, professor calls 2016 election]…*act of terrorism, president-elect a white supremacist"* -ORANGE COAST COLLEGE, COSTA MESA, CA, PROF. OLGA PEREZ STABLE COX.[351]

We can thank the intentional indoctrination of our students on the left for what is now known as the "mob". It consists of groups such as Antifa, Black Lives Matter (BLM) and Occupy Wall Street. Note that one of the teachers quoted above called Trump a racist before he

---

[350] Ibid.
[351] Ibid.

even took office and well before his Charlottesville comment. Racist name-calling is just part of Alinsky's tactic of ridiculing used by the left for decades.

Antifa, short for "anti-fascists", consists primarily of white, entitled, college graduates saddled with tuition debt, many of whom live at home with mommy. They are the most violent of all, dress in black and wear masks. Wallowing in the worst kind of hatred, they've been taught that America is evil. They will become the future "Brownshirts" of America. History tells us the violence will only get worse in the decade to come. "Antifa" is the militant arm of the political left, much as ISIS and Al Qaeda are for the Muslim Brotherhood. If we do not put safeguards in place now, most assuredly we'll be paying for that in years to come.

Before we can understand what "Antifa" is, a definition of "fascism" is helpful. Merriman-Webster Dictionary defines fascism as: "a political philosophy, movement, or regime...that exalts nation and often race above the individual and...stands for a centralized autocratic government headed by a dictatorial leader, severe economic and social regimentation, and forcible suppression of opposition."

In breaking that definition down, let's compare it to what we know about our president versus the "mob".

First, "Trump-ism" is a political philosophy (populism), a movement (MAGA), and a regime (a government in power, with Trump as its duly-elected leader). The "mob" is also a political philosophy (leftism/socialism), a movement (destroy the "evil" America), and a regime (a mob backed by unelected leftist billionaires, e.g., George Soros and other anti-Trump, anti-capitalist, socialists).

Does Trump "exalt nation and...race above the individual"? To believe that, one would have to think Trump is an anti-Constitutionalist and anti-rule of law. His nomination of Justices Gorsuch and Kavanaugh to the SCOTUS should put that one to rest. Yes, he writes executive orders. But, so have all previous presidents. Importantly, he has reversed (or tried to) the most egregiously anti-rule of law and over-regulatory executive orders signed by Obama. The "mob", on the other hand, has demonstrated repeatedly that it dismisses our rule of law, most recently by creating chaos on the Supreme Court steps when refusing to accept the Kavanaugh confirmation. More revealingly, the left believes in globalism, open borders, abolishing ICE, and an evolving Constitution. The dividing line could not be clearer.

Trump believes in nationalism (i.e.: putting our nation first, before other nations). Whereas, the left believes in globalism (i.e., putting the world first, before our nation). Globalism smacks of socialism. Being a nationalist hardly makes Trump a "white-supremacist", as the left would have us believe.

Just ask African-American commentator, Deroy Murdock, who wrote a piece entitled, "Republicans, yet again, do right by black Americans". A few statistics Murdock hopes his fellow blacks will learn are: both unemployment and poverty levels among blacks have fallen to historical lows, and "1.2 million more black Americans have found work".[352] Trump's policies have directly led to those accomplishments.

---

[352] Leroy Murdoch. "Republicans, yet again, do right by black Americans" *FOX News* (Nov. 3, 2018)

Even more telling, the "GOP's Tax Cuts and Jobs Act, which *every single Democrat* in Congress opposed, includes Opportunity Zones ... tax incentives for businesses to invest in economically distressed communities, making them a powerful vehicle for economic growth and job creation....[353] [Emphasis his.]

"Among his earliest acts, President Trump welcomed to the Oval Office the heads of historically black colleges and universities [HBCUs]. He launched a White House office to assist HBCUs. These educators identified year-round Pell Grants as one initiative that sprang from their dialogue with this alleged 'racist'.

"'President Trump has kept his promise to make HBCUs a priority..., signing the HBCU executive order just six weeks into his presidency...,' *HBCU Digest* reported in September. ...Trump made Dr. Martin Luther King Jr.'s burial site a national historic park. Obama had *eight years* to sign such a proclamation, but he couldn't be bothered."[354] [Emphasis his.]

The second part of the definition of fascism is even easier to quantify: "A centralized autocratic government headed by a dictatorial leader". As defined, an "autocrat" is "a person (such as a monarch) ruling with unlimited authority." That explains why so many on the left love to accuse Trump of being like a "King", a ludicrous analogy. The left hopes that, if Americans hear it often enough, they'll start to think Trump believes himself to be one. Fortunately, Deplorables aren't that dumb. But,

---

https://www.foxnews.com/opinion/republicans-yet-again-do-right-by-black-americans.
[353] Ibid.
[354] Ibid.

others are. Actions taken by Trump to-date favor a de-centralization of government.

"Dictator" is defined as "a person with unlimited governmental power; and, one ruling in an often oppressive way."

Obama broadened intelligence agencies to oppress Americans, as when his IRS targeted Tea Party groups, successfully silencing many of its members just prior to the 2012 elections. His FBI spied on journalists like Sharyl Attkisson. She wrote that "[t]he government [under Obama] subsequently got caught monitoring journalists at Fox News, The Associated Press, and, as I allege in a federal lawsuit, my computers while I worked as an investigative correspondent at CBS News."[355]

Trump has cut more regulations from government than any predecessor I'm aware of. That action has freed up businesses and individuals from the oppressive bureaucracy of government overreach.

Trump is also known to hold more frequent, more transparent, and longer-lasting press conferences than any president in recent memory. Trump frequently holds round table discussions with various groups of every persuasion to broaden his options. Many witnesses have testified to his amazing ability to bring people together and get things done.

The tactics used by the left fit the definition of "oppressive" far more logically than those used by Conservatives.

---

[355] Sharyl Attkisson. "It looks like Obama did spy on Trump, just as he apparently did to me" *The Hill* (Sept. 20, 2017) https://thehill.com/opinion/campaign/351495-it-looks-like-obama-did-spy-on-trump-just-as-he-did-to-me.

The left's militant arm, the "mob", is known for blocking highways, destroying property, holding violent protests, shutting down conservative speakers on college campuses, intimidating its opponents by confronting them with threats at their homes, places of business, restaurants, malls and "whenever and wherever they are", as Maxine Waters so disgracefully incited. If anyone is suppressing opponents, it's the "mob", created and encouraged by the left. The "mob's" vile actions speak volumes as to which group should be entrusted with the future of our country: i.e., left vs. right/mobs vs. jobs.

As a 2010 member of an offshoot group of the national Tea Party movement (the South Pinellas 912 organized by local patriot Barb Haselden), I heard the left spew the same ugly epithets they now hurl at Trump and Deplorables: terrorists, nazis, fascists, Hitlers, white-supremacists, xenophobes, racists, etc. There's no difference except now their target is Trump and his Deplorables. Our Tea Party rallies were peaceful, law-abiding, orderly, clean and fun. The only problems we encountered were when leftists showed up at our rallies, full of venom, disrespectful, destructive, using filthy language and trashing the areas.

The final third of the definition of fascism is, "severe economic and social regimentation, and forcible suppression of opposition." Economic and social regimentation equate to heavy regulations.

As Trump proves by his actions that he wants less government in Americans' lives, the left calls for unsustainable green energy, Medicare and college free-for-alls. They'd be happy bankrupting our country.

Reporter James Rosen is another journalist who could tell us a lot about the suppressive actions and chilling effects of Obama's administration.

While Trump banned one *CNN* reporter from White House press briefings, it was a first. The reporter had repeatedly exhibited disrespectful behavior over a long period of time; and, many were happy to see him go.

"'Don't confuse "mob" rule and protest: The Constitution only protects peaceable demonstration,'[356] explains Bernard Kerik, a former New York City Police Commissioner. 'In an op-ed masquerading as "news," *Washington Post* political reporters inform us that Republican criticism of left-wing "mobs" is merely "fearmongering" designed to rile up 'white voters, particularly men'.[357]

"'The "angry mobs" that Republicans have been denouncing, they claim, are nothing more than high-minded activists engaging in the "freedom to assemble" because they're "appalled" by GOP policies.'"[358]

Kerik lists a few illegal acts frequently committed by the "mob": shutting down public roadways, disrupting public institutions, and unlawful assembly. I never witnessed the Tea Party participating in such activities, although the "fake news" media did a good job of getting the American people to believe we did.

Kerik sums up by saying, "'[t]he Democratic-Media Complex's characterization of unruly--and frequently

---

356 Bernard Kerik. "Don't confuse mob rule and protest: The Constitution only protects peaceable demonstration" *USA Today* https://www.usatoday.com/story/opinion/2018/10/16/mob-protestors-activists-constitution-antifa-liberal-riots-first-amendment-column/1642922002/.
357 Ibid.
358 Ibid.

violent--mob action as mere 'activism' demonstrates not only a shocking ignorance of basic constitutional principles, but also a callous disregard for the well-being of those individuals who have the misfortune to become collateral damage in the left's unhinged, self-righteous crusade.'"[359] So long as their actions continue to be met with denials by the left and dismissals by the right, the "mob" will continue to increase in violence and frequency. We must crack down on their lawlessness while we still can, before they grow even more emboldened. We witnessed what happened with ISIS after Obama called them a "JV team" and dismissed them. They became a global killing machine, growing exponentially by numbers and evil deeds. Because they went unchallenged, they caused untold misery and death.

A counter-balance to the "mob" has emerged. While the media consistently portray this conservative group as "white supremacist", "Unite the Right" has had the courage to stand up to Antifa and other violent leftist groups by holding peaceful rallies, and not backing down, in an effort to protect our declining freedoms.

During one such rally held in Washington, D.C. on August 12, 2018, even the liberal *VOX* had to admit that "'Antifa' counter protesters did engage in violence, throwing eggs and water bottles and shooting fireworks at police officers and some journalists who were covering the demonstrations."[360] If you google whether

[359] Ibid.
[360] Jennifer Williams. "Antifa clashes with police and journalists in Charlottesville and DC" *VOX* (Aug. 12, 2018)
https://www.vox.com/identities/2018/8/12/17681986/antifa-leftist-violence-clashes-protests-charlottesville-dc-unite-the-right.

the Tea Party ever behaved this way, you'll be hard-pressed to find a *factual* account. I'm imagining it's the same with "Unite the Right". Where they obtain proper permits to gather, Antifa counter-protesters show up without, and for one purpose only: violent revolt. They should be arrested on the spot.

The *VOX* adds that the D.C. rally was "not the first time Antifa protesters have been violent. In August, 2017, about 100 anarchists and Antifa members assaulted far-right demonstrators who were marching peacefully in Berkeley, California, with pepper spray, water bottles, and direct physical assault."[361] (Keep in mind that their adjective, "far-right", is subjective.)

Cloward-Piven (C-P) helped create the "mob". They drew upon Alinsky's tactics to activate local militant groups that could maximize chaos. The ultimate goal, as explained in their 1966 article, "The Weight of the Poor: A Strategy to End Poverty", was to destroy the American system as we know it by calling on "'cadres of aggressive organizers' to use 'demonstrations to create a climate of militancy.' Intimidated by threats of ... violence, politicians would appeal to the federal government for help. Carefully orchestrated media campaigns, carried out by friendly, leftwing journalists ... Washington would have to act."[362]

C-P partnered with the Democratic Party decades ago. It didn't take long for C-P to infiltrate the party. They did so by using Alinsky-ite community organizers

---

[361] Ibid.
[362] Major Resource: *The Shadow Party*, by David Horowitz and Richard Poe (Nashville, TN: Nelson Current, 2006), pp, 106-128. https://www.discoverthenetworks.org/organizations/clowardpiven-strategy-cps/.

to flood welfare rolls. Once achieved, the welfare cause would then extend to other leftist causes that Dems were all too happy to support. So long as C-P was able to continue creating programs that overloaded our systems, leading our country towards eventual socialism, they were thrilled. The Dems were able to flood their voter rolls with both poor black and white people who realized they could get what they wanted by voting Democrat."[363] Having the Democratic Party as an ally gave C-P captive militants from both groups for the next crisis, manufactured or not. Votes were only useful to C-P to keep the cooperating Dems in sync with C-P's political goals.

An African-American author of the book "The Unhyphenated American", Lloyd Marcus, explains the rise of the "mob" mentality in a recent article. He says "we have young adults in positions of power and influence who literally hate their country. Like sleeper cells, leftist young enemies-within operatives are seeking to bring down by any means necessary America as founded, openly advocating violence and treason."[364]

Unlike the mobs who were brainwashed by C-P and Alinsky in the 60s, Antifa and Occupy Wall Street consist of many college-aged, middle- to upper-class kids indoctrinated and funded by the left. "Mark Bray, a Dartmouth lecturer who has defended antifa's violent tactics, recently explained in The Post, 'Its adherents are predominantly communists, socialists and anarchists' who believe that physical violence 'is both ethically

---

[363] Ibid.
[364] Lloyd Marcus. "Enemies Within" *American Thinker* (9-11-2018) https://www.americanthinker.com/articles/2018/09/enemies_within.html.

justifiable and strategically effective.'"[365] The degree of militancy used by current-day mobs is growing stronger and is itself totalitarian in nature.

David Bossie who, along with Corey Lewandowski, co-wrote a best-selling book entitled, "Let Trump Be Trump", recently wrote an article called, "Chaos is the Democrats' only strategy for 2018 and beyond". He has it exactly right saying, "We've never had a political phenomenon like Donald Trump in the White House and we've never seen a thoroughly crazed "resistance" trying to destroy a president and everyone around him at all cost. These Democrats would do harm to their own country if it meant taking down President Trump in the process."[366]

We cannot count on the Dems to help curb the violence. They are implicit in its spread.

Can we count on Republicans to stand up to such tactics? In the past, there wasn't much hope. But, according to Laura Ingraham, host of "The Ingraham Angle" on *FOX News*, times have changed with Trump as president. He is a real leader who fights the left using their own tactics, and he teaches others to do the same.

Laura believes that, "If the GOP gives into the rabid mob mentality…, they will just embolden the worst instincts of the left. President Trump gave Republicans

[365] Marc A. Thiessen. "Yes, antifa is the moral equivalent of neo-Nazis" *The Washington Post*
https://www.washingtonpost.com/opinions/yes-antifa-is-the-moral-equivalent-of-neo-nazis/2017/08/30/9a13b2f6-8d00-11e7-91d5-ab4e4bb76a3a_story.html?noredirect=on&utm_term=.bb7d948e9ec4
[366] David Bossie. "Chaos is the Democrats' only strategy for 2018 and beyond" *FOX News* (Oct. 9, 2018)
https://www.foxnews.com/opinion/dave-bossie-chaos-is-the-democrats-only-strategy-for-2018-and-beyond.

a master class in retaliating against the tactics of the left on Tuesday [during the Kavanaugh hearings], and GOP senators would do well to take notes.... Mr. Trump decided it was time to do what he does best -- fight back. 'The Democrats are playing a con game, C-O-N. A con game,' Trump said. '...They are winking. They know it's a con game.'"367 We should be thankful we finally have a president who understands that, and is taking real action.

Lest you think the "mob" is a group of spontaneously-gathered protesters with real concerns, think again. When asked even basic questions about their causes, most of the mob's own members are clueless, instead repeating mindless chants over and over again.

Thomas Lifson, writing for *American Thinker*, lays out who is behind the well-organized "mob", saying that Trump is right to call attention to who is funding it. In his article entitled, "Trump goes full Alinsky in the midterm race", Lifson explains why he thinks our president is winning against the left. He points out a recent tweet by Trump that we should "'look at all of the professionally made identical signs. Paid for by Soros and others.'"368 Soros, the self-made billionaire who covertly funds leftist causes with the purpose of

367 Laura Ingraham. "Laura Ingraham: The critical lessons of the Kavanaugh battle" *FOX News* (Sept. 26, 2018)
https://www.foxnews.com/opinion/laura-ingraham-the-critical-lessons-of-the-kavanaugh-battle.
368 Thomas Lifson. "Trump goes full Alinsky in the midterm race" *American Thinker* (Oct. 8, 2018)
https://www.americanthinker.com/blog/2018/10/trump_goes_full_a linsky_in_the_midterm_race.html.

replacing free-market societies with socialism is someone we should all watch and fear.

Asra Q. Nomani, a respected journalist (and liberal feminist) for the *Wall Street Journal,* has been keeping tabs on leftist funders of the "mob". She agrees with Trump that these well-organized protesters are backed by Soros, et al. She claims the Women's March, held just one day after Trump's inauguration, is a prime example. Noticing the fine print on protesters' signs at the Kavanaugh hearings, she says they were "from a familiar list of Democratic interest groups that have received millions from Mr. Soros: the American Civil Liberties Union, the Leadership Conference on Civil and Human Rights, Planned Parenthood, NARAL Pro-Choice America, the Center for Popular Democracy, Human Rights Campaign and on and on."[369] These groups bind together and use deceiving titles that sound oh-so benevolent. It's up to us to stay one step ahead of them.

Just prior to the cloture vote on Kavanaugh, a "Colombian-born [self-described] sexual-assault victim cornered Sen. Jeff Flake in a Senate elevator last month and screamed 'Look at me!' It turns out that she is co-executive director of the Center for Popular Democracy. Her salary was listed as $156,333, with a bonus of $21,378, in a recent Internal Revenue Service 990 form."[370] She was calling attention to herself as a victim protesting Kavanaugh's cloture vote while the cameras rolled. We can no longer allow ourselves to be used by such trickery, as Flake and others so often do. It simply emboldens the plight of the left.

---

[369] Ibid.
[370] Ibid.

Applying Alinsky's eleventh tactic, *"if you push a negative hard and deep enough it will break through into its counterside"* to the "mob" and its actions, one can easily see that the ultimate goal of the left is to create chaos anywhere and anytime, as Rep. Maxine Waters urged. Once that chaos reaches fever-pitch, the left intends to make their final push to complete the transformation of America. That's their positive "counterside" to the negative side of "mobs". Our very freedoms are at stake.

We are up against a sophisticated, well-funded, group of far-left socialists who want to end those freedoms. That is well-established fact. The left will call it a "conspiracy theory." That's part of their Alinsky-shaming strategy to confuse moderate, uninformed Americans. We cannot allow ourselves to become complacent, especially now that we finally have a president fighting for us and our Republic.

In the next chapter, "Build That Wall", find out how, and why, these leftist billionaires are funding the multiple invasions of illegal immigrant caravans heading to our southern border. If we don't win this fight, we can kiss our country bye-bye. Fight back, while our votes still count. There really is precious little time left.

BUILD THAT WALL

TACTIC #12: *"The price of a successful attack is a constructive alternative."*[371]

"Are you aware of the perception of many about how the power and the discretion at ICE is being used to enforce the laws and do you see any parallels [with the KKK]?," asked 2020 presidential hopeful, Democratic Senator Kamala Harris of President Trump's newly-nominated head of ICE (Immigration and Customs Enforcement).

Ronald Vitiello dutifully responded, *"'I do not see any parallels.'* ... *'Are you aware of a perception that the way that they...'* Harris went on, before [he] snapped back saying, *'I see none.'* ... *'Are you aware that there is a perception that ICE is ... causing fear and intimidation, ... among immigrants ... specifically ... coming from Mexico and Central America?'* she asked again."[372]

Part of the left's strategy is to abolish ICE.

Harris' questioning drew intense fire. The gall of this former prosecutor to ask such public, biased, and accusatory questions of a respected law enforcement officer about one of our most esteemed agencies is despicable. Unfortunately, such behavior has become all

---

[371] Ibid. Alinsky, pg. 130.
[372] Lukas Mikelionis, "Kamala Harris compares ICE to KKK, gets slammed for 'disgusting,' 'horrifying' remarks" *FOX News* (Nov. 16, 2018) https://www.foxnews.com/politics/kamala-harris-under-fire-after-comparing-ice-to-kkk.

too common on Capitol Hill, lately. Dems haven't always been anti-ICE and pro-open borders. While Obama was still a senator, he said, *"[w]e all agree on the need to better secure the border and to punish employers who choose to hire illegal immigrants. We are a generous and welcoming people, ... but those who enter the country illegally, and those who employ them, disrespect the rule of law and they are showing disregard for those who are following the law. ... We simply cannot allow people to pour into the United States, undetected, undocumented, unchecked and circumventing the line of people who are waiting patiently, diligently and lawfully to become immigrants in this country."* [373] What a concept.

This chapter explores what Obama and the Democrats have done to fix our illegal immigration system, even as they ridicule Trump for trying to do just that. If Obama had followed his own advice about immigration after becoming president, Americans would have been thrilled. Instead, he sent literal welcome mats to immigrants. Because of that, they are now coming to our border in record numbers.

Because Trump is finally taking steps to fix immigration, the left is calling him heartless, racist, xenophobic, and loony. They are clearly putting politics over country.

Long considered one of the deepest red states in America, Texas is fast-becoming purple. The number of Dems fleeing self-imposed, crime-ridden, illegal

---

[373] Dan MacGuill. "Did Barack Obama Express Opposition to Undetected, Undocumented, Unchecked' Immigration?" *Snopes* (Last Updated Aug. 2, 2018) https://www.snopes.com/fact-check/barack-obama-2005-immigration-quote/.

immigrant-heavy, sanctuary-friendly, highly taxed welfare states like California, is staggering.

Most libs and illegal immigrants aren't interested in assimilating once they relocate. Rather, they change once-prosperous states into the same failing homes they are leaving. They believe that by moving to an area that is thriving they can continue their failed policies and succeed in turning the prosperous new location into a more liberal one. As their numbers grow, their "new" state begins to fail. It will infect the entire country if we don't put an end to the trend now.

Relocations by liberals and illegal immigrants are not by accident. Leftist groups, intent on transforming America into a socialist country, are behind the effort.

With his twelfth tactic, *"the price of a successful attack is a constructive alternative",* Alinsky says the effective activist "cannot risk being trapped by the enemy in his sudden agreement with your demand and saying 'You're right – we don't know what to do about this issue. Now you tell me.'"[374] Today's left is always ready with back-up plans to "keep the pressure on"

Dems know that if they lack real solutions to problems they'll lose credibility. How would it look if Trump asked them for help fixing a problem and they had no solution of their own? That's exactly what happened when Republican congressional members missed the opportunity to repeal and replace the Affordable Care Act's individual mandate when John McCain gave it his infamous "thumbs-down" vote. After years of promising a "constructive alternative", the GOP came up empty-handed when it held the majority.

---

[374] Alinsky, pg. 130.

It may well have cost them the House in the 2018 midterm elections.

Since Trump became president, every attempt he's made to fulfill his campaign promises to build the wall, cease the immigration lottery, end chain migration and birther babies, get Deferred Action for Childhood Arrivals (DACA) under control, reform sanctuary city laws, and deport MS-13 gang members, has been met with opposition, even from some in his own Republican party. Republicans should be ashamed.

Anti-Trumpers and uninformed libs don't understand the full scope of the left's plan to collapse our system. And, they have no idea just how dangerously close the left is to doing that.

Open borders is just one aspect of the left's sinister plot, albeit a critical one. It's through illegal immigration that Dems hope to earn enough votes to maintain a perpetual majority control. But, the radical left has a darker motive: to transform America into a socialist nation. That's why the current migrant "invasion" should matter to every law-abiding American today.

C-P created the blueprint for upending our elections. In a "December 1982 article, 'A Movement Strategy to Transform the Democratic Party,' ... They sought to do to the voting system what they had previously done to the welfare system. ... [f]lood the polls with millions of new voters. ... The result would be a catastrophic disruption of America's electoral system, the authors predicted."[375]

---

[375] *Discover the Networks*. Major Resource: *The Shadow Party*, by David Horowitz and Richard Poe (Nashville, TN: Nelson Current, 2006), pp, 106-128. *Discover the Networks* (Last updated Nov. 16,

We are witnessing the undeniable success of C-P's strategy unfolding today with invasions of future, illegal voters approaching our borders. It will create chaos in our voting system. Complacency is not an option.

In the 2018 midterms, the Democrats successfully turned the elections in several key states into total confusion. Georgia, Florida and California were prime examples. While the American people are being told that these states' voting problems were anomalies needing minor corrections, they were not. The left doesn't need to commit *provable* voting fraud. All they need is to look incompetent while achieving their goals, and they know it. We are losing our democracy right under our noses.

Originally, C-P hadn't counted on the Dems in their illicit scheme to overwhelm our voting system. They predicted that "the flood of new voters would provoke a backlash from Democrats and Republicans alike, who would join forces to disenfranchise the unruly hordes, using such expedients as purging invalid voters from the rolls, imposing cumbersome registration procedures, stiffening residency requirements, and so forth. This voter-suppression campaign would spark 'a political firestorm over democratic rights,' they wrote. Voting-rights activists would descend on America's election boards and polling stations..."[376] What C-P had not predicted was that Dems would *join* the evil plan in their own self-interest. That really changed the game.

The C-P "voting rights" movement was carried out by three organizations, one of which was the fraudulently-convicted, now-bankrupted ACORN (which

---

2018)https://www.discoverthenetworks.org/organizations/clowardpiven-strategy-cps/.
[376] Ibid.

employed Obama during his community organizing days).

"All three ... set to work lobbying energetically for the so-called Motor-Voter law, which President Bill Clinton ultimately signed in 1993. At the White House signing ceremony..., both Richard Cloward and Frances Fox Piven were in attendance. The new law eliminated many controls on voter fraud, making it easy for voters to register but difficult to determine the validity of new registrations. ... [S]tates were required to provide opportunities for voter registration to any person who showed up at a government office to renew a driver's license or to apply for welfare or unemployment benefits. 'Examiners were under orders not to ask anyone for identification or proof of citizenship,' notes *Wall Street Journal* columnist John Fund in his book, *Stealing Elections.* 'States had to permit mailing voter registrations, which allowed anyone to register without any personal contact with a registrar or election officials'. Finally, states were limited in pruning 'deadwood' – people who had died, moved, or been convicted of crimes – from their rolls."377

"'The Motor-Voter bill did indeed cause the voter rolls to be swamped with invalid registrations signed in the name of deceased, ineligible or non-existent people — thus opening the door to the unprecedented levels of voter fraud and 'voter disenfranchisement' claims that followed in subsequent elections during the 1990s, and culminating in the Florida recount crisis in the 2000 presidential election. On the eve of the 2000 election, in Indiana alone, state officials discovered that one in five

---

377 Ibid.

registered voters were duplicates, deceased, or otherwise invalid. ... The cloud of confusion hanging over elections serves leftist agitators well. 'President Bush came to office without a clear mandate,' the leftwing billionaire George Soros declared. 'He was elected president by a single vote on the Supreme Court'."[378] The left uses chaos and misinformation well.

Did you know that, aside from Bill Gates and his foundations, Soros is the second biggest contributor to change in the world? Americans should make it a point to know who George Soros is, and in what direction he is taking our country. His tentacles are global.

Born and raised in Hungary, Soros survived the Holocaust as a young Jewish teenager who was taken in by a Christian family. He later became rich as a successful stock broker. When he shorted England's pound sterling, it propelled him into billionaire status and earned him the description as "the man who broke the Bank of England". He later repeated his winning strategy in Thailand, bankrupting the entire country. A lot of people lost their fortunes.

In one of his books, Soros wrote: "The main obstacle to a stable and just world order is the United States ... And I think that's rather shocking for Americans to hear."[379]

He's made it clear that he is no fan of nationalism, rather he is a globalist. He has said that "nationalism is spreading throughout the world. It is a very unstable world. After the collapse of the Soviet Union, there was

---

[378] Ibid.
[379] Susanna Schrobsdorff. "Soros on American Fallibility" *Newsweek* (June 27, 2006) https://www.newsweek.com/soros-american-fallibility-110647.

a brief moment when the United States emerged as the undisputed leader of the world. But it abused its power. Under the neocons, who argued that the United States should use its power to impose its will on the world, President George W. Bush declared 'war on terror'"[380]

Soros seems to enjoy playing judge, jury and executioner. But, what if he's wrong? Being rich doesn't make one right. He says, "[I]f we want to be the dominant power in the world, then we have a unique responsibility to consider the common needs of humanity in addition to pursuing our national interests."[381] That assumes we don't already consider others' well-being in our policies and that simply isn't true. In fact, we take in more immigrants and are more charitable than any other country. Why else would immigrants from all over the world want to come here?

Soros said, "'[c]hanging the attitude and policies of the United States remains [his] top priority, [including a] quest to crack the conservative hold on American politics.' He spent more than $25 million trying to unseat President Bush in 2004."[382]

Far-left groups behind the illegal immigrant caravans of 2018 and 2019, are said to be funded by Soros. "'The caravan is organized by a group called Pueblo Sin Fronteras [People Without Borders], [b]ut the effort is supported by the coalition CARA Family Detention Pro Bono Project, which includes Catholic Legal Immigration Network (CLIN), the American Immigration Council (AIC), the Refugee and Immigration Center for Education and Legal Services (RICELS) and the

---

[380] Ibid.
[381] Ibid.
[382] Ibid.

American Immigration Lawyers Association (AILA) – thus the acronym CARA,' WND reported. 'At least three of the four groups are funded by George Soros' Open Society Foundation.'"[383] Soros' left-wing influences don't end there.

According to *InfoWars.com*, "last year, Judicial Watch said the U.S. Agency for International Development [USAID], a federal agency which works closely with the State Dept., was giving grant money to Soros-linked groups which were pushing leftist agendas in various countries. Six US senators also asked then-Secretary of State Rex Tillerson to investigate the relationship between USAid and the Soros-funded foundations."[384] Since some of the recent caravan members in October 2018 were seen carrying the familiar USAID yellow bags, I wanted to know more.

Judicial Watch president, Tom Fitton, says the following on their website: "This is our second FOIA lawsuit to uncover the truth about the scandal of Obama administration's siphoning tax dollars to the Soros operations in Europe. ... Soros' association with the State Department in Albania goes back at least to 2011 when Soros urged Hillary Clinton to take action in Albania over recent demonstrations in the capital. ... *Fox News* reported on August 17, 2016 that: 'Newly leaked emails and other files from billionaire George Soros'

---

[383] Daniel John Sobieski. "Illegal Caravans Encouraged by Honduras and Soros" *American Thinker* (Oct. 18, 2018) https://www.americanthinker.com/articles/2018/10/illegal_caravan s_encouraged_by_honduras_and_soros.html.
[384] Alex Jones. "Judicial Watch Calls for Criminal Investigation of Soros Funding Behind Caravan" *InfoWars.com* (Oct. 29, 2018) https://www.infowars.com/judicial-watch-calls-for-criminal-investigation-of-soros-funding-behind-caravan/.

web of organizations are shedding light on the liberal powerbroker's extensive influence in political and diplomatic affairs. One email chain shows the Wall Street titan in 2011 personally wrote then–Secretary of State Hillary Clinton, urging intervention in Albania's political unrest. Within days, an envoy he recommended was dispatched to the region.'"[385]

As alarmingly, in "February [2017], Judicial Watch reported: Barack Obama's U.S. Ambassador to Macedonia ... has worked behind the scenes with Soros' Open Society Foundation to funnel large sums of American dollars for the cause, constituting an interference of the U.S. Ambassador in domestic political affairs in violation of the Vienna Convention on Diplomatic Relations.

"The Open Society Foundation has established and funded dozens of leftwing, nongovernmental organizations (NGOs) ... The groups organize youth movements, create influential media outlets and organize violent protests to undermine the institutions and policies implemented by the government. One of the Soros' groups funded the translation and publication of Saul Alinsky's 'Rules for Radicals' into Macedonian. The book is a tactical manual of subversion, provides direct advice for radical street protests and proclaims Lucifer to be the first radical."[386]

---

[385] *Judicial Watch.* "Judicial Watch Sues State Department and USAID for Records about Funding of George Soros' Open Society Foundation – Albania" (May 31, 2017) https://www.judicialwatch.org/press-room/press-releases/judicial-watch-sues-state-department-usaid-records-funding-george-soros-open-society-foundation-albania/.
[386] Ibid.

Obama and Hillary "colluded" with the radical left-wing George Soros using American taxpayer money to replace conservative leadership in sovereign countries with left-wing socialists. It's almost too incredible to believe. But, thanks to the unparalleled and tireless work of Tom Fitton and *Judicial Watch*, suing for information under the Freedom of Information Act, we now know the truth. The real question remains: Is Soros' group, Open Society Foundation, interfering in the governments of Central America and coordinating the caravans as a way of disrupting America? The answer appears to be, yes.

The Pueblo Sin Fronteras group is thought to be an offshoot of a group that was "a Chicago, Illinois-based illegal immigration advocacy group formed in 2001 by [an] illegal immigrant...." It operates with the assistance of Centro Sin Fronteras (Center Without Borders) out of the same church in Chicago. That Center is run by a left-wing community organizer who ... planned to lead two activist campaigns: 'one for mass citizenship training for undocumented immigrants, and another for mass voter registration.' As she put it, '[w]e need to change America, we are all America.'"[387]

Both groups operate way over budget, with most of their funding coming from known far left-wing groups. Disturbingly, they've been caught doing business from "the Lincoln United Methodist Church as a rallying point for illegal immigration activism, using a tax-exempt

[387] Hayden Ludwig. "The Open Border Activists Behind the Illegal Immigrant Caravans" *Capital Research Center* (Oct. 24, 2018) https://capitalresearch.org/article/the-open-border-activists-behind-the-illegal-immigrant-caravans/.

church as cover to advocate for foreign violation of our country's border laws."[388]

According to Hayden Ludwig, research analyst at Capital Research Center, Pueblo Sin Fronteras "is one of the key organizers behind the caravan."[389] This original caravan of 2018 was not the "spontaneous" movement the "fake news" media tried to convince us it was.

"The tenth rule of the ethics of means and ends," according to Alinsky, *"is that you do what you can with what you have and clothe it with moral arguments. ...* Availability of means determines ... whether you will move for extensive changes or limited adjustments... The absence of any means might drive one to martyrdom in the hope that this would be a catalyst, starting a chain reaction that would culminate in a mass movement."[390]

George Soros understands that. That's why he and the left continue to remind Dems that former President George Bush "stole the election." It wasn't true, but on a moral level, "Cloward, Piven, and their disciples had introduced a level of fear, tension, and foreboding to U.S. elections previously encountered mainly in Third World Countries."[391] Soros won't be the martyr, though. He'll leave that proud title to immigrants who suffer the inhumane scars left by danger along their journey. The women and children who will be raped, kidnapped by human traffickers, injured, or become sick along the way will, unwittingly, do Soros' bidding for him.

---

[388] Ibid.
[389] Ibid.
[390] Ibid. Alinsky, pg. 36.
[391] Ibid. *Discover the Networks.*

The left is constantly observing, analyzing and discrediting every election they lose because they understand the power of setting the stage for the next one. When they cry "foul", their real goal is to create new laws that expand the voting base without proper ID, which would facilitate "opportunities for fraudulent voters to cast ballots under other people's names".[392]

The "Voting Rights movements depend heavily on financial support from George Soros' Open Society Institute and his 'Shadow Party', through whose support the Cloward-Piven strategy continues to provide a blueprint for some of the Left's most ambitious campaigns to overload, and cause the collapse of,..." our electoral system.[393] We cannot let that happen!

Charlie Kirk, founder and executive director of Turning Point USA, an advocacy group for young Conservatives, isolates three issues that most affect valid votes: 1) voter fraud; 2) election tampering; and, 3) voter suppression.[394] He says Democrats are responsible for nearly all of the voter fraud and election tampering. Yet, they cry "voter suppression" against the Republicans in almost all of their election losses. They do this to create a shiny object they hope voters will follow, rather than the real fraud. And, they maximize their losses to create new rules that will make voter fraud easier to accomplish in future elections. How anyone can be against voter ID in our voting system is baffling, unless you agree with the left's real agenda.

---

[392] Ibid.
[393] Ibid.
[394] Charlie Kirk. "Charlie Kirk: Democrats come out the big losers in Florida's election mess" *FOX News* (Nov. 17, 2018) https://www.foxnews.com/opinion/charlie-kirk-democrats-come-out-the-big-losers-in-floridas-election-mess.

The 2018 Florida midterms should convince most that voting fraud by Democrats is alive and well. If a person knows the history of Florida's elections, it's difficult to deny the tactics that are at work.

Russian dictator Joseph Stalin has been quoted as saying the following: *"I consider it completely unimportant who in the party will vote, or how; but what is extraordinarily important is this—who will count the votes, and how."*[395]

Florida's Broward County Democratic Supervisor of Elections, Brenda Snipes was the laughingstock of the country during the 2018 midterms. Snipes has had multiple election abnormalities in the past. As a Florida resident, and a voter paying close attention, I feel qualified in saying that her missteps were too numerous, and too timely in fashion, to not be suspect.

Predictably, Snipes waved the other shiny object, racism (she is black), as a reason for all the negative publicity directed at her. But, one only needs to look at her actions to know otherwise. Even former Governor Jeb Bush, who nominated Snipes almost twenty years ago, is calling for her removal from office saying that, "[t]here is no question that Broward County Supervisor of Elections Brenda Snipes failed to comply with Florida law on multiple counts,...."[396] Snipes has been accused of destroying ballots, altering election documents, missing deadlines many believe intentionally to favor

---

[395] David Emery. "Joseph Stalin: 'It's Not the People Who Vote That Count' *Snopes* (Oct. 14, 2016) https://www.snopes.com/fact-check/stalin-vote-count-quote/.
[396] Barnini Chakraborty. "Broward election boss says racism may be behind clamor against her" *FOX News* (Nov. 17, 2018) https://www.foxnews.com/politics/broward-election-boss-says-racism-may-be-behind-clamor-against-her.

Democrats, losing ballots, "finding" ballots, and allowing non-citizens' votes to count. Astonishingly, even the Dems' attorneys, called in for oversight, motioned for illegal votes to be counted!

Florida's Palm Beach County fared only slightly better. Together, the two created unimaginable chaos in our states' voting system. Could Snipes, an experienced elections official making some $180k/year, really be so incompetent and dumb? Or, as some Republicans fear, is she crazy like a fox? Many are worried this is a "dry run" for the 2020 presidential elections. The DOJ has been called in. Given its recent biased performance, I'm not holding my breath. We can only hope they hold Snipes and other wrong-doers accountable. Only then can we be assured of fair elections going forward ... especially with invasions of illegal immigrants arriving at our borders in the tens of thousands.

Liberal San Franciscans have already been registering illegal aliens to vote in their school board elections. They spent over $300k to implement their new plan. "The program resulted in 49 new voters, which turned out to cost the city $6,326 each, *The San Francisco Chronicle* reported. The paper called the effort "pretty much a bust the first time out."[397] But, that's not the point. This genie will be hard to put back in the bottle. Incredibly, they aren't the first. "In Maryland, where an estimated 15 percent of residents are foreign-

---

[397] Edmond DeMarche. "San Francisco spends about $6,326 for each non-citizen voter to sign up for local election, report says" *FOX News* (Oct. 29, 2018) https://www.foxnews.com/politics/san-francisco-spends-about-6326-for-each-non-citizen-voter-to-sign-up-for-local-election-report-says.

born, at least six cities allow noncitizens to vote in local elections."[398] That should alarm us all.

European countries have been harsh in their criticism of President Trump's promise to "build that wall", including Pope Francis himself, who is well-protected by a wall at the Vatican. The open border policies of Germany's Angela Merkel and other countries in the EU just a few short years ago have been quickly reversed as millions of illegals who were allowed entry caused total chaos. "The U.N. and others condemn [the immigration policy] as massive humanitarian failures."[399]

A lesson not lost on those of us paying attention is that, "[U]ntil the message is made abundantly clear that illegal economic migrants will not be processed, that boats will be turned back, thousands ... more sad and desperate lives will be lost in vain, all for your feelings of virtue," said Nathan Gill, a British member of the European parliament, accusing fellow legislators ... of being soft on immigration. "You're not really helping people."[400] Trump has been pleading the same argument of compassion here at home. But, will we listen?

Even a member of Doctors Without Borders, hardly a conservative group, had this warning: "a quarter of the minors [in camps] had either attempted suicide, had suicidal thoughts or were harming themselves."[401]

---

[398] Ibid.
[399] Frank Miles. "Europe's migration 'fixes' trigger disgusting humanitarian crises" *FOX News* (Sept. 19, 2018) https://www.foxnews.com/world/europes-migration-fixes-trigger-disgusting-humanitarian-crises.
[400] Ibid.
[401] Ibid.

Another was even more foreboding, revealing that Moria (the over-crowded "refugee" camp in Greece) "was as grim as 'an old-fashioned mental asylum, not seen in parts of Europe since the mid-twentieth century.'"[402] Will America repeat the EU's irreversible mistake?

Health care professionals fully understand the dangers of diseases spreading as illegal immigrants overwhelm our borders. One who has worked for years on medical projects in Central and South America is Dr. Elizabeth Lee Vliet. She wrote in 2014 that many are carrying "diseases the U.S. had controlled or virtually eradicated: tuberculosis (TB), Chagas disease, dengue fever, hepatitis, malaria, measles, plus more."[403] She blames the Obama administration for messaging those countries that our borders are "open" and offering "free stuff". Dr. Vliet claims the policy follows "textbook Cloward-Piven strategy to overwhelm and collapse the economic and social systems, in order to replace them with a 'new socialist order' under federal control."[404] Folks, you can't make this stuff up.

While most of the detectable diseases health care professionals are seeing at the border refugee centers are scabies, lice or chickenpox, Texas "doctors providing medical care for immigrants being released by U.S. Border Patrol ahead of their court dates say those recent detainees were not appropriately screened or treated for illness while in federal custody. ... Worse,

[402] Ibid.
[403] Elizabeth Lee Vliet, M.D. "Deadly diseases crossing border with illegals' *Colorado Alliance for Immigration Reform* (June 20, 2014) http://www.cairco.org/news/deadly-diseases-crossing-border-illegals.
[404] Ibid.

there is 'no testing for vaccinations or tuberculosis.'"[405] Many of these immigrants are then bused, without notification to the city of destination, and dumped onto their streets. Who knows if they'll ever be tested?

A new disease has popped up since 2012, called acute flaccid myelitis (AFM) that paralyzes some of its victims, particularly children. The Center for Disease Control (CDC) tells us they have no idea where it comes from, or its cure. Most doctors and media outlets warn us not to blame immigration, but the lack of testing gives me little comfort. Would they tell us the truth? The virus is spreading. Is it a coincidence that Obama loosened our borders at about the same time?

With potentially disastrous effects on our elections, hospitals, welfare, and school systems, are open borders good for America? Trump says no. Deplorables agree. It's not compassionate (as Dems like to pretend) to our citizens, legal immigrants, minorities or for the illegal immigrants themselves, who face incredible dangers along the way.

Thanks to Trump's persistence and hardline approach, some in the original caravan have returned home or sought asylum in Mexico. Trump has sent the message loud and clear that he intends to "enforce existing rule of law. He's sent troops. He's sent reinforcements. He's thrown up the razor wire. He's warned the invaders that they will not be treated at all differently from all the other people asking for asylum, and they will have to wait their turn in line. What's more,

---

[405] Alexa Ura. "Texas Health Officials: Immigrant Surge Presents a Medical Crisis" *The Texas Tribune*
https://www.texastribune.org/2014/06/24/health-officials-docs-raise-concerns-about-immigra/.

if they get into the U.S., there won't be the freedom to do what they want for a while, no catch and release, because they will have to wait in tent cities for their cases to be adjudicated, same as other people."[406] That's far more than Obama ever did.

Trump wins every time he turns one of Alinsky's tactics against the left, especially this one: *"[T]he price of a successful attack is a constructive alternative."* Trump's constructive alternatives to the invasion on our southern border have been genius. The left thought the caravan would make it to our border in time to create chaos for the midterms. Instead, Trump used the looming disaster to his favor.

When the left whines about our lack of compassion and supposed voting suppression, we need to remember that they are simply following their tenth rule of ethics of means and ends: *"you do what you can with what you have and clothe it in moral garments."* There is nothing immoral about wanting closed borders and fair elections. We cannot give in to their ridicule.

What we need is to start playing hard ball. Charlie Kirk said, "Republicans need to understand there is no high road to take here. We need to be as aggressive as we legally can be, and any politician subjected to Democratic tactics designed to improperly win elections cannot ever concede or withdraw."[407] I totally agree.

Find out how we can accomplish exactly that, over the next two years, leading up to President Trump's re-

---

[406] Monica Showalter. "Trump's resolve is breaking the migrant caravan up fast" *American Thinker* (Nov. 5, 2018) https://www.americanthinker.com/blog/2018/11/trumps_resolve_is _breaking_the_migrant_caravan_up_fast.html.
[407] Kirk. Ibid.

election. In the following chapter, "Divided, They Fall", our next, and most important mission, is to conquer the Democratic Party by exploiting the divisions they've created for themselves. The hard-left (the Democratic Socialists of America) and the old-guard moderates of the Democratic Party (like Schumer and Pelosi), are heading for a perfect storm. Trump and Deplorables can make sure that, when the fracture is complete, we have some converts on our side. Only then will we be able to destroy their growing stranglehold on truth and save our country from the evils within.

DIVIDED,
THEY FALL

TACTIC #13: *"Pick the target, freeze it, personalize it, and polarize it."*[408]

"'WE ARE THANKFUL TO Leader Pelosi for her years of service to our Country and to our Caucus,'" the letter from both incumbent and newly-elected Democrats read. *"'However, we also recognize that in this ... [midterm] election, Democrats ran and won on a message of change.'* ... Announcing plans to oppose Pelosi, the lawmakers wrote: *'Our majority came on the backs of candidates who said that they would support new leadership because voters in hard-won districts, and across the country want to see real change in Washington. ... We are committed to voting for new leadership in both our Caucus meeting and on the House floor,'* the letter stated."[409]

President Trump weighed in saying this about Leader Pelosi: "'She's tough and she's smart, but she deserves to be speaker.' He added: 'I don't imagine she'd need too many but whatever number of votes she needs, if it's 50, or 10, or two, or one, she's got them

[408] Ibid. Alinsky, pg. 130.
[409] Brooke Singman. "16 House 'Never Nancy' Dems oppose Pelosi for speaker, demand 'new leadership'" *Fox News* (Nov. 20, 2018) https://www.foxnews.com/politics/16-house-dems-announce-plans-to-oppose-pelosi-for-speaker-as-they-demand-new-leadership.

from me—automatic. So tell her opposition they're wasting their time.'"[410] Americans on both sides of the aisle thought Trump had gone mad. As usual, they simply do not understand his logic.

Alinsky's thirteenth tactic is to *"pick the target, freeze it, personalize it, and polarize it."* When Trump glorified Nancy Pelosi, his intent was to drive a wedge between her and her newest, far-left and moderate colleagues who promised their constituents they'd vote against the leader. Pelosi has been forced to lean ever more left as her party's differences between the expanding Democratic Socialists of America (DSA) and the old-school moderates force a self-imposed schism. It will drive moderates ever closer to the radical left. Either way, Conservatives will emerge the winners, if we can *unite*. Trump gets it. By zeroing in, and heaping praise on Pelosi, he is further polarizing her party. It's exactly what all Republicans need to be doing.

John Perazzo summarizes Alinsky's tactics in an article for *FrontPage Mag*. The main goal of the thirteenth tactic, he claims, is "asserting that the primary task of radical activists and political figures is to cultivate in people's hearts a visceral emotional revulsion to the mere sight of the enemy's face, or to the mere sound of the enemy's voice."[411] We know from previous chapters of *Rules for* Deplorables that the left has been attacking our president, with great success,

---

[410] Ibid.
[411] John Perazzo. "The Party of Saul Alinsky & Its War on Trump" FrontPage Mag (Jan. 24, 2018)
https://www.frontpagemag.com/fpm/269085/party-saul-alinsky-its-war-trump-john-perazzo

using the thirteenth tactic since before Trump was even elected. Now, Trump is using it against them.

Perazzo also refers to a second Alinsky book called *Rules for Reveilles.* "'The organizer who forgets the significance of personal identification,' said Alinsky, 'will attempt to answer all objections on the basis of logic and merit. With few exceptions this is a futile procedure.'"[412] That's where never-Trumpers do our country a real disservice. They try to use logic, ethics and merit to make sense of the left's constant negative reporting about Trump. Most people have trouble believing that reporters would blatantly lie, or omit relevant facts. Trump knows the left's arguments have nothing to do with logic, ethics or merit. Anti-Trumpers would do well to understand that, too.

When Trump targeted Nancy Pelosi, he didn't do it because he prefers her as House leader. He did it because, with Pelosi re-elected, Democrat voters who were promised new leadership will feel betrayed. Perhaps some will even stay away from the polls in 2020. That is Trump's long-term goal. Perazzo writes that, by ignoring logic and merit, "Democrats and media leftists invariably avoid addressing even the most glaring contradictions in the[ir] narratives ... typically turn[ing] a deaf ear to anyone who tries to elicit from them a logical or reasoned clarification."[413] Conservatives should not allow them to get away with that behavior. Trump doesn't.

Even financial journalists can no longer be trusted. According to an editorial in *Investor's Business Daily,*

---

[412] Ibid.
[413] Ibid.

"[D]espite journalists' denials ... journalism is one of the most left-wing of all professions. But until recently, that wasn't thought to be true of financial journalists — who have a reputation for being the most right-leaning and free-market-oriented among mainstream journalists. ... Researchers from Arizona State University and Texas A&M University questioned 462 financial journalists around the country. ... The journalists worked for the Wall Street Journal, the New York Times, Washington Post, Associated Press [and others]."[414] They found "a ratio of 13 'liberals' for every one 'conservative.' ... Please remember this as you watch the business news or read a financial story in the paper. ... That's especially true if the piece seems unduly harsh on the free-market system and its many proven benefits. Or if it lauds socialism as an 'answer' to society's ills."[415] Free-market systems still "trump" socialism. It's the crony capitalism we should focus on, much of which is caused by dirty politicians. When Dems blame the free-market for society's ills, they do so mainly to deflect attention from their own greed.

The left has now successfully polarized all journalists between those who believe in capitalism versus socialism. This is a very dangerous trend for our democracy. Beware of those who try to convince you that Trump's progress on trade negotiations isn't working, especially with China. Don't fall for the naysayers who claim his talks will start a trade war. We've been getting

---

[414] "Media Bias: Pretty Much All Of Journalism Now Leans Left, Study Shows" *Investor's Business Daily* (Nov. 16, 2018) https://www.investors.com/politics/editorials/media-bias-left-study/.
[415] Ibid.

ripped off for decades. We now have a president brave enough to reverse unfair trade contracts. But, he needs our *undivided* support to do it.

"The sixth rule of the ethics of means and ends is that the less important the end to be desired, the more one can afford to engage in ethical evaluations of means."[416] In other words, the more important the goal, the less ethical one need be. That's why lying is acceptable to the left. Conservatives, on the other hand, hold themselves to a higher standard, often to our country's detriment. It's a losing strategy.

Republicans believe the rule of law can only be maintained if lying is avoided at all costs. That's commendable. But, it will not win this war. While I agree it's critical to maintain our credibility, Conservatives would do well to remember that this is a moment in time that we are on the verge of losing our country to socialist ideologies. If they realize how close we are to becoming the next Venezuela, they would overlook *all* of Trump's exaggerations and they'd be smart to do so. In the big picture, his indiscretions are so insignificant. Deplorables understand the urgency. That's why we give a pass to Trump's more offensive statements and behaviors.

The main focus now must be on dividing the Democratic Party whenever possible. It's the fastest route to winning in 2020. I believe President Lincoln would have agreed. He understood the powerful tactic of division. In referring to the slavery issue polarizing the north and south, he often quoted *Matthew 12:22–28 (NKJV):* "A house divided cannot stand." Republicans

---

[416] Ibid. Alinsky, pg. 34.

must unite ourselves, and divide Democrats, to win a war, once again.

In September, 2017, *Politico* published an article stating that, "[a]s [Bernie Sanders] enjoyed a meteoric ... rise as a self-described democratic socialist, the organization [DSA] grew fivefold over the past two years. And it's now feeling an even greater sense of purpose since the election of President Donald Trump. Last month it wrapped up its best-attended convention, in Chicago, by approving resolutions on single-payer health care, labor unions and a drive to get its candidates elected to public office."[417] Conservatives are losing ground at a rapid pace.

Ms. Ocasio-Cortez, less than a month in office, has put forth a radical 4-point socialist agenda. It specifically calls for: 1) a government-run, single-payer health care system; 2) a "Green New Deal", which would eliminate *all* fossil fuels, and socialize energy; 3) massive tax increases, up to 70%; and, 4) abolishing the electoral college, which would further erode our voting protections by ignoring voters in rural America. And, there are many more goals to facilitate the destruction of America, as stated by the young DSA member, including guaranteed incomes, raising minimum wages, free college for all, and abolishing ICE. Astonishingly, the freshman congresswoman was given a coveted position on the powerful House Oversight Committee, which will oversee investigations into President Donald Trump's administration. You can't make this stuff up.

---

[417] Elana Schor. "Democratic socialists struggle for relevance even as a defining cause gains traction" *Politico* (Sept. 12, 2017) https://www.politico.com/story/2017/09/12/democratic-socialists-bernie-sanders-242576.

Conservatives need to understand that the socialist policies recommended by AOC have already been drawn up and are ready to implement. Plus, they are gaining traction. Are these proposals acceptable to you? Do you understand what they mean for our survival as a nation? If you aren't sure, it's time to educate yourself. That you are reading this book means you are already concerned. If you'd be against the adoption of the left's proposals, Trump needs you to help him stop these radicals from taking control of our country. He can't do it with never-Trumpers, et al, constantly siding against him. Now is not the time for ethics, or division.

Before this never-Trumper was even sworn in to Congress after winning in the 2018 midterm elections, "Mitt Romney, the incoming senator from Utah and former Republican presidential nominee, revived his rivalry with President Trump ... with an op-ed essay in The Washington Post in which he said Mr. Trump 'has not risen to the mantle of the office.'"[418] This, after Romney requested and received, President Trump's endorsement, during his midterm race. That act, alone, exposes Romney's ignorance as to how perilous America's future really is. Let us pray that he and fellow never-Trumpers wake up soon.

Abolishing ICE has already begun at one college campus. According to Campus Reform, "Seattle University's law school hosted an externship fair, in which ICE offered students an externship for course credit. The university decided to suspend the program

---

[418] Sarah Mervosh. "Mitt Romney Says Trump 'Has Not Risen to the Mantle of the Office'" The New York Times https://www.nytimes.com/2019/01/01/us/politics/romney-trump-oped.html.

... after receiving backlash from students and community members concerned with the practices of the agency, according to the school's student newspaper...."[419] Apparently, school policy "condemns administration policies that have led to the unjust and inhumane treatment of asylum seekers and migrant families, practices that continue today and that directly affect members of our community."[420]

Like most of the left's propaganda, Seattle University subjectively mischaracterized the policies of ICE. Our administration does not treat asylum seekers and migrant families unjustly or inhumanely. Rather, our overwhelmed system to handle the sheer number of illegals entering our country does not lend itself well to top-notch treatment. Still, we can't forget that Illegal immigrants are in this country, *illegally*. Congress is responsible for passing the laws that ICE carries out. ICE should be commended, not ostracized, for enforcing those laws. It is irresponsible for a university to buckle under pressure put upon it by a few highly-trained, well-paid, radical community organizers riled up with enough hatred to gather some signatures on a petition. Logic-minded people must stop appeasing these bullies. Stop buckling every time one of these loons implants a negative thought about Trump and his policies into our brains. It only empowers the left to make more loony demands, which will never end. It's time for Republicans to fight back, using *any means necessary*.

[419] Kenneth Nelson. "Seattle University gives ICE the cold shoulder" *Campus Reform* (Nov. 15, 2018)
https://www.campusreform.org/?ID=11526.
[420] Ibid.

Even Democratic pollster, Doug Schoen, says that "Democrats have moved so far to the left that Republican attacks on them for being extremist and too far in the clutches of their tired, out-of-touch leadership have been working. … The Republican campaign now is simple: just focus on how far left the Democrats are, and how beholden its candidates – particularly Congressional candidates – are to the unpopular Democratic leadership in both the House and the Senate."[421] He could not be more right.

Schoen also sees Dems as on the wrong side of immigration. He astutely observes that "…they have not disavowed the attack that they are for open borders. Having a substantial number of their candidates supporting either the denuding or the elimination of ICE doesn't help either."[422] When a Democratic strategist speaks, Conservatives should listen. We need to hit them hard over the next two years about their views on immigration, ICE, and utopian vision of all things free.

The left does some pretty wacky things that hurt themselves in the eyes of intelligent voters, and a united right needs to pound them every time they do, just as the left pounds us. For example, "Minneapolis Mayor Jacob Frey … announced that mandatory placards detailing immigrants' rights will be displayed in police squad cars, and now some officers are pushing back. … Lt. Bob Kroll, president of the Police Officers Federation of Minneapolis, said … that this is an example of city leaders' … 'extreme, left-wing politics. … They refuse

---

[421] Doug Schoen. "Democrats, we have a problem" *FOX News* (Oct. 23, 2018) https://www.foxnews.com/opinion/doug-schoen-democrats-we-have-a-problem.
[422] Ibid.

to accept the first word is 'illegal.' They're an illegal immigrant. It's obviously illegal to be here to begin with, and then secondly, further illegal activity is what's led them to the back of a squad car,' Kroll said."[423]

Kudos to Lt. Kroll. This battle will come down to the rule of law versus the rule of crazy law.

Doug Schoen believes that the Dems made a big mistake by refusing to compromise with Trump on health care and immigration. While the Dems still won 35+ seats in the House of Representatives, they lost the Senate. That was a huge, and almost unprecedented, victory for a first-time president's first midterm election. Schoen says that's because Dems went too far left: "The loud agenda of their Democratic socialist wing and the utterances of many of their potential 2020 presidential candidates only compound this perception."[424]

Conservatives must pay attention over the next two years on how the Dems use their newly-acquired House majority power. Anyone concerned with the threat of socialism should consider becoming active in politics. From what the Dems are saying, they already have over 85 investigations lined up against Trump. If that is what they are going to spend their time on, 2020 will look favorable for Trump. Of course, that is only if Republicans can quit their own in-fighting. The Dems are impressive in their ability to hang together, no matter what. Never-Trumpers are just not in it to win it.

[423] "Minneapolis Mayor Angers Police With Mandatory Placards Aimed at Helping Illegal Immigrants" FOX News Insider (Oct. 12, 2018) http://insider.foxnews.com/2018/10/12/minneapolis-mayor-angers-police-mandatory-placards-aimed-helping-illegal-immigrants
[424] Ibid. Schoen.

A good example of how the Democratic Party can be divided occurred during the 2018 midterms. Sen. Claire McCaskill (D-Mo.), who has eked out challenging wins over twenty years, came out with a radio ad in which the voice-over assured the voters of Missouri that, "Claire's not one of those crazy Democrats."[425]

In the process of distinguishing herself from radicals, McCaskill attacked one of her fellow Democratics, Missouri state Sen. Maria Chappelle-Nadal. In defining what she thought "crazy" looks like, McCaskill told *FOX News*' Bret Baier in an interview that, "... we have a state senator here in Missouri that actually advocated for the assassination of President Trump. That's a crazy Democrat."[426] That began a divide, and the response was immediate.

"'Claire McCaskill is desperate,' state Sen. Maria Chappelle-Nadal tweeted. 'She's a piece of s---. Instead of knowing why people of color are angered by this administration, she chooses to put us and our families in harm's way. If my family is harmed, blame it on Claire McCaskill. She deserves to lose. She is not a Democrat.'"[427] In other words, McCaskill is a racist because she thought calling for the assassination of a sitting president was "crazy". McCaskill did, in fact, lose.

Republicans don't have to work very hard to turn radical Dems against moderate ones. The Dems are doing that all by themselves. But, it would be wise for

---

[425] Adam Shaw. "Missouri Dem lashes out at McCaskill for 'crazy Democrats' comment, in profanity-laced tirade" *FOX News* (Oct. 31, 2018) https://www.foxnews.com/politics/missouri-dem-calls-sen-mccaskill-a-piece-of-s-t-for-distancing-herself-from-crazy-democrats.
[426] Ibid.
[427] Ibid.

the right to have a back-up plan, given how the Dems have a history of sticking together when the going gets tough.

Alinsky says "the job of the organizer is to maneuver and bait the establishment so that it will publicly attack him as a 'dangerous enemy'"[428] This philosophy is especially interesting given that Trump has consistently, against all objectors, called the "fake news" media the "enemy of the people". Alinsky says use of the word 'enemy' is enough to put one on the side of the people. I believe that Trump is right to call the "fake news" media the "enemy" for that reason alone. By doing so, Trump awakens the "other-than-Deplorables" to pay closer attention to the "fake news" that is being reported.

Another interesting concept Alinsky shares is that, according to him, he won the black population over because they felt that if "the fat-cat white newspapers are ripping the hell out of Alinsky – he must be all right!"[429] Since we know that Trump has been gaining numbers in the black community, let's hope it's because they are seeing the injustices of "fake news" attacks against our president. Never mind that Trump is white. Unlike what the left tries to tell us, intelligent blacks are way beyond an ignorant mind-set. As they see the injustices lobbed against him, and the successes he has made on their behalf, we should see their pro-Trump numbers increase exponentially prior to 2020.

The minority community's growing exodus from the Democratic Party is best revealed by a provocative

---

[428] Ibid. Alinsky, pg. 100.
[429] Ibid.

movement that started with a six-minute YouTube video posting in May, 2018. "'We're walking away from the Democratic Party and literally walking toward freedom,' #WalkAway founder Brandon Straka told Fox News. ... 'People are fed up with what's happening on the left,' he said, adding that interest skyrocketed after the hearings into sexual misconduct allegations against Supreme Court Justice Brett Kavanaugh. 'These were really the kind of die-hard loyalists. People in their 60s and 70s who had been Democrats their whole life who said 'This was the final straw for me.'"[430]

Straka, a gay man, added that members of his movement consist of many Latinos, African-Americans and the LGBTQ community. According to *FOX News*, "...video testimonials posted to the #WalkAway Campaign Facebook page give a variety of reasons for switching political allegiances. Some said the Democratic Party has become hate-filled and hostile to opposing points of view while moving further to the left. Others say they were tired of the party's 'politically correct' culture."[431]

Even more intriguing is how a *CNN* contributor spins #walkaway: "David Love called the movement fake and a Russian ploy to divide key Democrat voting blocs, the *Washington Times* reported. ... 'Republicans want to split up the Democratic political opposition and divide black and Latino voters. And Russia looks like it wants to help here, too,' Love wrote. 'The most recent example

---

[430] Louis Casiano. "#WalkAway movement urges disgruntled Democrats to leave the party behind" *FOX News* (Oct. 28, 2018) https://www.foxnews.com/politics/walkaway-movement-urges-disgruntled-democrats-to-leave-the-party-behind.
[431] Ibid.

of this strategy is the #WalkAway hashtag, which is presented as a grassroots effort by former Democrats who are critical of the party's alleged intimidation, confrontation and lack of civility and want people to walk away from the party.'"[432]

While Love's fear that the right is dividing the Democratic Party is telling, to call the movement a Russian "ploy" is yet another dirty tactic by the left to refocus the public's attention on the Trump-Russia "collusion" witch hunt. It's disgraceful. It also proves that Dems are aware of the fracture in their own party. That's why they're so desperate to keep our borders open, even if it destroys America's sovereignty. They'll be needing new votes to replace those they've lost from other, now more enlightened, minority groups. That the votes would come from illegal immigrants makes no difference to the left. They are using the same "keep them dumbed down" philosophy that worked so well hundreds of years ago, when enslavement of "negroes" was necessary for the survival of the Democratic Party. Today, illegal immigrants are the left's new "negroes". It's abhorrent.

When the left used Alinsky's thirteenth tactic, *"pick the target, freeze it, personalize it, and polarize it"* to destroy Kavanaugh and his family, many never-Trumpers finally had enough. In *The New Republic*, staff writer Jeet Heer states that "one of the core insights of the Trump era is that the president can maintain control of the Republican Party by presenting all politics as a binary choice of friend versus enemies: Once Republicans realize that they have to choose between

---

[432] Ibid.

Trump or the dastardly Democrats, they will rally to the GOP standard bearer no matter how much they dislike him. With the binary choice of yes or no to Kavanaugh, Trump seems to be winning over some of his remaining foes on the right."[433] Binary choices like ICE, the wall, guaranteed incomes, free college, single-payer health care, etc., are what will win moderate Democrats over, too.

So great was the revulsion over Kavanaugh's treatment, that even *The Wall Street Journal* editorial board chimed in saying, "[t]he left's all-out assault on the judge is clarifying because it shows that the "'resistance"' is really about anything and everything conservative in America. Mr. Trump is its foil to regain power."[434]

When liars believe they are infallible, they make mistakes. Democrats will find out, over the next two years, that their zeal to impeach Trump will fail. If Conservatives stick together to divide the Democratic Party, we will win half the battle. But, anti-Trumpers must *all* unite if we are to win the other half. In the next and final chapter, "United, We Stand", the last stages of the plan to save our country are laid bare. It's not nearly as hard as you might think. But, there is no time to delay. The future of America depends on every single one of us.

---

[433] Jeet Heer. "The Kavanaugh Debate Is Dividing Never Trump Conservatives" *The New Republic* (Oct. 4, 2018) https://newrepublic.com/article/151567/kavanaugh-debate-dividing-never-trump-conservatives.
[434] Ibid.

UNITED,
WE STAND

"When someone shows you who they are,
believe them the first time. " – Maya Angelou

"OUR COUNTRY IS IN SERIOUS trouble. We don't have
victories anymore. ... When was the last time anybody
saw us beating, let's say, China in a trade deal? They kill
us. ... When do we beat Mexico at the border? They're
laughing at us, at our stupidity. And now they are
beating us economically....We need somebody that can
take the brand of the United States and make it great
again....I'll bring back our jobs, and...our money....I
would repeal and replace...Obamacare....I would build a
great wall on our southern border....Nobody would be
tougher on ISIS...I will stop Iran from getting nuclear
weapons....I will immediately terminate President
Obama's illegal executive order on immigration....fully
support and back up the Second Amendment....end
Common Core....rebuild the country's infrastructure. ...
Save Medicare, Medicaid and Social Security without
cuts....And strengthen our military and take care of our
vets....if I get elected president I will bring it back bigger
and better and stronger than ever before, and we will
make America great again."[435]

Billionaire Donald J. Trump told America he was
going to fix our problems when he and wife, Melania,

---

[435] Time Staff. "Here's Donald Trump's Presidential Announcement
Speech" *Time Magazine* (June 16, 2016)
http://time.com/3923128/donald-trump-announcement-speech/.

descended the escalators at Trump Tower to announce his run for the highest office in the world. Most laughed out loud, some snickered to themselves, others thanked God. The latter group, of which I was one, was later to be called "a basket of Deplorables" by Trump's presidential opponent, Hillary Clinton.

Like most people, Trump had a honeymoon period with his new job. Some of his subordinates, especially Obama holdovers and leftists, sabotaged his efforts. Never-Trumpers viewed him with suspicion and tried to prevent him from accomplishing what they deemed to be unpopular campaign promises. Still others treated him with the dignity that a president deserves and assisted in his transition.

There's no question candidate Trump fought like a dog for the presidency. He scratched. He got down and dirty. He even called people names. Every one of those tactics was okay by Deplorables and long overdue by a party that has allowed itself to be bullied by the left far too long. Anti-Trumpers were disgusted by his behavior, or pretended to be in order to turn public opinion against him.

People who don't like President Trump can be separated into three categories, not just here in America, but all over the world.

First, there is the left. This group includes socialists, globalists, and ultra-environmentalists who have been ingrained with socialist ideologies from school, the "fake news" media, and moderate Democrats more hungry for power than for the health of our country. They would treat any president attempting to save our free-market economy from global socialism with contempt.

Second, are the unengaged. Rush Limbaugh calls them "sheeple". They go along to get along, so long as a policy doesn't affect them negatively. They won't wake up and "activate" until they're personally affected. Once that happens, it may be too late to save our country's slide into socialism. The "sheeple" are dangerous because they are so passive that they base their political opinions on emotion, rather than knowledge, leaving the rest of us to do the heavy lifting. Their counterparts in Nazi Germany last century, and Venezuela today, are the ones who enabled the total destruction of their countries.

Third, are the self-righteous never-Trumpers. Of the three groups, this one has done the most preventable damage to America. Republicans had a unique opportunity to reverse a lot of the transformative destruction caused by the Obama Administration when they ruled both houses of Congress under a Republican president. They squandered that luxury. We may never again have such an easy opportunity to save America. I am convinced that the reason these never-Trumpers feel about our president the way they do is because they really have no idea how perilously close we are to a socialist precipice.

Never-Trumpers who cannot put their animosity of this president aside for the good of our country had better wake up. If Trump fails, it will be because of them, and Deplorables know it. Former Republican Senators Jeff Flake and Bob Corker, along with House Speaker Paul Ryan, did more damage under Trump's first two years than most Democrats. Current Senators Ben Sasse, Mitt Romney, and Marco Rubio are also doing little to help Trump achieve his agenda. They speak out against him and his policies even when it would be easier to just stay silent. In doing so, on even the most mundane of issues, they embolden the Dems whether they mean to or not.

It's well-known that Trump's personality is what offends never-Trumpers. That's an unfortunate reality. Deplorables care very little about how he gets things done. We are far more concerned with the divisions in our country, political-correctness run amok, rising health care costs, rampant illegal immigration, skyrocketing debt, trade imbalances, crime, money-controlled mobs, voter fraud, unequal justice, social security, and the rapid spread of socialism. You know, *things that matter.*

Never-Trumpers have contributed little to solve these issues, even as they get richer while in office. Trump, on the other hand, has made incredible progress, especially given the unprecedented obstructionism leveled against him. How much more he could achieve, with Republicans united, is anybody's guess. No doubt, quite a bit.

When Trump revealed his intentions to run for office, it was understandable that many had doubts. But, after two years of promises made/promises kept, it's time for us to say, *when someone 'shows' you who they are, believe them the first time.*

Rules for Radicals' "power is not only what you have but what the enemy thinks you have" tactic has been used by the left for decades. While famed sociologists, Cloward-Piven provided the blueprint to transform America into a socialist state, Alinsky provided the means, one of which was the perceived projection of power. Now Trump is using that same tactic against the left. It's why he especially needs the support of never-Trumpers, who harm Trump's real, or perceived, power every time they publicly disagree with him. To Deplorables, they prove their own ignorance, at a great cost to our country, every time they speak against him.

An article by Paul Bedard, in the *Washington Examiner*, is a great reminder of some of Trump's successes. It lists over 289 achievements in his first twenty months. According to Trump's 2016 campaign pollster John McLaughlin, "'[t]hey told him he couldn't be president and beat the establishment and he did. For two years the establishment is telling him he can't do things in Washington and he's succeeding in spite of them. He never retreats. He doesn't back up. He's relentless. He just wins,' he added."[436]

Trump's achievements would make any leftist's head spin. His "'successes in reducing the cost of taxes and regulations, rebuilding our military, avoiding wars of choice and changing the courts, rival those of all previous Republican presidents,' said Grover Norquist, president of Americans for Tax Reform. 'They include 173 major wins, such as adding more than 4 million jobs, and another 116 smaller victories, some with outsize importance, such as the 83 percent one-year increase in arrests of MS-13 gang members ... And shockingly the NAFTA achievement is presented as a sidebar to the larger achievement that reads, 'President Trump is negotiating and renegotiating better trade

---

[436] Paul Bedard. "Trump's list: 289 accomplishments in just 20 months, 'relentless' promise-keeping" *Washington Examiner* (Oct. 12, 2018)https://www.washingtonexaminer.com/washington-secrets/trumps-list-289-accomplishments-in-just-20-months-relentless-promise-keeping.

deals, achieving free, fair, and reciprocal trade for the United States." Under that umbrella are eight trade deals cut with Japan, South Korea, Europe and China.'"[437] You would never know about Trump's achievements if you are listening to biased news. The way to stay strong in the midst of this battle, is to discontinue following news sources that are misleading. They hope to confuse you. They are very successful at turning public opinion against Trump with insignificant and, oftentimes, false news stories. Don't give them that power.

The left fears that Trump's successes are setting back their agenda to overwhelm the American system by decades. His every success delays the left's march towards socialism. That's why they are so "deranged". It's also why we cannot allow ourselves to become disillusioned every time we hear something negative that may, or may not, be true about Trump. He needs our *undivided* support. To do otherwise is detrimental to the security of America.

This president also understands the importance of Alinsky's second tactic, *"[n]ever go outside the experience of your people."* The youngest member of Congress, Alexandria Ocasio-Cortez, and many 2020 Democratic presidential hopefuls are now vocalizing their support of socialist policies. While many never-Trump Republicans dismiss the left's platforms as far-fetched, these radicals' constituents do not.

According to another article in the *Washington Examiner*, if AOC was old enough to run for president today, she'd win. A stunning 75% of Democratic voters, according to an Axios/Survey Monkey poll, would

---

[437] Ibid.

definitely vote for her, mostly the young and minorities.[438] That, alone, should worry every American who cherishes our unique freedoms.

In a push for her "Green New Deal", AOC has been warning Americans that, "'Millennials and people, you know, Gen Z and all these folks that will come after us are looking up and we're like: 'The world is gonna end in 12 years if we don't address climate change and your biggest issue is how are we gonna pay for it?' Ocasio-Cortez said."[439] Former VP-turned-climate-change-doomsayer, Al Gore, became rich after the false prophet said the exact same thing in 2006. His expiration date for the world was 2016. How did that work out? Tragically. "Political leaders in a college town in central Texas won wide praise from former Vice President Al Gore and the larger Green Movement when they decided to go '100 percent renewable' seven years ago. Now, however, they are on the defensive over electricity costs that have their residents paying more than $1,000 per household in higher electricity charges over the last four years."[440] The residents are stuck in a 25-year contract

[438] Dominick Mastrangelo. "Poll: Lots of Democrats open to voting for Alexandria Ocasio-Cortez for president" *Washington Examiner* (Jan. 27, 2019) https://www.washingtonexaminer.com/news/poll-lots-of-democrats-open-to-voting-for-alexandria-ocasio-cortez-for-president.

[439] Joseph A. Wulfsohn. "Ocasio-Cortez calls climate change 'our World War II,' warns the world will end in 12 years" (Last Update Jan. 22, 2019) https://www.foxnews.com/politics/ocasio-cortez-calls-climate-change-our-world-war-ii-warns-the-world-will-end-in-12-years.

[440] Chuck DeVore. "Texas town's environmental narcissism makes Al Gore happy while sticking its citizens with the bill" *FoxNews* (Jan. 29, 2019) https://www.foxnews.com/opinion/texas-towns-environmental-narcissism-makes-al-gore-happy-while-sticking-its-citizens-with-the-bill.

that costs them more money every time the wind isn't blowing or the sun doesn't shine. That is exactly what radicals want to do nationwide. The political leader in charge of that Texas college town was a Republican who got snookered; and, now his constituents are paying dearly for it.

Instead of griping about all-things Trump, Republicans should start getting messages of the left's failed policies out to the public. Even Democratic presidential hopeful, former New York City Mayor Mike Bloomberg, called AOC's "Green New Deal" unrealistic.

Fortunately, some Conservatives do keep these issues front and center. They are the ones our politicians should be listening to more often. One of those is Dan Bongino, a former Secret Service agent who speaks up loudly, and often. After AOC announced her plan to raise taxes on the rich by 70%, Bongino responded, "by the way liberals, if you want to pay the 70 percent marginal tax rate, go right ahead. It's voluntary. Just pay It! ... Everyone should sign a pledge to commit to a 70 percent tax rate. ... But I know you won't do it because you're big frauds. You're hypocrites. You've always been hypocrites. You're ideologues and you don't stand for a darn thing. ... I challenge you to donate your salary, Ms. Ocasio-Cortez. Show us how it's done and step up."[441]

AOC's base may be dumb enough to believe her many exposed falsehoods, but that's only because she speaks in elementary terms about complex issues. She

---

[441] Dan Bongino. "Dan Bongino: Hey, Rep. Ocasio-Cortez, show us how it's done and donate 70 percent of your income to the government" *Fox News* (Jan. 17, 2019) https://www.foxnews.com/opinion/dan-bongino-hey-rep-ocasio-cortez-show-us-how-its-done-and-donate-70-percent-of-your-income-to-the-government.

never goes outside her people's expertise. That's probably also because she doesn't understand the issues herself. Bongino points that out when he says: "[T]he reason she prefers to use a marginal tax rate as a talking point is because she believes it wouldn't affect the overwhelming majority of Americans and that she can get public support for it. She assumes that most Americans will say, 'Hey, it's not gonna affect me.'"[442]

Trump also knows how to communicate within the experience of his own supporters. On November 5, 2018, he tweeted that, "Republicans have created the best economy in the HISTORY of our Country – and the hottest jobs market on planet earth. The Democrat Agenda is a Socialist Nightmare. The Republican Agenda is the AMERICAN DREAM!"[443]

The GOP needs to take lessons from Bongino and Trump and start challenging the Dems, rather than finding reasons to bash Trump's every move.

The left is expert in using Alinsky's third tactic: *"Wherever possible go outside the experience of the enemy".* The GOP's naïveté and sanctimony allow the left to take advantage of them time and again. It's what made Jeff Sessions such a failure as Trump's first attorney general. He caved to the left's demands that he recuse himself from the Trump–Russia collusion investigation, leaving our president's most vulnerable flank wide open. Some on the right, even today, insist that Sessions was right to recuse himself. Hogwash. Right or wrong, I can pretty much guarantee that, given the exact same circumstances, former–AG Eric Holder

---

[442] Ibid.
[443] *@realdonaldtrump (Nov. 5, 2018)*

would have never done the same, leaving his president exposed.

It's a shame that Trump's most ferocious defenders come, not from within the Republican Party itself, but from Conservatives in the media. Gregg Jarrett is another proven warrior for Trump. The *FOX News* legal analyst and author of the best-seller, *The Russia Hoax: The Illicit Scheme to Clear Hillary Clinton And Frame Donald Trump,* has worked tirelessly, along with *FOX News* host Sean Hannity, to expose the suspect activities of the FBI and DOJ. When the *New York Times* reported in January of 2019 that, in May, 2017 the FBI actually investigated Trump as a possible Russian spy, Jarrett claimed that, "[T]hey invented facts and ignored the law to subvert our system of justice and undermine the democratic process. They compromised essential principles and betrayed the nation's trust. ... And they did it to depose Trump."[444]

The GOP's blind trust in Democrats' political intentions has allowed our agencies to become stacked with radicals who have nearly gotten away with a soft coup against a duly-elected president. The FBI and DOJ deliberately set the stage for Trump's impeachment based on a phony dossier that enabled them to conduct illegal wiretapping of Trump and his campaign. Once the "suspicions" were shared with the press, giving the public a healthy dose of doubt, our agencies felt brazen enough to assign a special counsel to investigate our

---

[444] Gregg Jarrett. "An FBI that is corrupt and dishonest -- Latest reports offer only more proof" *FOX News* (Jan. 14, 2019) https://www.foxnews.com/opinion/gregg-jarrett-an-fbi-that-is-corrupt-and-dishonest-latest-reports-offer-only-more-proof.

president. The *Yahoo News* reporter now says it is "likely false". But, the damage is already done.

On November 27, 2018, Trump tweeted that, "[t]he Phony Witch Hunt continues, but Mueller and his gang of Angry Dems are only looking at one side, not the other. Wait until it comes out how horribly & viciously they are treating people, ruining lives for them refusing to lie. Mueller is a conflicted prosecutor gone rogue".[445] By taking certain actions and tweeting things that are "un-presidential", as his detractors like to say, Trump has the left in a constant scramble to figure out what his next move will be as he educates Americans on the truth. That's Alinsky 101. When the left tells you Trump and his administration are in total chaos, rejoice. It is exactly the message he should be sending.

"Make the enemy live up to their own book of rules", Alinsky's fourth tactic, is something at which Trump especially excels. When the left wreaked havoc on the nomination process of now-Justice Kavanaugh, using character assassination, they intentionally used his high ethics, morality, and values against him, calling his stellar reputation into question. To their credit, Republicans finally followed Trump's hardline approach against the Dems and were able to get the judge confirmed by a single vote. Trump is now teaching Republicans how to street fight; and, the Kavanaugh confirmation was their first victory.

Disturbingly, a newly-elected "freshman Democrat on the House Judiciary Committee told constituents the panel will 'likely' investigate Supreme Court Justice Brett Kavanaugh for purportedly committing perjury during

---

[445] *@realdonaldtrump (Nov. 27, 2018).*

his confirmation hearings last fall. ... 'There's no question [he] committed perjury..." [Rep. Joe] Neguse said, responding to a question about the possibility of impeaching Kavanaugh."[446] There's that pesky "due process" interpretation of the law again. No doubt, the Republicans have a real fight on their hands ahead. Let's hope the GOP will stay strong with Trump on this, and other issues, over the next two years.

On October 10, 2018, Trump tweeted, "Despite so many positive events and victories, Media Research Center reports that 92% of stories on Donald Trump are negative on ABC, CBS and ABC [sic]. It is FAKE NEWS! Don't worry, the Failing New York Times didn't even put the Brett Kavanaugh victory on the Front Page yesterday–A17!"[447] Not only does Trump call the "fake news" media untrustworthy, he also explains why. Our president really is brilliant. Republicans must now prove to voters whether they are capable of sharpening the street fighting skills Trump is teaching them. For the sake of our nation, they'd better be.

The Alinsky tactic I believe Trump loves using against the left most is the fifth one, *"[R]idicule is man's most potent weapon"*. The left has been ridiculing Conservatives effectively for decades by calling us "racists", "Islamaphobes", "fascists", "homophobes", "xenophobes", "sexists", and every other name they can think of, including the now-infamous "Deplorables". The GOP has cowered under the ridicule, so much so

---

[446] Andrew O'Reilly. "House Judiciary Democrat says Justice Kavanaugh will 'likely' be investigated for perjury" *FOX News* (Jan. 21, 2019) https://www.foxnews.com/politics/house-judiciary-democrat-says-that-justice-kavanaugh-will-likely-be-investigated-for-perjury.

[447] *@realdonaldtrump (Oct. 10, 2018).*

that they back away from issues rather than face them for one reason alone: self-preservation. That's why the GOP has been so ineffective, especially the never-Trumpers. Trump will have none of it. He has been ridiculing his opponents since day one. And, his strategy is working.

Several of the newest, most radical members of the House have drawn a lot of fire in their first month in office. U.S. Rep. Ihan Omar, an outspoken anti-Israel Muslim, alleged that Republican Sen. Lindsey Graham was "compromised", perhaps even blackmailed, by Trump because he has been more supportive of our president's policies than usual lately. She was purportedly alluding to unsubstantiated claims by the left that Graham is gay. "Graham critics point out that the senator previously held a negative view of Trump, even calling him 'a race-baiting, xenophobic, religious bigot' during the presidential campaign."[448]

The Dems got a swift counterpunch, thankfully. The RNC's national committeewoman, Harmeet Dhillon, "slammed Omar's comment for bigotry: 'Breathtaking bigotry, homophobia from a member of Congress. It's not funny, and puzzling why Dems get away with outdated stereotypes and dumb conspiracy theories like this."[449] They get away with it, Harmeet, because Republican legislators are mostly wimps, who weaken

[448] Lukas Mikeliionis. "Hard-left Dem accused of 'breathtaking bigotry' after claim that Lindsey Graham is 'compromised' FOXnews.com (Jan. 17, 2019)
https://www.foxnews.com/politics/democrat-ilhan-omar-accused-of-breathtaking-bigotry-after-saying-lindsey-graham-is-compromised.
[449] Ibid.

their own party by attacking our president; and, the American people are beginning to realize it.

When the Dems originally embraced *Rules for Radicals'* sixth tactic, *"[a] good tactic is one that your people enjoy"*, they didn't foresee that the younger generation being dumbed down by the left would someday become the future lawmakers of the Democratic Party. Now, these new radical Dems are pushing the moderate ones even too far left for a majority of their own constituents to stomach. That's good news for Republicans, unless the GOP starts capitulating to them, too.

A new favorite on the Democrat's socialist team now considering a 2020 presidential run, Beto O'Rourke, has remained visible ever since he nearly ended Texas Republican Senator Ted Cruz's career in the U.S. Senate during the 2018 midterms. For some odd reason, he decided to livestream his recent routine dental visit for all the world to see. It appeared to be his Corey Booker "Spartacus" moment that fell totally flat. But, he enjoyed his new tactic. His lack of wisdom, fortunately, doesn't end with bad Instagram decisions.

During a more substantive interview in *The Washington Post*, Beto exposed himself to be a totally uninformed and dangerous candidate. When answering basic questions about issues pertaining to illegal immigrants who overstay their visas and the Syrian withdrawal, Beto's answers were: "I don't know" and "I don't necessarily understand." But, the real controversy came when, alluding to our Constitution, he wondered aloud whether our country could "'still be managed by the same principles that were set down 230-plus years ago.' Even a senior political reporter for the very liberal

Huffington Post conceded that, '[T]his last bit – where he suggests we might need to ditch the Constitution? – is wild.'"[450]

To her credit, Republican U.S. Representative for Wyoming, Liz Cheney, astutely observed that Beto's comments "'may make it difficult to take any future oath of office to 'preserve, protect and defend the Constitution'.'"[451] The Dems give Republicans all the fodder needed to divide their party. So, why continue to criticize Trump? His policies, with which some Republicans may disagree, are based on information that even some in his own party may not be privy to. Even so, the extreme agenda of the left far exceeds any of Trump's in sheer stupidity and damage to our country. It's time never–Trumpers picked a side and stuck to it.

"A tactic that drags on too long becomes a drag" is Alinsky's seventh. Ever since the Dems won a majority of House seats in the midterms, they've been talking non–stop about investigations against our president to impeach him. They claim they had eighty–five such plans ready to go the first day they took control. At least they had a plan, unlike our majority in 2016.

Within hours of being sworn in, the second of two Muslim women to ever be elected to the U.S. Congress, Rashida Tlaib said, "'President Donald Trump is a direct and serious threat to our country. On an almost daily basis, he attacks our Constitution, our democracy, the

---

[450] Gregg Re. "Beto O'Rourke mocked after offering few answers in wide-ranging policy interview" *FOX News* (Jan. 16,, 2019) https://www.foxnews.com/politics/beto-orourke-mocked-after-offering-few-answers-in-wide-ranging-policy-interview.
[451] Ibid.

rule of law and the people who are in this country,.... The time for impeachment proceedings is now.'"[452] Fair enough, let's see the evidence, Rashida. Instead, she threatened, while her young children were present, "'...when your son looks at you and says, 'Momma, look you won. Bullies don't win.' And I said, 'Baby, they don't, because we're gonna go in there and we're gonna impeach the mother****er.'"[453] It is certainly refreshing to know that the evidence for impeaching a duly-elected, sitting president is because he is a "mother****er."

As usual, Trump is one step ahead of the left, as he proved when he tweeted, on November 7, 2018, one day after the elections: "If the Democrats think they are going to waste Taxpayer Money investigating us at the House level, then we will likewise be forced to consider investigating them for all of the leaks of Classified Information, and much else, at the Senate level. Two can play that game!"[454] Kudos to Trump. But, does his majority-held Senate have his back? That's debatable.

Alinsky's eighth tactic to *"[k]eep the pressure on"* could have been written by Donald Trump, himself. He's got it mastered. One of his campaign promises was to "lock her up" (referring to Hillary); and, it became a highly-charged chant at every one of his rallies. If there is one promise Trump wants to keep, along with "build that wall", it's to make sure Hillary Clinton faces consequences for her past illegal actions. It now appears

---

[452] By Louis Casiano and Bradford Betz. "Rashida Tlaib calls Trump an expletive during pitch to impeach" *FOXNews.com* (Jan. 4, 2019) https://www.foxnews.com/politics/democrats-call-for-impeachment-on-first-day-of-new-congress.
[453] Ibid.
[454] *@realdonaldtrump* (Nov. 7, 2018).

obvious that she committed plenty of them. Unfortunately, the Trump–Russia witch hunt has effectively sidelined that campaign promise, as was its intended purpose. The entire country should unite in hoping that an honest, effective attorney general replacement will be confirmed. The Sessions' catastrophe should ensure that Trump selects more wisely this time by ignoring advice from untrustworthy political holdovers. Hopefully, that appointee will feel duty–bound to drain the swamp and return our agencies to the neutral arbitrators they were meant to be. Once that is accomplished, Trump will refocus on the wrongful actions of Comey's FBI and Rosenstein's DOJ. He is already laying the framework.

On November 25, 2018, Trump tweeted: "Clinton Foundation donations drop 42% – which shows that they illegally played the power game. They monetized their political influence through the Foundation. 'During her tenure the State Department was put in the service of the Clinton Foundation.' Andrew McCarthy."[455] I believe Trump will do everything he can, when the time is right, to go after those on the left who have committed crimes. Our institutions are filled with left–leaning socialists and it is critical to clean them out. Becoming a banana republic is the inevitable outcome if we do not. But, that cannot succeed unless Republicans are united.

The left constantly uses the ninth tactic, *"[t]he threat is usually more terrifying than the thing itself"*, to their full advantage. What they've never experienced is a Republican president who threatens back, refusing to

---

[455] *@realdonaldtrump* (Nov. 25, 2018).

be bullied. You can bet some of Trump's unveiled threats are terrifying to the left.

I'm sure Trump's tweet on November 27, 2018 has Hillary, Mueller, and former leaders of the FBI and DOJ a tad nervous, when he wrote: "The Phony Witch Hunt continues, but Mueller and his gang of Angry Dems are only looking at one side, not the other. Wait until it comes out how horribly & viciously they are treating people, ruining lives for them refusing to lie. Mueller is a conflicted prosecutor gone rogue.... The Fake News Media builds Bob Mueller up as a Saint, when in actuality he is the exact opposite. He is doing TREMENDOUS damage to our Criminal Justice System,.... Heroes will come of this, and it won't be Mueller and his...terrible Gang of Angry Democrats. Look at their past, and look where they come from. The now $30,000,000 Witch Hunt continues and they've got nothing but ruined lives. Where is the Server? Let these terrible people go back to the Clinton Foundation and "Justice" Department!"[456] Trump plans to drain the swamp. The GOP must get on board.

"The major premise for tactics is the development of operations that will maintain a constant pressure upon the opposition". Alinsky's tenth tactic was also dominated by the left until Trump became president. Trump's constant tweeting keeps his enemies in fear of what he'll say and do next. It's one of his most powerful weapons.

Unfortunately, the "resistance" against Trump is everywhere. The left has been grooming academia and the media as their "pressure" partners against

---

[456] *@realdonaldtrump* (Nov. 27, 2018).

Conservatives since the 60's. But another danger comes from covert anti-Trumpers, some even inside the White House, who are against either his personality or his policies yet pretend to be loyal subjects.

The day after Trump's Secretary of Defense, Jim Mattis, resigned over the president's announced pull-out from Syria, "Brett McGurk, the U.S. envoy for the global coalition to defeat Islamic State (ISIS)"[457] followed suit. People blamed Trump for not listening to his advisers. Is that fair, though? Deeper research reveals some interesting background that may explain from just how many directions the "resistance" keeps pressure on our president.

"McGurk, who was an Obama appointee in 2015, had said in a Dec. 11 press conference that it would be 'reckless' to consider ISIS defeated and that the 'enduring defeat of a group like this means you can't just defeat their physical space and then leave.'"[458] Is it logical policy to stay in Syria, for example, until every single ISIS member is defeated? What about all the other countries they operate in worldwide? Should we be in those, as well? Consider, too, that McGurk was the lead negotiator in the Iranian prison swap and ransom payment. "McGurk previously served as a deputy assistant secretary of state for Iraq and Iran, and led secret side talks with Iran about the release of American prisoners during the negotiations for the Iran nuclear

---

[457] Adam Shaw. "Brett McGurk, US envoy to anti-ISIS coalition, resigns in wake of Trump decision to pull troops from Syria *foxnews.com* (Dec. 22, 2018) https://www.foxnews.com/politics/brett-mcgurk-us-envoy-to-anti-isis-coalition-resigns-in-wake-of-trump-decision-to-withdraw-from-syria.
[458] Ibid.

deal...."[459] If Trump did not agree with the policy these men were proposing, it just may have been for good reason. After all, his campaign promises included getting us out of Syria and discontinuing our practice of nation-building. Mattis and McGurk were in positions that mandate they serve at the pleasure of the president. If either disagreed with Trump's campaign promises, they were more wrong to resign, than they were to have taken their jobs in the first place.

Ever the transparent president, in response to the fallout from the Mattis and McGurk resignations, Trump tweeted, "'[I]f anybody but your favorite President, Donald J. Trump, announced that, after decimating ISIS in Syria, we were going to bring our troops back home (happy & healthy), that person would be the most popular hero in America,' he continued in a follow-up tweet. 'With me, hit hard instead by the Fake News Media. Crazy!'"[460] So true.

"If you push a negative hard and deep enough it will break through into its counterpart" is Alinsky's eleventh tactic. What I like most about Trump is that he refuses to take "no" for an answer. Instead, he pushes ahead until he gets a positive result.

While the radical left calls for the elimination of ICE and spreads obscene rhetoric to incite violence against law enforcement, Trump understands that getting people back to work is the best way to calm mobs of discontent. On October 23, 2018, he tweeted that, "[B]illions of dollars are, and will be, coming into United States coffers because of Tariffs. Great also for

---

[459] Ibid.
[460] *@realdonaldtrump* (Dec. 22, 2018).

negotiations – if a country won't give us a fair Trade Deal, we will institute Tariffs on them. Used or not, jobs and businesses will be created. U.S. respected again![461] He has succeeded in getting people back to work, eliminating NAFTA and negotiating better deals between the U.S., Mexico and Canada.

As Trump works around the clock for fairer trade with China, some Americans are getting nervous. They are the same ones who would agree to war only to back out when the going gets tough, costing our country precious American lives and money. We no longer have what it takes to win. We can no longer allow China to rip off our technology or the $800 billion a year in unfair trade. If anyone can pull this off, it's Trump. There may never be another president as capable of tough negotiations. China is hurting itself financially right now purely because of ego. When their economy suffers even more, they'll buckle. Trump knows that or he wouldn't be taking the risk. Have faith, be strong, and unite!

Alinsky's twelfth tactic, *"the price of a successful attack is a constructive alternative"*, is another that Trump uses well. If not for the idiotic never-Trumpers who should, without exception, always be united with him, he would have had the wall built by now. Instead, we have illegal caravans lining up on our southern border ready to overwhelm our country at the first chance they get. While our brave border patrol agents are being pelted with cinderblocks, bottles, and other projectiles at work, the left denigrates them at home. If we had a wall, this would not be happening. If we had politicians with guts, we'd have a wall already.

---

[461] *@realdonaldtrump.* Oct. 23, 2018.

During the midterm elections, as Trump was trying desperately to find a solution to the looming crisis on our southern border, former Republican House Speaker Paul Ryan found the need to publicly contradict the legality of Trump's attack on birthright citizenship. In doing so, he weakened the president's multi-pronged illegal immigration plan by giving the left ammunition with which to attack him. With friends like that, who needs a Republican Party? I applauded Trump's October 9, 2018 rebuttal, in which he tweeted: "Paul Ryan should be focusing on holding the Majority rather than giving his opinions on Birthright Citizenship, something he knows nothing about! Our new Republican Majority will work on this, Closing the Immigration Loopholes and Securing our Border!"[462]

Thanks to Ryan's sanctimonious focus on attacking our president, he lost the House majority.

Fortunately for America, Ryan, Flake, and Corker are now gone. Unfortunately, we have new Republican Trump-resisters, like Mitt Romney, ready to pounce every chance they get. They are a disgrace to conservative ideals.

Ryan failed to get the wall built or to pass a "repeal and replace" Obamacare bill, two of Trump's most important campaign promises. As Alinsky explains in *Rules for Radicals*, if you're not part of the solution, you are part of the problem. Ryan, and others like him, are part of the problem standing in the way of Trump and his supporters' agenda.

Alinsky's thirteenth, and final, tactic is, that in order to win a war, you must *"pick a target, freeze it,*

---

[462] *@realdonaldtrump*. (Oct. 9, 2018).

personalize it, and polarize it". Both the left and its "fake news" media arm have successfully used this tactic against Trump since day one, precisely because his own GOP doesn't unite behind him. Now the Dems are threatening to go after his finances from decades ago. Will Republicans protect him? Don't count on it.

Demonstrably proving the division between the Republican Party and our president, in mid-January, 2019, "eleven [Senate] Republicans ... joined with unanimous Democrats to keep alive a resolution opposing the Trump administration's decision to diminish sanctions against Russia."[463] Today's Dems are 100% indivisible, not because they always agree, but because the end goal, government control/socialism, is the bigger prize. Our guys keep wanting to fight with old rules. One of those eleven was my own senator, Marco Rubio. I made sure to call his D.C. office and leave a message explaining my dissatisfaction, saying, *"It's not enough anymore to believe you are right, and Trump is wrong. We are in danger of losing our country to socialism. In the old days, sticking to your values when voting was commendable. Today, it's suicidal."* You can bet I'll be sending him a copy of this book, too!

Revealingly, in just the first three weeks "[I]n the new Congress, the Republican Senate has failed three times to begin debate on a measure backed by [Senate Majority Leader] McConnell. But the first measure on which the Senate actually was able to begin debate in the new Congress is the one backed by [Senate Minority

[463] Gregg Re. "Senate Republicans rebuke McConnell, Trump on Russia sanctions resolution" *foxnews.com* (Jan. 15, 2019) https://www.foxnews.com/politics/senate-republicans-rebuke-mcconnell-trump-on-russia-sanctions-resolution.

Leader] Schumer."[464] That's disgraceful. Once again, our naïve, "holier-than-thou", Republican senators have shown they are clueless about the seriousness of our country's slide towards socialism. But, the Democrats are fully aware and ready for their fight. If President Trump thought a bigger majority in the Senate was going to help him, he may be in for a disappointing surprise.

Fortunately, though, our president knows how to pick and polarize targets, too. On October 28, 2018, he tweeted that, "[T]he Fake News is doing everything in their power to blame Republicans, Conservatives and me for the division and hatred that has been going on for so long in our Country. Actually, it is their Fake & Dishonest reporting which is causing problems far greater than they understand!"[465] Once again, he has it exactly right. If we cannot get our educational systems and our media back to an honest assessment of facts, our march towards socialism will continue. That genie will take decades, if ever, to put back in the bottle. Venezuela is facing that uphill battle today.

Cloward-Piven and Saul Alinsky did one helluva job guiding the left towards their stated goal of socialism. Germans didn't pay attention to what Hitler wrote in his best-selling book, *Mein Kampf*, even though it outlined his entire plan to exterminate the Jewish race. Their country paid dearly for that mistake. Americans, today, face a similar challenge for our survival.

Rules for Deplorables was written to alert the American people to the left's rapid advance to socialism.

---

[464] Ibid.
[465] *@realdonaldtrump*. (Oct. 28, 2018.

I sincerely hope this book makes clear the vulnerable situation our country faces and what is needed to fight the evils of socialist programs advanced by radicals. Now, it's time to get involved.

We can no longer afford to miss elections. We should only trust news from reliable sources; and, we must verify claims that sound too crazy to be true. We should ensure that the schools educating our children teach the truth about our history and the difference between free markets versus socialism. Finally, we must give our president the support he needs by voting out politicians who are not staunchly united behind him.

Write letters to, and call, your Representatives on important issues. Put his/her phone number in your cell phone contact list for easy access. You can call the main switchboard number (202-224-3121) at the Capitol in Washington, D.C., to find out your Congressperson's direct number. Volunteer for campaigns when solid pro-Trump Conservatives are running. Just start getting involved! Trump needs every single one of us.

Thank you President Donald J. Trump, Melania, Ivanka and husband, Jared, and the rest of the Trump family and loyal staff, for your sacrifices to *Make America Great Again*. Never in my lifetime have I witnessed such committed and gracious people occupying our White House. *God Bless America...and, May God Bless President Trump forever!*

IF YOU FOUND MY BOOK MEANINGFUL, PLEASE SIGN UP TO RECEIVE
MY BLOGS AND PODCASTS AND SHARE WITH OTHERS. IT'S
CRITICAL THAT WE KEEP THIS DIALOGUE GOING.
OUR COUNTRY IS AT A CROSSROADS AND IT'S UP TO
EVERY ONE OF US TO BECOME INVOLVED.

Blogs/Podcasts: **www.TheDeplorableReport.com**
Website: **www.RulesforDeplorablesBook.com**
Email: **Contact@RulesforDeplorablesBook.com**

Made in the USA
Monee, IL
28 March 2021